KING JOHN

THE MEDIEVAL WORLD

Editor: David Bates

KING JOHN

Ralph V. Turner

LONGMAN
London and New York

Longman Group UK Limited,
Longman House, Burnt Mill,
Harlow, Essex CM20 2JE, England
and Associated Companies throughout the world.

*Published in the United States of America
by Longman Publishing, New York*

First published 1994

ISBN 0582 06727 8 CSD
ISBN 0582 06726 X PPR

British Library Cataloguing-in-Publication Data

A catalogue record for this book is
available from the British Library

Library of Congress Cataloging in Publication Data

Turner, Ralph V.
King John / Ralph Turner.
p. cm. – (The Medieval World)
Includes bibliographical references and index.
ISBN 0-582-06727-8. – ISBN 0-582-06726-X (pbk.)
1. John, King of England, 1167?-1216. 2. Great Britain–History–John,
1199-1216. 3. Great Britain–Kings and rulers–Biography.
I. Title. II. Series.
DA208.T87 1994
942.03′3′092–dc20 [B]   93-7778 CIP

Set by 5P in 11/12pt Baskerville
Produced by Longman Singapore Publishers (Pte) Ltd.
Printed in Singapore

CONTENTS

LIST OF GENEALOGICAL TABLES AND MAPS

EDITOR'S PREFACE

The reign of King John is one of central importance to all with an interest in the English Middle Ages. It was a decisive time in England's history because the kingdom was conclusively separated from the vast majority of the lands which its rulers had previously held in France and because John's granting of Magna Carta established England as a limited monarchy in which the king's power was definitively confined within certain legal limits. The reign is also a fascinating one because of the way in which the king's personality exercises a mesmeric effect on all who study it. For some medieval chroniclers, and for many nineteenth-century historians who took their verdict literally, John was evil incarnate. Even if twentieth-century scholarship has accurately pin-pointed the limitations of the chroniclers' approaches – and above all their requirement that political failure had to be explained on a basis of personal moral failings – the dilemma which has to be confronted when any individual's place in History is assessed remains. How far were the disasters of John's seventeen-year reign the king's own fault?

Ralph Turner's contribution to the Medieval World Series is a welcome one for many reasons. His extensive publications on the Angevin period make him an established authority who is able to tackle John's reign on the basis of long familiarity with the records of twelfth- and thirteenth-century government. It is also important that there has been no major comprehensive treatment of John's reign since the early 1960's. Professor Turner is therefore able to draw on the scholarly and interpretative advances of the intervening period. He brings clearly into focus and weighs judiciously the factors which have always been seen as central to a verdict on John and his reign, such as the king's personality, his financial and military legacy from his brother Richard, the nature of baronial ambition, the strengths and weaknesses of the so-called Angevin Empire, the impact of economic change and of papal disapproval. He deals authoritatively with the controversies between those historians who stress John's political and military failings and those who stress his administrative ability. Out of this emerges a coherent portrait of John which is of itself a contribution to historical understanding. One dominant theme of the reign is a ruthless and remarkably consistent attempt to finance war. Another, is the insufficiency of the financial resources at John's disposal. The loss of the continental possessions colours and controls everything that follows. Their recovery was the dominant theme of the king's policy. Had he lived longer, John might well have defeated his English enemies and Magna Carta might not have become a permanent feature of the English political scene. In some areas, John faced impossible difficulties. In others, he came close to success. John is able, but flawed. Like the recent US presidents with whom Ralph Turner draws some illuminating parallels, John's failure should command a measure of our sympathy. But, as perhaps also with them, the humanity is lacking which might persuade us to see the failure as a tragic one.

David Bates

ACKNOWLEDGEMENTS

When I began studying under Sidney Painter at the Johns Hopkins University over thirty years ago, it never occurred to me that one day I would write a biography of King John. My own work has made me more respectful of Painter's *Reign of King John*, a masterful study of early thirteenth-century England published in 1949 that he plainly stated is not a biography but 'essentially a political and administrative history'. My attempt to present a new portrait of King John also has made me mindful of Kate Norgate's unequaled knowledge of the chronicles displayed in her 1902 biography, *John Lackland*, and of W.L. Warren's judicious balancing of narrative accounts and administrative sources in his 1961 biography. My book cannot replace these earlier studies, but builds upon them, taking advantage of more readily available sources and of recent scholarship that suggests new approaches to a deeper awareness of John and his reign.

This book relies not only on earlier works on King John, but on the scholarship, friendship, and encouragement of many fellow historians on both sides of the Atlantic, notably David Bates, editor of Longman's 'Medieval World' series, for his confidence in my work and for his perceptive comments. Special thanks go to John W. Baldwin, Professor Painter's successor at Johns Hopkins, author of an important study of John's contemporary, Philip Augustus, and a mentor who has consistently encouraged my scholarly efforts. He read an earlier version of a chapter of this book, as did C. Warren Hollister and Charles R. Young. Also I acknowledge my debt to Sir James Holt, not only for his writings on the Angevin period but also for his friendship. Many others have given generous assistance, among them RaGena de Aragon, Fred A. Cazel and Sue Ann Walker, who sent me copies of papers otherwise unattainable, and all members of the Charles Homer Haskins Society, who patiently listened to exploratory papers on King John at its Houston, Texas, annual conferences.

Several agencies assisted me with grants that made available research travel and time for writing. The Florida State University's Council on Faculty Research and its Committee on Sabbatical Grants, the National Endowment for the Humanities, the Henry E. Huntington Library, San Marino, California, and the American Philosophical Society, all supplied funds. The Department of History at Florida State afforded me the necessary extended stretches of time for writing. Many libraries besides the Strozier Library at Florida State made their resources available to me, among them the British Library, the Institute of Historical Research, University of London, and the libraries of Duke University, Emory University, and the University of North Carolina.

Ralph V. Turner
Tallahassee
8 December 1992

Chapter 1

KING JOHN IN HIS CONTEXT: A COMPARISON WITH HIS CONTEMPORARIES

After so many scholars have sifted the same evidence, are any new approaches to King John possible? A comparative approach to John, placing him alongside his father Henry II, his brother Richard Lionheart, and his great rival Philip Augustus, should enable us to see him more clearly and in context. Two controversial British historians, H.G. Richardson and G.O. Sayles judge such contemporaries of John bad; they add, 'And it was in association with all this badness that John grew to manhood and in turn became a bad man.'[1] Bad or simply misunderstood, John was a loser, losing Normandy in 1204, losing his quarrel with the Pope, forced by his barons to grant them a charter of liberties, and at his death struggling not to lose his kingdom to an invading foreign prince.

King John failed at the greatest task he set for himself: regaining the continental lands that he had lost to his French rival. At the battle of Bouvines in 1214, a decade's furious activity went down the drain. When he died about two years later, he was fighting a stalemated civil war against his English barons, whose discontent had been fanned by his efforts to extort wealth from England for the recover of Normandy. In contrast, his brother Richard I had won glory crusading in the Holy Land and combating Philip Augustus's threat to the Angevin territories. Although Henry II died tragically fighting his

---

1. Richardson, H.G., Sayles, G.O. (1963) *The Governance of Mediaeval England*, Edinburgh UP, p. 330.

faithless sons, he had largely achieved his aims of restoring his grandfather's strong rule over England and protecting his continental empire from its Capetian overlords. John's failure has led historians to paint him not as a tragic figure, but as a contemptible or hateful one.

A key to comparing John's reputation with that of his father, his brother Richard, or his enemy Philip is to set them in their context, seeing how their contemporaries perceived them. It is essential to be aware that the standards of writers in John's own time were not those of later historians. The chroniclers who first fixed the portraits of these rulers had very different standards from twentieth-century academics; like later historians, they were subject to prejudices or preconceptions that could distort their perceptions. They were churchmen, following the lead of other clerics who had set standards for judging medieval kings, painting a conventional portrait of the 'good' king. Yet the barbarian tradition of the warrior king, victorious in battle against foreign foes and internal rebels, remained strong; and romance writers' praise of prowess reinforced it. Chroniclers also praised monarchs who provided royal protection for the Church and its property, and who proved submissive to papal authority.

Chroniclers distinguished hardly at all between a king's public role and his private morality, expecting him to be an exemplar of piety and virtue; 'conventionally pious' is the usual phrase. Monastic writers' verdict on a ruler was 'essentially a moral judgment upon an individual sinner';[2] and because Victorian scholars adopted this moralistic approach, it has continued to influence estimates of medieval monarchs. John, like his father and grandfather, earned chroniclers' condemnation for adulterous affairs. In his case, however, his lust for his barons' wives and daughters may have had consequences beyond morality, contributing to political difficulties with his great men. Because Richard Lionheart was a Christian knight, a crusader, tireless in attending religious services, and

2. Galbraith, V.H. (1945) 'Good kings and bad kings in English history', *History* 30, reprinted (1982) *Kings and Chroniclers*, Hambledon Press, p. 120.

generous to the Church, his faults could be overlooked by contemporary writers. Yet monarchs such as William Rufus or John were condemned for leading grossly immoral lives, and they were likely to be accused of irreligion as well as sexual improprieties.

Most chroniclers stressed the king as defender of the oppressed, the poor, widows and orphans. Often this was expressed negatively as not oppressing his subjects, not taxing the Church too harshly, not being too greedy. Greed, a vice that chroniclers often found in monarchs, was significant because early medieval government was predatory, living off the land, much like the government of modern Haiti. Medieval monarchs and Haitian dictators are comparable in ruling rural societies with little commerce or industry, lacking means of producing wealth other than subsistence agriculture. Since the means of increasing the wealth of the royal family, the nobility, and their retainers was squeezing some surplus from their subjects' sparse resources, administrative agents functioned more for efficient raising of revenues from the populace than for performance of public services. The surest path to financial success, then, was to join the royal household or to secure some lesser post, sharing in the plunder; government was a gigantic shakedown. Conflict between the king and nobles often amounted to competition over means of shaking down the common people, that is, conflict over control of instruments for exploiting the countryside ranging from castles to law courts.

Because of this, administrative innovations to make royal government more efficient were unlikely to arouse the admiration among contemporaries that they do among historians today. Gerald of Wales expressed a common view when he compared the king to 'a robber permanently on the prowl, always probing, always searching for the weak spot where there is something for him to steal'.[3] Modern scholars' admiration of kings such as

---

3. Gillingham, J. (1978) *Richard the Lionheart*, Weidenfeld & Nicolson, p. 133. Translation of Gerald of Wales, Brewer, J.S., Dimcock, J.F. Warner, G.F. (eds) (1861–91) *Giraldi Cambrensis Opera* (8 vols), Rolls Series, vol. 8, p. 316.

John for attention to administration is anachronistic, applying standards of the twentieth century rather than the thirteenth. Few authorities today would deny that John applied himself to administrative work with energy and ability, although some may overpraise him simply because his activity is so well documented. His predecessors had ruled England as absentees, however; and his English subjects did not always appreciate his presence, regarding his close supervision as oppression. The best loved Angevin king was Richard Lionheart, allegedly the least concerned with administration, yet recent studies find him a competent enough administrator in the area most vital for him, marshalling resources for war.

A growing influence on thinking by the feudal nobility about kingship in the twelfth century was chivalry, with its definition of the perfect knight's quality of prowess, physical strength and courage. Monastic writers no longer monopolized judgment of a king's qualities, as laymen writing verses in the vernacular joined in praising valiant warriors. Characteristics of importance to these poets, besides prowess, were loyalty, courtesy, and especially largess, gift-giving. Ever since the barbarian invasions, reciprocal gift-giving had strengthened bonds between lords and men.

Generosity is closely related to patronage, for young knights sought lands, wives, and other favours from the king. With growth of royal government, however, office was providing the route to influence, power, and wealth. Competition arose between professionally competent 'new men' and aristocrats, who assumed superior status alone entitled them to gifts from the king. Chroniclers and poets mirrored the conflict with their contempt for *curiales*, courtiers whom they claimed Henry II and his sons were choosing from lowborn, even servile-born servants. With John, an added accusation was that his intimates were not only low-born but also aliens. Any successful king had to balance his barons' expectations of reward with distribution of patronage to his servants, satisfying both without creating any over-mighty subjects.

By the later twelfth century, Henry II's reforms had tipped the balance of power from the barons toward the king and royal government. The Angevin kings were becoming powerful enough to discipline their greatest tenants by disseizing them of their lands, and much medieval political thought supported such strong royal authority. Some notion of the 'public power' or the king's obligation to rule for the common good was taking root with revival of Roman law concepts of the *respublica*. We can see this positive view of the civil servant in the writings of Ralph Diceto and Roger of Howden in the last decades of the twelfth century, 'a golden age of historiography in England'.[4] These two chroniclers, though not 'official' historians, combated the anti-government bias of most monastic writers. Neither was a monk: Ralph Diceto was a canon of St Paul's Cathedral, Roger a clerk in the king's service. Ralph wrote of Henry II, 'The king sought to help those of his subjects who could least help themselves, having found that the sheriffs were using the public power in their own private interests.'[5]

Gerald of Wales's character sketches of Henry II illustrate medieval writers' confusion, mixing personal vices and virtues with public qualities. He first wrote favourably of Henry, but later failure to gain office at the Angevin court made him more critical. He chronicled Henry's downfall, contrasting the tyrannical Angevins with the pious and law-abiding French monarchs. Gerald found Henry 'strenuous in warfare', 'most diligent in guarding and maintaining peace', and 'very prudent in civil life'; but unlike historians today, he found little to praise in the king's administration of justice, writing that Henry 'judged that to be right or wrong, lawful or unlawful as it served his purpose'. Gerald condemned Henry for being 'an open violator of the marriage bond'; and he faulted the king for lack of religious fervour, 'devoting scarcely an hour to the divine mysteries of the sacred Host, and that very time . . . he passed more in taking counsel and in discussion than in his devotions'.

4. Smalley, B. (1974) *Historians in the Middle Ages*, Scribner's, New York, NY p. 113.
5. Ralph Diceto. Stubbs, W. (ed.) (1876) *Radulphi de Diceto, Opera Historica* (2 vols), Rolls Series, vol. 1 pp. 434–5; Douglas, D.C., Greenaway, G.W. (eds and trans.) (1968) *English Historical Documents*, vol. 2, *1042–1189*, Eyre & Spottiswoode, Cambridge, pp. 481–2.

He also condemned Henry for exploiting vacant churches' wealth, 'bestowing on the impious soldiery the moneys which should have been given to the priesthood'. Gerald's summation of Henry's character is that he had many good qualities, but his disobedience to God and Church denied him success or happiness.[6]

William of Newburgh, a Yorkshire cleric and chronicler, proved less prejudiced against Henry II than Gerald. Although he agreed that the king was 'especially inclined to lust', had exploited vacancies, and never repented sufficiently of his severity towards Thomas Becket, surprisingly, he found Henry to have been 'the champion and defender of ecclesiastical interests and liberties, as became evident after his death'. The Newburgh chronicler, writing in the time of Richard I, recalled Henry's reign fondly, finding it preferable to his son's rule. He concluded, 'Indeed the experience of present evils has revived the memory of [Henry's] good deeds, and the man, who in his own time was hated by almost all men, is now declared to have been an excellent and profitable prince.'[7] William of Newburgh, reacting against Richard I's endless thirst for money, first to finance his crusade and then to raise his ransom, found Henry II less extortionate than his son. Roger of Howden held a similar view, asserting that once Richard was crowned, 'He put up for sale everything he had – offices, lordships, earldoms, sheriffdoms, castles, towns, lands, the lot.'[8]

Gerald of Wales, like many modern scholars found differences only in degree between the greed of Richard, his father, and his brother. He alleged that all three turned frequently to extraordinary levies, when ordinary

6. Gerald of Wales, *Opera*, vol. 5, pp. 303–5 *[Expugnatio Hibernica]*; vol. 6, p. 145 *[Itinerarum Kambriae]*; Douglas, D.C., Greenaway, G.W. (1968) (trans.), pp. 386–8.
7. William of Newburgh. Douglas, D.C., Greenaway, G.W. (eds) (1968) (trans.), pp. 371–3; Howlett, R. (ed.) (1885–90) *Historia Rerum Anglicarum of William of Newburgh*. In *Chronicles, Stephen, Henry II and Richard I* (4 vols), Rolls Series, vol. 1, pp. 280–3.
8. Roger of Howden, *Chronica*. Stubbs, W. (ed.) (1868–71) *Chronica Rogeri de Hovedene* (4 vols), Rolls Series, vol. 3, p. 13; Benedict of Peterborough. Stubbs, W. (ed.) (1867) *Gesta Regis Henrici Secundi Benedicti Abbatis* (2 vols), Rolls Series, vol. 2, p. 90.

sources of revenues failed them. Contemporaries could not appreciate that by the beginning of the thirteenth century inflation, combined with larger and longer military campaigns, was rendering traditional sources of royal income inadequate. John had no choice but to search for every possible expedient for raising revenues, including the thirteenth of 1207, a measure that approached general taxation. His financial desperation drove him to measures that his subjects considered oppressive novelties, and because he involved himself personally in extorting money his subjects could not excuse him by blaming 'evil counsellors'. No one who raises taxes is popular, as politicians today know too well.

Most writers much preferred Richard to Henry II; an example is Roger of Howden's contrast of the two: 'Those whom the father had disinherited, the son restored to their former rights; those whom the father had forced to flee, the son recalled; those whom the father had held in chains, the son permitted to go unfettered; those whom the father had burdened with various punishments in the cause of justice, the son released in the cause of pity.'[9] Vernacular writers found Richard to be a perfect chivalric prince as well as a brilliant general. The Norman author of the verse *Estoire de la Guerre Sainte*, called Richard 'the finest knight/ On earth, and the most skilled to fight'.[10] The early thirteenth-century author of the *Histoire de Guillaume le Maréchal* proclaimed that Richard, 'the courageous and the well-bred, the generous and the good giver, the enterprising and the conqueror', would have made himself master of the whole world, both Saracen and Christian, had he lived.[11] Richard of Devizes and Ralph of Coggeshall, two monastic chroniclers influenced by the poets, also treated the Lionheart as a romance hero.

9. Howden *Chronica*, vol. 3, p. 6; Benedict of Peterborough, vol. 2, p. 76.
10. Hubert, J.H., La Monte, J.L. (ed. and trans.) (1941) *Ambroise, The Crusade of Richard Lion-Heart [Estoire de la Guerre Sainte]*, Columbia UP, New York, NY, p. 441, lines 12134–7.
11. Meyer, P. (ed.) (1891–1901) *Histoire de Guillaume le Maréchal* (3 vols), Société de l'Histoire de France, Paris, vol. 2, p. 61, lines 11820–9.

Unfortunately for King John's reputation, the golden age of medieval English historiography ended in his first years. No chronicler after the deaths of Diceto and Howden early in his reign took a positive view of royal government. After the twelfth century ended, we learn of Angevin administration chiefly from its critics. If those years mark the end of the great age of historiography in England, in France the early thirteenth century saw the creation of official royal histories. The abbey of Saint Denis became, in effect, 'the official custodian and interpreter of royal history'.[12]

Philip Augustus's successes contrast strongly with John's losses. Philip expelled the Angevins from Normandy, expanded the royal domain, increased his revenues, and improved the central administration; and he found two historians – Rigord and his successor Guillaume le Breton – to glorify and sanctify his image, laying the groundwork for later Capetian royal ideology. Of Philip's Angevin opponents, he is certainly more comparable to King John than to Richard I. Hardly heroic or a model of chivalry, he shared unattractive traits with John: lustful, authoritarian, cynical, suspicious and duplicitous. But Philip's image as a model monarch, shaped by his historians, took hold. Robert Fawtier's widely cited 1942 work on the Capetian monarchs describes him as 'tirelessly active, a brave and daring war leader, a prudent and skilful diplomat, reorganising his kingdom internally after a fashion that influenced the character of the French monarchy for centuries'.[13]

Rigord and Guillaume le Breton saw Philip's mission of enlarging and strengthening the French monarchy as justifying his evil deeds. Rigord's *Gesta Philippi Augusti*, a narrative to 1206, was the first of a number of semi-official chronicles written by monks at Saint Denis for the French kings; it first depicts Philip as a protector of the Church, using the phrase 'defense of the Church' to justify royal policies. Later, however, Rigord had to

12. Spiegel, G.M. (1978) *The Chronicle Tradition of Saint Denis: A Survey*, Classical Folio Editions, Brookline, Mass., p. 7.
13. Fawtier, R. (1960) *The Capetian Kings of France*, translated by Butler, L., Adam, R. J., Macmillan, pp. 24–5.

recognize his patron's faults, especially his scandalous repudiation of his Danish bride, his bigamous marriage, and his plundering of ecclesiastical property.

Rigord's continuator Guillaume le Breton, was one of Philip Augustus's clerks who enjoyed the post of official royal historian, and the monks of Saint Denis later incorporated his work into their chronicles. In his *Gesta Philippi* and verse *Philippide*, he also portrayed the French king as a protector of the Church, even depicting the battle of Bouvines as in the Church's defence, because the enemy leaders were excommunicates and allies of Albigensian heretics. Guillaume pictured Philip as a monarch who ruled his people peacefully and with paternal affection. According to him, the king and his people competed to see which loved the other more.

How does Philip II in fact compare with his Angevin enemies? Contemporaries found only Richard Lionheart a sufficiently generous king; the Capetian monarch earned condemnation for parsimony, and poets and other writers seeking largess at his court were likely to be disappointed. Two accounts of the Third Crusade, one in French verse and another in Latin prose, contrasted Richard's magnanimity with Philip Augustus's meanness. Even Gerald of Wales, harsh critic of the Angevin kings, found Richard I praiseworthy for his 'immense gift-giving and almsgiving'.[14] Two English monastic chroniclers, Richard of Devizes, a Winchester monk, and Ralph, abbot of Coggeshall, also contrasted Richard I's generosity on crusade with Philip Augustus's miserliness. Rigord excused the French king's lack of patronage for poets and singers, claiming that he preferred giving to the truly needy poor.

Neither did Philip demonstrate the chivalric virtue of prowess; he looks decidedly unheroic beside Richard Lionheart. Indeed, his awareness that he could not compete with Richard for military glory may have caused his early departure from the Holy Land. The French king often appears paranoid, even fearing that Richard had hired fanatical Arab assassins to kill him. Philip won his victories more by diplomacy or scheming than by armed

14. Gerald of Wales, *Opera*, vol. 8, p. 248.

might. He proved a master at sowing dissension, as seen in his success in splitting Henry II from his sons and John from his crusading brother, earning him an unsavoury reputation as a plunderer of a crusader's property. Philip Augustus did not prove to be a particularly bold warrior in his conflict with Richard, 1194–99, or his campaign in Normandy against John, 1202–04. Philip's victory in Normandy is sometimes attributed more to John's shortcomings than to his own military skills. Recently, scholars have turned to France's superior financial resources to account for Philip's easy conquest of Normandy; whether he or John had greater revenues for conduct of the war is a much debated question. Chroniclers, seeking an explanation in personal morality, blamed John's loss on his marriage to Isabelle of Angoulême. The battle of Bouvines in 1214 enabled Capetian partisans to skip over Philip's earlier unimpressive military record to concentrate on this victory over John's coalition, depicting him as a great warrior. Guillaume le Breton transformed Bouvines into a mythical struggle of good versus evil, a massive trial by combat, and also a national victory, fought for all 'children of France'.[15]

Unlike John, Philip took care to cultivate good relations with the Church, although the conflict over his rejection of his Danish wife complicated matters. Philip Augustus won the French Church's support with a promise of free elections in his new province of Normandy, contrasting with previous Angevin policy there. Only twice did he interfere in episcopal elections to install his own candidate, both times early in his reign. He yielded to the temptation to plunder ecclesiastical property during the interdict of 1200, however, confiscating property of bishops who enforced the ban on religious services. Later he renounced regalian rights over vacant bishoprics, but soon reverted to a policy of exploiting vacancies little different from the Angevins' exercise of that privilege. The fruit of his cultivation of friendly relations with the Church was his depiction in French chronicles as its defender.

Philip could not escape entirely charges of greed, but

---

15. Duby, G. (1990) *The Legend of Bouvines*, translated by Tihanyi, C., pp. 154–5.

lucky circumstances brought him great profit without burdening his subjects too heavily with taxes. In his first decade, two windfalls vastly increased his revenues: his savage spoliation of the Jews, 1180–82, yielded possibly 15,000 silver marks; and Richard I paid relief of 24,000 marks following his father's death.[16] The feudal incidents proved as lucrative to Philip Augustus as to the Angevin kings; sums paid to him as relief are as spectacular as any paid to the English kings. John himself had paid a 20,000-mark relief in 1200 as part of the settlement at Le Goulet. Although documentation is sparse, Philip apparently exploited as shamelessly as the Angevins his right to wardship of minors. The mother of the young count of Troyes offered 15,000 *l. parisis* and other concessions to have custody of her son. Such enormous sums could add a quarter to a third to a year's royal revenues. During 1190–1203, Philip succeeded in increasing his revenues by 50 per cent, giving him an ample war chest for his final push to oust John from Normandy. With such superior resources, he could afford to forego the frequent financial extortions that were earning John his subjects' hatred.

Philip II's policies toward his vassals parallel those of his Angevin rival. Like John, he sought new lands for himself and for his *familiares* by controlling the marriages of heiresses of his major vassals and by intervening in noble inheritances whenever uncertainty of succession afforded an excuse for royal acquisition. Also like John, Philip appeared distrustful, demanding guarantees of his magnates' loyalty by giving charters of fealty and hostages. His tendency to deny great men any place in his councils, restricting his counsellors to a handful of new men, aroused complaints from otherwise admiring French chroniclers. One vernacular writer echoed complaints levelled at John, accusing Philip of relying upon common soldiers for advice. A contrast appears in the Angevins' and Capetians' rewards to their counsellors drawn from sons of lower-ranking knights. The Angevin monarchs'

16. A word about medieval money: a mark was $\frac{2}{3}$ of a pound, or 13s. 6d. £1 sterling equalled 4 *livres angevins*; 1 *livre parisien* (*l. parisis*) equalled 1.46 *livres angevins*. The pound was divided into 20 shillings (s.), the shilling into 12 pence (d.).

patronage to such servants aroused resentment among their magnates. While under King John men of obscure origin acquired baronies or bishoprics, Philip Augustus proved much less generous. None of his knights broke into the baronage, and out of seventy-five bishops elected during his reign, only five were royal clerks.

King John, unfortunately, lacked official historians to put a good light on his failures. Instead, monastic authors, sitting in strongholds of local privilege, unsympathetic to royal government, suspicious of any change that threatened social stability, would write the history of his reign. The only contemporary author approaching John without blatant bias is the anonymous Barnwell annalist (or 'Walter of Coventry'), writing c. 1202–25. The best that he could say of John is that, 'like Marius, he experienced the ups and downs of fortune'. He concluded that the king's own men abandoned him because he was 'a pillager of his own people'.[17]

The chroniclers most influential in creating John's bad historical reputation are the two St Albans writers, Roger of Wendover and Matthew Paris. England is unique in having its greatest medieval histories, the St Albans chronicles, written with an anti-royalist bias. Roger of Wendover wrote in retrospect, viewing John's reign in light of the struggles of Henry III's minority. By the time that he began writing, a 'myth' of John's wickedness apparently already had taken shape in clerical and monastic circles. He did not first draw this sinister portrait, but he added shading and colour. Wendover handed on a pro-baronial bias to Matthew Paris who succeeded him as historian at St Albans in 1235. Matthew Paris, in his borrowings from Wendover, made no change in the basic picture of Bad King John, since he viewed Henry III's conflict with his barons as a continuation of John's earlier quarrel. He simply added darker shading to blacken the portrait further. V.H. Galbraith said, 'Paris' portrait is a creation of literature: as fictitious as Shakespeare's Falstaff;' and he concluded, 'Paris' additions

17. Barnwell Chronicle. Stubbs, W. (ed.) (1872–3) *Memoriale Walteri de Coventria* (2 vols), Rolls Series, vol. 2, p. 232.

to Wendover for [John's] reign are not merely worthless, but very misleading . . .'.[18]

Not all John's wickedness was imagined by idle monks. His need for money drove him to arbitrary rule; but his distasteful, even dangerous personality traits, among them a streak of pettiness or spitefulness, also impelled him towards tyranny. He thirsted for revenge and crowed at the humbling of his rivals. Especially damning was John's spite against his great men for real or imagined slights; typical is his taunting of the highly respected William Marshal during 1205–08 when he was out of royal favour, seeking to harass him by harming his retainers. Members of the royal entourage could contrast the king's petty conduct with the earl's dignity.

We cannot doubt King John's capacity for cruelty, which chroniclers described and often embellished. He was responsible for political murders on at least four occasions: the strangling or drowning of his nephew, Arthur of Brittany, possibly by his own hand; the deliberate death by starvation of the wife and son of his former friend, the Welsh marcher lord William de Braose; the hanging of twenty-eight hostages, sons of Welsh chieftains; and the hanging of the prophet Peter of Wakefield with his son. Several others died in his dungeons, whether at his command or simply due to harsh conditions; among them was a former exchequer official, Geoffrey of Norwich, who may or may not have been crushed under the weight of a leaden cope.

John's cruelty must be put in context, however. In a brutal age, he did not stand alone among monarchs for acts of cruelty, or even murders. His brutality differed little from that of fellow rulers with much better reputations, and his crimes in no way compare with the carnage wreaked by twentieth-century dictators. Yet John went beyond the lax standards of his own age with his role in Arthur of Brittany's death. The murder of one's own nephew, even if he was a dangerous political rival, disgusted medieval aristocrats with their strong

18. Galbraith, V.H. (1944) 'Roger Wendover and Matthew Paris'. David Murray Lecture, University of Glasgow Publications. Reprinted in (1982) *Kings and Chroniclers*, Hambledon Press, pp. 35, 37.

sense of family solidarity. John again moved beyond acceptable bounds of noble conduct in his pursuit of William de Braose, when he caused the deaths of his wife Matilda and their son through cruel conditions of imprisonment. Medieval monarchs who limited their cruelty to non-Christians were less likely to suffer condemnation by chroniclers. Richard Lionheart's massacre of nearly 3000 Muslim prisoners at Acre in 1191 aroused no complaints. Neither did Philip Augustus's savage expulsion of the Jews from his domain in 1180–82, first stripping them of their property and then exiling them. The chronicler Rigord only complained of the king's later decision to allow their return.

Chief among King John's faults in contemporaries' eyes were his failures on the battlefield. In contrast to his brother Richard Lionheart, he appeared as incompetent in warfare, failing to defend Normandy 1202–04, failing in his effort to regain it in 1214, and dying during a stalemated war against rebel barons. Yet warfare was a central concern for John; he was at war or planning for war throughout his reign. His reputed lack of courage comes chiefly from comments by chroniclers, who had little interest in details of warfare. Contemporaries spoke of John in his youth as lacking the warrior's vigour, 'somewhat slack of spirit, and loving quiet' or 'more given to luxurious ease than to warlike exercise'.[19] Particularly damaging was the epithet applied to John, 'Softsword' (*Mollegladium*),[20] assumed today to derive from his loss of Normandy. In fact, the chronicler Gervase of Canterbury states that John's detractors, hostile to the peace he had made with Philip Augustus, first applied it in 1200. Gervase himself thought the king had been wise in preferring peace to war. Most damning to John's reputation was his failure to defend Normandy, depicted by Roger of Wendover as due to his lazing about in bed with his young bride.

Some modern historians have succeeded in looking beyond chroniclers' anecdotes about John's military in-

19. Robert of Auxerre, *Recueil des Historiens des Gaules et de la France*, vol. 18, p. 263; Gerald of Wales, *Opera*, vol. 5, p. 200.
20. Gervase of Canterbury. Stubbs, W. (ed.) (1879–80) *Gervase of Canterbury, Historical Works* (2 vols), Rolls Series, vol. 2, pp. 92–3.

capacity. They recognize that victory in medieval warfare went not to the chivalric hero heedlessly pursuing glory, but to the cautious commander who plundered his enemy's resources and besieged his castles, avoiding pitched battles. They find that John was no coward, and that he showed competence as a military planner, especially at strategy; his attempted relief of Château Gaillard, and on a grander scale, the two-pronged 1214 campaign against Philip Augustus bear them out. Unlike many medieval generals, John showed himself skilled both as builder and besieger of castles; his success at Rochester Castle in November 1215 reveals his siegecraft. As one scholar has written, 'John's military skill has not seldom been severely underestimated by historians and much too much prominence has been given to his alleged title of "Softsword".'[21]

Although John had potential for success, with intelligence, administrative ability, a flair for military strategy and for diplomtic intrigue, too many personality flaws limited him. One of John's faults was a lack of proportion, a propensity for pushing things too far, so that an action that should have brought success ended in failure. As W.L. Warren phrased it, John 'could not resist the temptation to kick a man when he was down'.[22] For example, his marriage to Isabelle of Angoulême may have been a brilliant move on the chessboard of Poitevin politics, allying him with a family that controlled the roads between Poitiers and Bordeaux; but he lost any advantage through his contemptuous treatment of her fiancé, Hugh de Lusignan, refusing him any compensation. Another example, combining character faults, is John's action following his victory at Mirebeau in 1202. His arrogance after the battle, his cruelty to his captives cost him any advantage won from his military achievement, provoking defections by important Loire valley vassals. Definitely pushing things too far was the

---

21. Brown, R. A. (1989) *Castles, Conquest and Charters: Collected papers*, Boydell & Brewer, Woodbridge, pp. 203–4. Reprint of (1951) 'Framlingham Castle and Bigod 1154–1216'. *Proceedings of the Suffolk Institute of Archaeology*, 25.
22. Warren, W.L. (1961) *King John*, California UP, Berkeley, Ca./Eyre Methuen, p. 71.

murder of his chief captive. Arthur of Brittany, his own nephew and rival claimant to the Angevin inheritance.

Also illustrating John's lack of proportion are his efforts at one moment to enhance the royal dignity, undone by his 'indecent levity' at another.[23] He sported splendid trappings that his father and brother had neglected, celebrating feastdays with crown-wearing and chanting of the *Christus Vincit* and keeping two trumpeters in his household. John loved fine clothing and jewelry; and he gave great attention to the royal gem collection, adding to it with gifts and purchases, perhaps betraying an aesthete's sense usually associated with his son, Henry III.

If John sought at times to enhance his royal majesty with splendour, at other times he could undermine respect with a lack of dignity and a coarse and crude sense of humour. His savage tongue, which sometimes still speaks out when reading his writs, 'could wound the more because it was informed by wit and observation'.[24] John's oscillating between gravity and crudity indicates a characteristic inconsistency. He can be compared to a twentieth-century US president, the Texan Lyndon B. Johnson, a cunning politician, who grasped at a statesman's dignity, but who clumsily undermined his quest for respect with crude conduct.

Clearly, John lacked the likeable qualities of his two predecessors that had enabled them to earn popularity in spite of arbitrary acts and financial extortions little different from his. Subjects of Henry II and Richard had frequently suffered from royal anger or ill-will. Those rulers could display on occasion, however, the chivalric courtesy that John lacked. The author of the *Histoire de Guillaume le Maréchal* despised King John and always sought to show him in as unfavourable a light as possible. Nonetheless, he appears correct in depicting John as a resentful and suspicious ruler, whose pride blinded him, who would not listen to reason, and who lost his barons' affection even before the loss of Normandy. Chancery

23. Norgate, K. (1902) *John Lackland*, Macmillan, p. 62.
24. Powicke, F.M. (1929) 'England: Richard I and John'. Chapter 7 in Tanner, J.R., Prévite-Orton, C.W., Brooke, Z.N. (eds) *Cambridge Medieval History*, vol. 6, Cambridge UP, p. 219.

records document John's secretive, suspicious nature, his conviction that conspiracies threatened him.

Since John could not win his barons' affection, he sought to rule them through fear. In his view, the tie of homage and fealty was an insufficient guarantee of barons' loyalty. He demanded charters of prospective fealty by which they surrendered any right to their land should they fall under suspicion or fail to perform services. In effect, they had to disclaim in advance any right to due process. John also demanded hostages as guarantees of faithful service, not an uncommon practice in his age, one that Stephen Langton sanctioned. Baronial fear and distrust of John, however, confronted them with a dilemma when he demanded their sons as hostages. Handing over hostages was difficult once rumours spread of Arthur of Brittany's disappearance while in his uncle's custody, and news of John's hanging of twenty-eight sons of Welsh nobles in 1211 made it more difficult.

Despite John's inability to win the trust or respect of some powerful subjects, he did succeed in recruiting capable and loyal servants. He retained some of his predecessor's ablest administrators; his chancellor Hubert Walter and his justiciar Geoffrey fitz Peter remained at their posts until their deaths. Some of the most respected barons, such as William Marshal or Ranulf of Chester, remained loyal to the king despite occasional quarrels. John also recruited to his service capable new men, administrators such as Hubert de Burgh or Peter des Roches as well as mercenary captains, although their low or foreign origins alienated the English aristocracy. What was it that won John such loyalty? In William Marshal's case, he owed all that he had to the Angevin monarchs. Perhaps for others, such as the earl of Chester, engrained loyalty to an anointed king and sworn lord took priority over any grievances. While for Poitevin mercenaries and clerks of humble origin, promise of patronage must have outweighed the menace of John's unpleasant personality.

John's barons never coalesced into a monolithic block of opponents. Although an opposition party eventually took shape, a few barons were courtiers, seeking advantage from their proximity to the king, while others remained preoccupied with local affairs, little concerned with high politics. John's suspicion of his barons prevented his seeking their advice as a corporate body, however, and turned him toward taking counsel with trusted intimates of his *familia*, or household. William Marshal's biographer pictures the king preferring the counsel of his 'bachelors' or household knights over that of his barons. John's reliance upon his household came at a time when many barons were voicing concepts of government *per consilium* that stressed their right to counsel and consent as spokesmen for the *regnum* as a whole.

Historians agree that one of John's most serious failures was his inability to manage his magnates. Mutual mistrust characterized his relations with a number of them, and periodically he or one of his barons manifested untrustworthiness that simply fuelled the other's suspicion. John's mistrust made him turn to his mercenary captains for counsel, and that reliance increased their suspicions of the king. No king could afford to alienate his great men by passing over them in favour of alien or low-born newcomers when seeking counsel or distributing spoils of government. Even though Angevin policies of royal centralization had weakened the baronage, it was still a formidable force, with armed men and castles, capable of exercising control over the countryside, with means to mount an armed rebellion. Any monarch needed to keep them contented, if his realm was to remain peaceful. John's failure to secure the devotion of more than a handful of magnates contributed heavily to his other failures. Defections of Angevin and Norman nobles in 1202–03 made impossible any effective resistance to Philp Augustus's advance; English barons increasingly opposed John's military plans for recovery of his continental lands, 1205–14; and Poitevin nobles' unreliability in 1214 spoiled his plan for a giant pincer movement to trap the French.

Also capable of mounting fierce opposition, although not by material means, was the Church. Should these two act in concert against a monarch, they could present an almost irresistible force. Although Henry II and Richard I quarrelled with individual magnates and churchmen, their personalities made possible relatively rapid healing of wounds. King John, of course, quarrelled with both of these groups, first with the Church over the appointment of the archbishop of Canterbury. The baronage gave no support to their clerical cousins, 1205–13, enjoying a pause in royal financial demands due to John's seizure of church property. Once barons resolved to resist the king with force in the months preceding Magna Carta, elements of the two coalesced, with English ecclesiastics' emphasis on government *per judicium* providing theoretical underpinning for baronial opposition to John's arbitrary acts. In any comparison with his contemporaries, King John falls short. Certainly he experienced massive failures, seeing careful plans miscarry. Yet thirteenth-century poets and chroniclers exaggerated John's moral flaws and underestimated his skills as a soldier, and later generations have likewise emphasized or ignored aspects of his personality or his political ability in accord with changing fashions in historiography. Although new perspectives, sharpened by study of administrative records, may present us with a clearer picture of John, his own context – the outlook of his own contemporaries – cannot be ignored when seeking an accurate view of him.

Chapter 2

YOUNG JOHN IN HIS BROTHERS' SHADOWS

. . .

JOHN'S CHILDHOOD AND YOUTH

Today's image of the family took form in the nineteenth century, when children were seen as happy little innocents, protected by a benevolent despot of a father and a nearly angelic mother. In the early twentieth century, Freudian psychology taught that a child's earliest years shape his or her adult personality, making the modern world 'obsessed by the physical, moral and sexual problems of childhood'.[1] This has led to growth of a subdivision of historical studies, psychohistory. Because too few scraps of information about King John's childhood survive, no psycho-historical study of him is possible. Nonetheless, his suspicious and devious character invites speculation about early influences that shaped his adult personality.

A key to John's character is the fact that he was the youngest child of Henry II and Eleanor of Aquitaine, the last of five sons and three daughters, nine years younger than his next brother, Geoffrey of Brittany (the eldest, William, had died in infancy). Eleanor gave birth to John at Oxford on Christmas eve 1167. Feudal custom decreed that the youngest son should inherit nothing, unless some expendable peripheral lands; yet John's father was determined to secure lands for him, inspiring his elder

1. Aries, P. (1960) *L'Enfant et la vie familiale sous l'Ancien Régime*, Librarie Plon, Paris (trans.) Baldic, R. (1962), p. 395.

brothers' jealousy and suspicion. Especially resentful was his eldest brother, Henry the Younger whom Henry II had crowned king in 1170 to ensure the succession; his royal title made him extremely conscious of his rights and privileges. This rivalry fuelled the three elder boys' revolt in 1173–74, the greatest challenge to Henry II's authority that he had to face. By the 1180s each brother was jostling the others in efforts to get as much of the Angevin lands for himself as he could, even at his brothers' expense. Henry's eldest son was engaged in another rebellion at the time of his death in 1183, and Richard was winning a war against his father when Henry died in 1189, just after learning that John had joined in the revolt.

John's position as lastborn son with uncertain prospects for land or power must have contributed to a negative estimate of his own worth; such self-doubts would have pressed him to assert strongly his will once he secured his crown. Perhaps John's childhood insecurity contributed to his adult personality, his jealousy, sensitivity to slights, thirst for revenge, and delight in humbling rivals. The glorious reputations of his father and his brother Richard added to whatever sense of inadequacy he might have had. The unexpectedness of his own succession may account for his love of banquets, jewelry, and fine clothing, his desire to surround himself with the splendid trappings of monarchy that his father and brother had ignored. Unlike his predecessors' successions, his was contested by his nephew, Arthur of Brittany; hence he felt a need to enhance his royal dignity with such symbols of sacral monarchy as ceremonial crown-wearings. John's childhood and adolescent experiences certainly contributed to his suspicious personality, his distrustful nature, and to his assertive and authoritarian character once he ascended the throne.

Medieval royal families had little in common with today's nuclear family. Indeed, twelfth-century Latin had no equivalent to the modern word 'family'; *cognati*, *consanguinei*, or *parentes* had looser meanings including kinfolk outside the nuclear group. The Latin *familia* is a false cognate, better translated as 'household'. Noble families did not centre on the nurturing and socialization of children. Instead, aristocratic families sometime after

A.D. 1000 took on a vertical appearance, what is termed in technical language an agnatic lineage or patrilineage, described by one scholar as 'a kind of fellowship of males, stretching backwards and forwards over time'.[2] Such a family pattern viewed the patrimony as an indivisible inheritance, succeeding by strict male primogeniture to eldest son. It fostered insecurity and competition within the family because the eldest son could not achieve full adult status or assume governing responsibilities as long as his father held lands and title, condemning the heir to remain a 'youth' for years past actual adolescence and tempting him to take up arms against his father.

Because little can be learned about John's upbringing, it seems best to focus on two spheres: first the 'social investment', the personnel and resources employed; and second the 'psychological investment', Henry's and Eleanor's personal involvement with him.[3] Medieval royalty had little time for child-rearing, and they, like the rich and powerful throughout history, turned their children when quite young over to the care of others. Few great ladies actually nursed their children, and like most noblewomen, Eleanor turned the newborn John over to a wet-nurse for suckling. Even though spiritual writers of the Middle Ages encouraged nursing, equating it with the maternal aspects of nurturing, the failure of noblewomen to do so does not necessarily indict them for child neglect. A noble lady's chief responsibility was ensuring continuity of her husband's line by giving birth, not rearing children; and it was commonly believed that breast-feeding prevented pregnancy.

The feudal nobility of both England and France often sent their children away to be reared in other noble households. English feudal custom recognized no special right for the mother to nurture her minor children in case their father's death placed them in their lord's custody.

2. Herlihy, D. (1985) *Medieval Households*, Harvard UP Cambridge, Mass., p. 82.
3. David Herlihy's terms, Herlihy, D. 'Medieval Children' in Ladner, B.K., Philips, K.R. (eds) (1978) *Essays on Medieval Civilization*, Texas UP, Austin, p. 120.

Children of royalty were separated from their parents even earlier and more often than most noble children. Since Henry II and Eleanor of Aquitaine were constantly on the move from castle to castle or across the Channel to and from the Continent, it often proved inconvenient for their children to accompany them. Eleanor frequently travelled with one or two of her children, but never with all of them together. Only on the occasion of the Church's feasts is it certain that royal parents and children came together. This meant that closest ties of affection for the royal children were not necessarily with their parents, but spread widely to other relatives, knightly retainers, and servants of lower rank.

Like most great ladies, Eleanor had responsibility for an elaborate household and even for governing in her husband's absence. She did not necessarily view rearing of children as her primary responsibility. Indeed, it was during Eleanor's childbearing years, before John's birth, that she was most active in English government. Her movements are uncertain after John's birth in December 1167, but she seems to have spent most of her time between 1168 and 1174 in Poitiers, apart from her husband Henry II and her younger children, busying herself with the politics of Aquitaine and plotting against her husband. She deposited John and his sister Joan, her two smallest children, at Fontevrault abbey, where he remained until aged six or so. Perhaps the intention was to prepare him for an ecclesiastical career, often the fate of younger sons in great families.

It is clear that royal parents made a heavy 'social investment' in their offspring, even if they failed to play a personal part. The most basic test of the care that they received is their mortality rate; only one of Henry's and Eleanor's children is known to have died in infancy, and four sons and three daughters attained adulthood. Pipe rolls record expenses for young Henry, especially for his coronation, and for daughters' marriages; but no expenditures on John were recorded before 1176. Then revenues of the vacant abbey of Peterborough provided £4 6s. 8d. for his expenses.

Although the parents did not consider personal supervision of their children's rearing an exclusively parental

23

responsibility, they chose with care the personnel who did supervise them. Wet-nurses were selected from women of free, not servile status, probably from wives of household servants. The wet-nurses must have resembled modern nannies in their relations with their charges, remaining with them long after weaning and winning their affection. Richard Lionheart's and John's wet-nurses earned their fond feeling; John had a nurse named Hodierna, and when king, he granted her a pension.

In addition, each of Henry II's sons had a *magister* or *praeceptor*, one of the *familiares regis* assigned primary responsibility for him, charged with spending on the child's needs and supervising the servants caring for him. Such a *magister* took charge of Henry and Eleanor's eldest son as early as his first year, 1156. The *magister* was not necessarily a cleric, and he did not give lessons; teachers – also called *magistri* – could be recruited from the clerks and chaplains present in any great household. After a noble youth reached adolescence, a knight took charge of his chivalric education, just as the young hero of a vernacular romance had his companion-guide.

John had left Fontevrault to join Henry II by the time that his elder brothers, inspired by their mother, revolted against their father, 1173–74; and he sailed to England with his father and his sister Joan in July 1174. In Henry II's household, the *curiales* or courtiers who depended on winning royal favour were discussing and practising the qualities needed to secure his patronage. Their critics depicted them in moralistic or satirical writings as ambitious, greedy, and sycophantic. They often needed to disguise their true feelings to fawn upon superiors or to plot against rivals. Such an atmosphere of jealousy, deceit, and intrigue must have taught young John lessons that he put into practice in adulthood.

Once Henry II and his sons were reconciled after the 1173–74 rebellion, he handed John over to young Henry's household, although he joined his father's court on great feastdays. Young Henry was charming and courteous, but incautious, shallow and irresponsible, committed to chivalric pursuits and to political plotting, hardly a model for John to emulate. His household was hardly an atmosphere in which the boy would imbibe maturity, responsibility, and trust. Indeed, it was filled with factions and informers, for a split developed between servants selected by Henry II and loyal to him and companions of the young king's own choosing, contemptuous of his father. The prince was so impecunious that his household piled up debts, which his father had to pay off periodically. Walter Map, a courtier who knew Young Henry well, described him as 'a prodigy of unfaith and prodigal of ill, a limpid spring of wickedness'.[4] He was a knight errant surrounded by a band of other landless youths, who like him were waiting impatiently to come into their inheritances. With his knightly companions, he amused himself by travelling from tournament to tournament, 'transformed from a king into a knight'.[5]

Young King Henry's mentor was William Marshal, assigned to teach him courtesy and martial arts, much admired for chivalry, but an illiterate with little interest in administration. The name of John's *magister* during his years of adolescence does not survive, but he was acquiring a staff of his own, even though living in the households of others. During 1177–78, while he was in Normandy, he had his own chamberlain, a servant in charge of his horses, and two serving women. In March 1185, when John was eighteen and lord of Ireland, preparing to take possession of his new lordship, he gained an elaborate establishment. Henry II arranged for experienced royal counsellors to accompany him to Ireland.

Young John first witnessed a royal charter in England early in 1182; and when Henry II crossed the Channel, he placed the boy in the household of the justiciar, Ranulf de Glanvill. John, then about fifteen, found himself in a veritable school for royal administrators, an environment quite different from Young Henry's household. One of John's companions in Glanvill's household was Hubert Walter, first Richard I's justiciar and then

4. James, M. R. (ed. and trans.) (1983) *De Nugis curialium*. Revised by Brooke, C.N.L., Mynor, R.A.B., Oxford UP (Oxford Medieval Texts), pp. 282–3.
5. Ralph Diceto. Stubbs, W. (ed.) (1876) *Radulphi de Diceto, Opera Historica* (2 vols), Rolls Series , vol. 1, p. 428; Hallam, E. (trans.) (1986) *The Plantagenet Chronicles*, Weidenfeld & Nicolson, p. 152.

John's chancellor. This was John's first long sojourn in England, and at such an age it must have made an impact. Among the administrators accompanying him to Ireland in 1185 were associates from Glanvill's household. John remembered Glanvill's household fondly enough to grant land to Ranulf and his nephew, Theobald Walter, while in Ireland and in 1202 to forgive a debt still owed by the justiciar's heirs. Perhaps John's later interest in details of royal government stems in part from the three years he spent in Glanvill's household.

A significant aspect of the 'social investment' in royal children is their education. Of course, they received the preparation for knighthood typical of noble youths. Roger of Howden wrote of Henry II's sons, 'They strove to outdo others in handling weapons. They realized that without practice the art of war did not come naturally when it was needed.'[6] Hunting sharpened knightly skills, and John shared his Norman ancestors' love for the chase. Among the earliest expenditures for him were purchases of horses and harness; when John sailed for Ireland in 1185, his huntsman required a separate ship for horses and hounds.

Sons of royalty needed to know more than skill in handling horses and weapons, however. Scholars and theologians throughout the Middle Ages urged that princes receive an education that would acquaint them with Scriptures and ancient history. Henry II had studied with the best teachers available, benefiting from a long tradition of learning among the counts of Anjou. Intellectual interests that he had acquired in childhood remained with him, and he attracted to his court a brilliant band of writers. Less is known about the schooling of Henry's sons than his own, but we can assume that he saw the value of education and sought the best for them. No formal office of royal schoolmaster existed, yet evidence indicates that the boys acquired a sound grounding in Latin grammar. Richard Lionheart's correcting of Archbishop Hubert Walter's Latin is a well-known example of his

6. Roger of Howden, *Chronica*, Stubbs, W. (1868–71) *Chronica Rogeri de Hovedene* (4 vols), Rolls Series, vol. 2, p. 166.

competence. John gained an interest in literature during his youth, and as king he built up a considerable library of classics and religious works. He deposited a number of volumes at Reading abbey for safekeeping, and he sometimes wrote to the abbot acknowledging receipt of copies. There is little doubt that John had more formal education than did Philip Augustus of France, whose literacy in Latin was limited.

It is more difficult to estimate royal parents' 'psychological investment' in their children. So little evidence survives for medieval aristocrats' personal feelings toward their young children that some scholars have speculated that they lacked the affection that parents today are expected to feel. The *Histoire de Guillaume le Maréchal*, indeed, indicates that William's father had no great affection for him, a younger son. When the boy was held hostage at age four or five, threatened with death, his father replied that he had 'the hammer and the anvils to make more and better sons'.[7] The psychological investment of medieval English royalty in their children seems generally not to have been great. Yet the family life of Henry II, Eleanor of Aquitaine, and their children had more than most royal families' share of hostility.

The stormy relationship between Henry II and his sons is almost a classic example of father-son relations in feudal society. They saw him preventing their attaining full manhood with lands and authority of their own, and their resentment pushed them into rebellion. Henry was a restless man with a violent temper, and his sons often bore the brunt of his impatience and anger. The estrangement between Henry and his queen by 1170 must have had an effect on their children's feelings, and the couple's hostility can account for some of the boys' lack of affection for their father. Once they reached adolescence, they lacked any loyalty to him; and their rebellions gave a tragic quality to his last years. Chroniclers saw the faithlessness of the king's sons as God's just punishment for his sins. Gerald of Wales sums up Henry's relations with his sons:

7. Crouch, D. (1990) *William Marshal: Court, Career and Chivalry in the Angevin Empire, 1147–1219*, Longman, pp. 16, 20.

On his legitimate children he lavished in their childhood more than a father's affection, but in their more advanced years he looked askance at them after the manner of a step-father; and although his sons were so renowned and illustrious he pursued his successors with a hatred which perhaps they deserved, but which none the less impaired his own happiness ... Whether by some breach of the marriage tie or as a punishment for some crime of the parent, it befell that there was never true affection felt by the father towards his sons, nor by the sons towards their father, nor harmony among the brothers themselves.[8]

William of Newburgh, a northern chronicler, wrote of Henry II's 'inordinate love for his sons' and accused him of trampling on others' rights 'while he exerted himself unduly for their advancement'.[9] Yet little concrete evidence survives for Henry's feelings toward his children except his schemes for succession to his lands. It is difficult to know whether Henry II was applying any principle in his partition of his territories, whether he had any vision of the Angevin domains as a unity or viewed them simply as a block of family lands to be used to provide for his offspring.[10]

Henry gave his sons honorific titles in 1169 when they were adolescents, hinting at an 'Angevin empire' with at least a loose structure held together by family ties. His eldest son and namesake, crowned king of England in 1170 at age fifteen, was to have the Anglo-Norman realm together with greater Anjou (Anjou plus Maine and Touraine); his second son, Richard, was proclaimed duke of Aquitaine, when he was fourteen; and Geoffrey became count of Brittany through marriage at age eleven; along with his continental county went the English earldom of

8. Gerald of Wales *Expugnatio Hibernica* in Dimock J.F. *et al.* (ed.) (1861–91) *Giraldi Cambreusis Opera* (8 vols), Rolls Series, vol. 5, pp. 302–6; translation Douglas, D.C., Greenaway, G.W. (1968) *English Historical Documents*, vol. 2, *1042–1189*, Eyre & Spottiswoode, Cambridge, p. 388.
9. William of Newburgh. Howlett, R. (ed.) (1885–90) *Historia Revum Anglicarum of William of Newburgh*. In *Chronicles, Stephen, Henry II and Richard I* (4 vols), Rolls Series, vol. 1, p. 281; translation Douglas, D.C., Greenaway, G.W. (1968) vol. 2, p. 372.
10. See below, pages 61–66.

Richmond. Little John 'Lackland' had no place in this tripartite partition.

Most scholars agree that Henry II followed feudal custom in rejecting strict primogeniture succession of Younger Henry to all his domains; he had both Angevin and Anglo-Norman precedent in feudal law for his scheme. Probably Henry held the hope that as his sons grew up, he could share the governing of the Angevin domains with them, withdrawing from day-to-day work into something like 'the chairman of a family consortium'.[11] Also he expected that after his death his sons would maintain an alliance, cemented by ties of vassalage, with periodic consultation among them and concerted action for mutual assistance. If so, he was to be sorely disappointed. His sons were unwilling to play the parts assigned to them; they felt that he never gave them adequate authority or incomes appropriate to their titles. He never granted his sons estates in their titular territories that would have supplied them with independent resources; neither did he grant Henry the Younger or Richard lordships in England, as he did Geoffrey and later John.

The birth of John in 1167 exacerbated relations between Henry II and his older sons, for he did not want his lastborn to remain 'John Lackland'. His periodic new schemes for partition of his empire angered Young Henry, Richard, and Geoffrey, feeding their jealousy of each other and of their youngest brother. Such schemes especially aroused Richard's resentment once his elder brother's death promoted him to senior rank among the sons. Any younger son had uncertain prospects; and since Richard and Geoffrey were ahead of John in any division of Henry II's acquisitions, his prospects were even less certain. He must have known from literature and from his own family's history that the youngest of several sons often got nothing. Twelfth-century vernacular poetry is filled with tales of younger sons forced to leave home to seek their fortunes as knights errant. Insecurity about his

11. Warren, W.L. (1973) *Henry II*, California UP, Berkeley, Ca./Eyre Methuen, pp. 560, 574.

future, rivalry with his brothers, and awareness of their resentment over his father's schemes to find land for him must have influenced John's character. No youth growing up in such an atmosphere of suspicion and treachery could fail to absorb some poisons.

In 1173, Henry II planned to use his lastborn son to seal an alliance he was seeking with Count Humbert III of Maurienne, part of a strategy to expand Angevin influence in the South of France. John was to marry Humbert's daughter and heir, Alais. The marriage contract called for him to hold extensive fiefs in Piedmont and Savoy from his father-in-law; and Henry in his turn promised the count 5000 marks and agreed to grant John the traditional appanage of a younger son of the counts of Anjou, the three castles of Chinon, Loudun, and Mirebeau. Nothing came of this project, since the count's daughter promptly died; nonetheless, it marked the beginning of much trouble between Henry and his sons.

Because John was only a child, aged five, the grant of the Angevin castles meant that they would actually be under Henry's control. Young Henry, who controlled no castles in his titular territories, viewed this transfer without his consent as an insult; it roused him to anger, and it led to his rebellion. The result was the great revolt of 1173–74 by his three elder sons, urged on by the French king and Eleanor of Aquitaine. Their mother, for all practical purposes separated from Henry by 1170, sought to use her sons for revenge against him. The fact that the boys had done homage to Louis VII as overlord and that he was young Henry's father-in-law enabled him to conspire with them against their father. Little John was at his father's side, a witness to his bitterness toward Eleanor and their faithless sons; the rebellion must have made a deep impression on him.

Following the revolt of 1173–74, Henry II and his elder sons made a peace settlement at Montmirail in October 1174. Henry agreed to what he doubtless considered generous terms, but which still left his elder sons landless. Young Henry was to have two castles in Normandy and an annual revenue of 15,000 *l. angevin* (£3750 sterling), and Richard received two unfortified residences in Poitou and half the revenues of that county. Geoffrey was to have half the revenues of Brittany until his marriage to its heir, Constance, then all her inheritance. Henry also provided for John, assigning him revenues from the English royal domain worth £1000, plus any escheats his father might grant him, the castle and county of Nottingham, the castle and lordship of Marlborough, plus two castles and 1000 *l. angevin* (£250 sterling) in Normandy, one castle each in Anjou, Touraine, and Maine, with another 1000 *l. angevin* from greater Anjou. This generosity to John can hardly have pleased the young king; as Kate Norgate comments, 'The scheme looks almost as if planned purposely to give John a foothold in every part of his eldest brother's future dominions – a strip, so to say, in every one of young Henry's fields.'[12]

Henry set about increasing John's holdings further. On the death of Reginald, earl of Cornwall, in 1175, his estates passed to John. Although the earl had daughters among whom his estates should have been divided, the king took them into his hand, disinheriting Reginald's married daughters of all but a small portion. In 1176, Earl William of Gloucester betrothed his unmarried daughter, Isabelle, to John; since his son had died a decade earlier, she was named his heir, although this disinherited her married sisters. In these two cases, Henry was violating the principle of equal partition among female heirs, which had become customary in England in his grandfather's time. His new principle was that daughters who wed before their father's death must be content with their marriage portions. At a royal council in May 1177, Henry made further provision for John, naming him lord of Ireland.

In 1182, inability of the Plantagenet heirs to work together as Henry had envisaged became clear. That autumn Young Henry, frustrated at his lack of any land of his own and angered at Richard, invaded Poitou supported by Poitevin barons who opposed Richard's 'tyrannical' attempts to impose his authority. Henry II summoned all his sons to the Christmas court at Caen

---

12. Norgate, K. (1902) *John Lackland*, Macmillan, pp. 5–6.

to try to make peace and to sort out once more a scheme for the succession. In January 1183, he asked Richard and Geoffrey to do homage to Young Henry, in the hope that the gesture might placate him. Although Geoffrey did so readily, Richard refused to do homage. Richard's homage to his brother would have appeared to drop him one degree in the feudal hierarchy, making Aquitaine a dependency of the Angevin territories; and it would have threatened his direct feudal tie to the French monarch. Richard withdrew from court in anger, and war soon broke out between the brothers in February 1183. Richard and his father had the Young King on the run, when his death on 11 June 1183 brought an end to the fighting.

Young Henry's death required new arrangements for the succession. Richard became heir to the English crown, to Normandy, and to the Angevin patrimony; and Henry intended to replace him as count of Poitou with John, who would do homage to his elder brother. Richard resisted giving up his actual power over Poitou, exercised for eight years, in exchange for his elder brother's empty title of king without any shadow of real power. He fled his father's court and rushed back to Poitiers. Henry tried throughout the winter of 1183–84 to pressure him into surrendering his duchy. Allegedly the king angrily told John, now seventeen, to lead an army into Richard's lands and to take them for himself by force.

John, on his own in Normandy, soon fell under the influence of his brother Geoffrey, nine years older. Geoffrey of Brittany and John shared personality traits; Gerald of Wales described the count as 'ready to deceive others . . . a hypocrite, never to be trusted, and with a marvellous talent for feigning or counterfeiting all things'.[13] Always the spoiler, he had joined Young Henry in invading Poitou in 1183. He and John raised an army to attack Poitou in August 1184, and Richard in retaliation invaded Brittany. Henry summoned his three sons to his Christmas court in England; and he forced them to make

13. Gerald of Wales. Dimock (ed.) (1861–91) vol. 5, p. 200, translation Norgate (1902) p. 10.

peace, but he had to abandon his scheme for making John duke of Aquitaine.

Henry now returned to his earlier plan for making Ireland a separate lordship for John that he could rule independently. In spring 1185, he knighted the eighteen-year-old youth at Windsor Castle and then sent him off to Ireland. This was a large-scale expedition, requiring a number of ships, horses, and food supplies for a force that included Flemish mercenaries and English administrators. Probably Henry's hope was that John could impose some order there, as his brothers were doing in other lands on the Angevin periphery. The nine months' expedition was hardly a success, however, and John clearly failed his first test in exercising authority. Gerald of Wales, who was a participant in the 1185 expedition, gives the fullest account, and he blames its failure on the immaturity and irresponsibility of John and his young companions. It appears that the campaign failed, however, less because of John's frivolous conduct than because of Anglo-Norman settlers' subversion. Lack of open armed resistance denied John a military confrontation with those opposing his rule, and he retired in frustration. John was waiting for a favourable wind to return to Ireland, when news of Geoffrey of Brittany's death in August 1186 caused his father to postpone any plans for Ireland. He needed John to play a part in new plans for disposition of his continental possession. Up to then Henry had been planning the boy's coronation as king of Ireland; in January 1187, papal legates arrived from Rome with a crown of peacock feathers, which went unused.

Geoffrey's death moved John up one step in the succession, and in 1186 it was not impossible that he might succeed to all the Angevin domains. His father was in his fifties, his brother Richard was unmarried and about to embark on a crusade with all its dangers, and his nephew Arthur of Brittany, posthumous son of Count Geoffrey, was not yet born. Henry sought to place John in a stronger position than any younger son could normally expect, and Richard felt so threatened that he imagined that his father was seeking to alter the succession, to supplant him as heir with John. Henry clearly felt closer to his youngest son than to Richard, perhaps simply because his much greater youth made him seem more compliant, perhaps because Richard was so obviously Eleanor's favourite. John did not appear very promising to contemporaries, but it may be that Henry saw something more in him, in W.L. Warren's words, 'a hard realism, a clear grasp of the complexities of politics and government, and a real interest in the mechanism of administration'.[14]

Richard's suspicions made him seek from his father a clear recognition as heir, but he failed to secure such a pledge. Henry, convinced that he had suffered from his premature acknowledgement of Young Henry as heir, resolved not to repeat the same mistake; and after 1185, he adopted a policy of keeping his sons uncertain about their futures that pushed Richard toward rebellion. It is impossible to know what Henry's actual plans were. Gerald of Wales wrote that the king in 1187 planned for Richard to succeed to England and Normandy and for all other continental lands to pass to John. While this violated the custom that the eldest surviving son should succeed to the ancestral lands, the rule was occasionally reversed when the acquisitions carried a more prestigious title or more power than the patrimony. As Norgate noted, 'Henry's schemes for John were probably in reality much less definite and less outrageous than Richard imagined.'[15] Yet Henry was certainly seeking larger shares for Richard's younger brothers than normal custom concerning succession would have secured for them. Most likely, Henry privately accepted that Richard should succeed, but was unwilling to acknowledge this publicly. Richard's uncertainty, however, drove him into alliance with the French monarch.

Philip Augustus of France proved more persistent and effective in exploiting the tensions between Henry II and his sons than Louis VII had been, but he could not turn his attention to them until several years after his accession in 1180. He had cultivated the friendship of Geoffrey of Brittany who died while at the French court. Philip then turned to Richard, who was at Paris

14. Warren (1973) pp. 599–600.
15. Norgate (1902) p. 23.

as Philip's guest in the summer of 1187; and as Roger of Howden reports, 'Between the two of them there grew up so great an affection that King Henry was much alarmed.'[16] Philip planted more doubts in Richard's mind about Henry's plans to supplant him as heir, and Richard demanded that his father publicly declare him his heir. By the autumn of 1188, Philip and Richard had reached a secret agreement. At a meeting of the two with Henry II at Bonmoulins on 18 November, Philip sought to promote conflict between father and son, and he supported Richard's demand. When Henry refused to recognize Richard as his successor, not wishing to yield to coercion, his son then knelt and did homage to the French king for his continental lands, asking his aid as lord in winning his rightful inheritance from his father.

Richard's recourse to the French royal court brought a break with his father, resulting in the rebellion that wore Henry II down to his death. Gerald of Wales hints that Richard's rebellion led Henry to seek to replace him as heir in the weeks before he died; according to Gerald, the king sought to ensure that in case any harm came to him, his strategic Norman castles would go to John. John broke his father's heart by deserting him and heading for Philip Augustus's court in June 1189, and the old king died at Chinon on 6 July. Henry never solved satisfactorily the question of inheritance of his possessions, and it proved his undoing. His hopes for the Angevin domains were doomed by the extraordinary hostility of his sons, perhaps explained by his unhappy marital situation.

The mother in a feudal family often took the role of protector and intercessor for her sons against their father. Eleanor of Aquitaine's relationship with her sons affords an extreme example of this. Her 'psychological investment' in them seems the opposite of their father's: distant in their early childhood years, only taking interest in them when they had reached an age to play some part in politics. Then she was willing to plot even against her husband for their advancement and for his

16. Benedict of Peterborough. Stubbs, W. (ed.) (1867) *Gesta Regis Henrici secundi Benedicti Abbatis* (2 vols), Rolls Series, vol. 2, p. 7.

discomfiture. We cannot know what scars early separation from his mother may have left on John's *psyche*. Elizabeth A.R. Brown, in a perceptive biographical study of Eleanor, suggests that John's separation from his mother in early childhood had unhappy effects on his personality, that his 'paranoia and unprincipled opportunism' may have resulted from 'the rejection and subsequent loneliness he must have suffered as a child'.[17] A problem is that John's brothers and sisters and most aristocratic children endured similar separations from their parents.

Eleanor's attitude apparently was similar to that of Jennie Jerome Churchill centuries later. She had shown little interest in her son Winston as a child, but once his political career started, she sought eagerly to hasten his advancement. Brown characterizes Eleanor's attitude towards her role of mother as 'hesitant', and she suggests that the queen's love of power meant that in relations with her children 'the domineering rather than the nurturant role of motherhood was strongest'.[18]

Eleanor concentrated her ambition on her sons during her residence in Poitiers, 1170–73, a time when she and Henry II were drifting apart and she was seeking power in her duchy. Although her boys were not yet knighted, they were capable of playing some role in politics. At fourteen, Richard was installed as duke of Aquitaine at Poitiers, June 1172. He remained continuously at his mother's court at Poitiers under her guidance. Two other sons – Young King Henry and Geoffrey of Brittany – sometimes joined them; but little John, aged less than six, remained at Fontevrault abbey. Some historians suggest that Eleanor's concern was due less to maternal interest in her sons' future prospects than to desire for vengeance against her husband. Both her contemporaries and modern scholars have accused her of fomenting the great rebellion of 1173–74. Soon after Young Henry's flight to the Capetian court in March 1173, she sent Richard and Geoffrey to Paris to join him. Her sons' youth and inexperience lend

17. Brown, E.A.R. (1976) 'Eleanor of Aquitaine: parent, queen, duchess' in Kibler, W.W. (ed.) *Eleanor of Aquitaine, Patron and Politician*, Texas UP, Austin, p. 24.
18. Brown (1976) pp. 10, 12.

support to suspicion of her direction; Young Henry was only eighteen, Richard sixteen, and Geoffrey fifteen. No doubt, she also applauded the young king's second revolt in 1183 and Richard's revolt in 1189, joined by John, even if confinement in Winchester castle denied her any active role. Eleanor's imprisonment did not entirely prevent contact with her children, and she may still have sought revenge against Henry through them.

Eleanor's strongest expressions of maternal feeling toward Richard I and John came during their adult years, when she struggled to secure their heritage for them and to preserve their power. She roused herself to action in 1199, when uncertainty over succession to the Angevin territories clouded John's chances of securing them all, reasserting her dominion over Aquitaine and allowing John to concentrate on gaining control of Anjou and Touraine. Richard and John returned her devotion, and during their reigns she took precedence over their wives as dowager queen, enjoying the status of a queen-regnant. The single boldest act in John's often feeble defence of Normandy was his dash to Mirebeau castle in July 1202, where his mother was being beseiged. An Angevin monastic annal describes John as so stricken by Eleanor's death in April 1204 that it led to his abandonment of Normandy. Although the compiler's chronology was weak he may have caught the depth of John's grief.

The family life of Henry II and Eleanor of Aquitaine fails to conform to today's child-centred ideal. Along with other medieval parents, they were unaware of the significance of earliest childhood for shaping adult personality that Freudian psychology teaches. They hardly had time for the tasks of child-rearing, and like the rich and powerful in all ages, they readily confided their young children to the care of others. John spent his earliest years at Fontevrault abbey; in adolescence he went to his eldest brother Henry's household, c. 1174–82, then to the household of Ranulf de Glanvill, c. 1182–85. Despite Henry II's affection for John, the boy joined his father only on great feastdays, where his mother was infrequently present, since Henry kept her imprisoned after the rebellion of 1173–74. John's experience in Glanvill's household was positive, possibly implanting in him an interest in practical work of government. The influence of two older brothers, first Henry and then Geoffrey, was less fortunate. Neither of them could set an example of responsibility or restraint; instead, they exemplified some of the worst features of the chivalric life. After their deaths, John's only remaining brother suspected, perhaps rightly, that Henry II was toying with plans for substituting him as heir to the Angevin domains.

John's childhood had little positive influence on his character; instead, the impact was largely negative. His early and frequent separations from his parents were not unusual, but the degree of hostility among the Plantagenets was unusual if not unique among aristocratic families. His parents' estrangement, his father's quarrels with his older brothers, their rivalries with each other, and their jealousy of him cannot have contributed to childhood happiness. The youngest of several sons in any feudal family had little certainty for the future, and young John must have experienced deep insecurity, uncertain of his inheritance, with little prospect of ever becoming king. His experiences could only give rise to feelings of inadequacy. The treachery that he witnessed within his own family, among his father's courtiers, and his brothers' retainers makes it no surprise that he grew up to be secretive and suspicious, a distrustful and autocratic ruler.

. . .

JOHN DURING RICHARD I's REIGN

Richard I succeeded to the Angevin domains following Henry II's death on 6 July 1189, and John accompanied him to his new English kingdom in August. Richard's chief task during this brief visit was to provide for government during his absence while on the Third Crusade. He refused to entrust his younger brother with a continental province or regency over England, yet he apparently assumed that John's character made him incapable of causing serious trouble. According to Roger of Howden, when news came to the captive Lionheart of his brother's rebellion in 1193, he replied, 'My brother John is not the man to conquer a country if there is a single person able to make the slightest resistance to his attempts.'[19] Richard so little feared his brother that his grants to him formed almost a separate state within England; he gave John a Norman comital title, control of six English shires and their revenues, and confirmed him in his title as lord of Ireland.

Yet Richard's generosity did not end John's uncertainty about his future, and the king soon learned that it is 'a younger brother's birthright' to plot.[20] John's conspiring with Philip Augustus in attempts to profit from his brother's captivity blackened his reputation, yet he did little that Henry I had not done during his brother's reign before securing the English crown or that Richard himself had not done during his father's last years. Richard's failure to produce a son and his vacillation between John and Arthur of Brittany as heir caused continued insecurity for John about his future. Their mother, Eleanor of Aquitaine, had a deep desire to see Richard married, doubtless in the hope that his marriage would soon produce a grandson to supplant both John and Arthur in the line of succession. In the spring of 1191, Eleanor travelled to Spain to fetch Richard's fiancée, Berengaria of Navarre, and to bring her to him in Sicily. The marriage, celebrated after Easter on Cyprus *en route* to Palestine, never resulted in any progeny, however.

When Richard set out to order his affairs before departing on crusade in the summer of 1190, he sought to safeguard his scattered possessions. He appointed trusted seneschals for his continental territories and joint-justiciars for England. The kingdom had an administration that had long run smoothly in Henry II's absence, and Richard I left most of his father's agents in place, although many had to repurchase their posts at high prices. In general, the English administration functioned remarkably smoothly during his absence on crusade and in captivity, yet his division of powers created confusion and conflict, 1190–92.

19. Howden, *Chronica*, Stubbs (1868–71) vol. 3, p. 198.
20. Brooke, C.N.L. (1961) *From Alfred to Henry III 871–1272*, Thomas Nelson, Walton-on-Thames, pp. 216–17.

A look at Richard's pattern of government is useful for judging John's later exercise of power in England. First, throughout the twentieth century, historians have contrasted the elder brother's preoccupation with warfare overseas with John's attention to administrative matters; and today's scholars tend to find John's apparent bureaucratic bent more attractive than Richard's talents as a soldier. Yet much of John's tightening of royal control over the kingdom first appeared under his absentee brother, put in place by his able justiciar, Hubert Walter. Second, the Lionheart's search for funds points toward his younger brother's financial demands as king. Massive sales of offices and privileges on Richard's accession in 1189 signalled the pressures of financing the crusade; then raising his enormous ransom forced an experiment with general taxation; and costs continued in his last years due to the struggle against Philip II of France. Ralph of Coggeshall, wrote during John's reign of Richard I, 'No age can remember or history tell of any king . . . who demanded and took so much money from his kingdom as this king extorted and amassed within five years of his return from captivity.'[21] Finally, Richard's absence from the kingdom required his agents to summon councils of great men to secure their support. Such meetings gave an opening for baronial participation in government that strengthened their political consciousness, possibly contributing to their collective resistance to John's rule.

Richard's settlement for his kingdom applied principles that he had absorbed during his years of ruling Poitou; he sought to divide responsibility and to balance powers. His original scheme for two joint-justiciars with shared authority – the earl of Essex and the bishop of Durham – represented 'a balance of feudal power in England',[22] but it soon broke down due to the earl's early death. William Longchamp, a Norman cleric of obscure birth, then became co-justiciar and soon managed to concentrate

21. Coggeshall. Stevenson, J. (ed.) (1875) *Radulphi de Coggeshall Chronicon Anglicanum*, Rolls Series, p. 93; translation, Gillingham, J. (1978) *Richard the Lionheart*, Weidenfeld & Nicolson, p. 303.
22. West, F.J. (1966) *The Justiciarship in England 1066–1232*, Cambridge UP, p. 66.

power in his hands, confining his colleague's authority to the North. Longchamp was 'a man with three titles and three heads',[23] exercising power as justiciar, chancellor, and papal legate. He proved unable to co-operate with four or five experienced royal servants named by Richard as *appares* or associate justiciars to share power with him in a primitive regency council. Although he tried to preserve the king's settlement, his greed, ambition, and authoritarian attitude soon aroused baronial opposition to government without their counsel or co-operation. The chronicler William of Newburgh noted that 'his arrogance in all things was almost more than a king's'.[24] John knew how to exploit baronial opposition to Longchamp's rule. Yet the barons' participation in councils represents a significant stage in growth of their consciousness as a corporate political body, which one day would be turned against him.

Richard I took particular care to guard against any potential rivals for the throne. Since his nephew Arthur, son of Count Geoffrey of Brittany, was only three years old and in the custody of his Breton kin, he was hardly a potential rallying point for troublemakers, and the king felt safe in naming him his successor. At Messina in autumn 1190, before sailing from Sicily for the Holy Land, Richard recognized Arthur as heir to all the Angevin domains should he die without issue. About the same time, the king's deputy in England, William Longchamp, was working to win the Scottish king's acceptance of Arthur as successor to the English throne.

Richard had two younger brothers who posed potential threats to him in England. His bastard half-brother, Geoffrey Plantagenet, was a clerk in minor orders, serving his father as chancellor. To remove any possibility of his seeking the throne, he received the archbishopric of York, requiring him to take priest's vows; and to prevent

23. Appleby, J.T. (ed. and trans.) (1963) *Chronicle of Richard of Devizes*, Thomas Nelson (Medieval Texts), Walton-on-Thames, translation Rothwell, H. (ed.) (1975) *English Historical Documents*, vol. 3, *1189–1327*, Eyre & Spottiswoode, Cambridge, p.52.
24. Newburgh. Howlett (1885–90) vol. 1, p. 333.

further trouble, he was barred from entering England for three years.

Richard treated his legitimate brother, John, in a way that was in one scholar's opinion, 'liberal to the extent of folly'.[25] Richard named him count of Mortain, Normandy, conferring on him the title that he would use throughout his brother's reign; he also confirmed to him Henry II's grants made in 1174 of the castle and county of Nottingham and the castle and honor of Marlborough; and he granted John a number of escheated honors, including the earldom of Cornwall, Lancaster, Wallingford in Berkshire, Tickhill in Yorkshire, Eye in Suffolk, and Peverel, Bolsover and the Peak in the Midlands. In addition, John held the earldom of Gloucester through his betrothal to Isabelle, the late earl's youngest daughter, whom he married on 29 August 1189. John controlled the administration of the six counties of Dorset and Somerset, Nottingham and Derbyshire, Devon and Cornwall. Although Richard curtailed his brother's military power by leaving those counties' key castles in his own hands, John nonetheless held a compact territorial base of four shires in the Southwest and two in the northern Midlands. Apparently Richard thought that he was doing no more than providing an income appropriate for his princely brother, and that he would not risk losing his vast lands by rebelling. As an added precaution, the king sought to bar him from the kingdom for three years. Due to the pleas of their mother, Eleanor, he relented, however, and allowed Count John to take personal possession of his English properties by early 1191.

The count of Mortain certainly considered himself next in line for the English crown despite Richard's designation of Arthur as heir. In the event of his brother's failure to return from the crusade, his powerful position would make it difficult for Arthur's supporters to dislodge him. He was an over-mighty subject, already possessing a household in his capacity as lord of Ireland that was prepared to serve as 'a ready-made ministry' much like

25. Poole, A.L. (1955) *From Domesday Book to Magna Carta*, 2nd edn, Oxford UP, p. 348.

a rival royal court.[26] John's household replicated on a smaller scale the *curia regis* with a chief justiciar, a chancery, and an exchequer probably housed at Marlborough castle. Furthermore, he controlled his English counties' revenues of possibly £4000 free from audits at Westminster. Clearly, his power was upsetting the balance that Richard had sought to maintain during his absence, and Longchamp's regime began to unravel.

A scholarly study of the justiciarship sees as the reason for Longchamp's fall 'John's power and ambition which were too great to be contained by a single justiciar'.[27] Longchamp had alienated potential baronial allies against the count of Mortain, who succeeded in depicting himself as defender of the magnates' interests. He told Longchamp, 'It was not fitting to take their custodies away from law-worthy men of the realm, well known and free, and hand them over to foreigners and unknown men.'[28] A confrontation that brought John and Longchamp to the brink of warfare arose over control of castles, for the chancellor was determined to place his castellans in royal strongpoints. When a dispute arose over Lincoln castle, where John's man Gerard de Camville was castellan, the count responded by seizing the royal castles of Tickhill and Nottingham. John took care to present himself as acting with the counsel of the great men of the kingdom, and he also was careful not to push too far his claims to power. The count and the chancellor met in July 1191 to reach a compromise, which quickly broke down. At a second meeting in August or September, John succeeded in securing Longchamp's promise to work for his succession should Richard fail to return from the crusade.

Contingency plans contained in a letter sent from Messina by Richard to Longchamp's *appares* reached England by the hand of Walter of Coutances, archbishop of Rouen, in April 1191. Longchamp steadily lost support, and Walter, a longtime royal servant, sought to restore

26. Norgate (1902) p. 29.
27. West (1966) p. 73.
28. Appleby (1963) p. 31.

stability The chancellor's mistake of moving unlawfully and violently against Geoffrey, John's and Richard's bastard half-brother, when he landed at Dover in September to claim his archbishopric of York, proved decisive. The archbishop-elect sought safety in a church, but was dragged from sanctuary, a shocking spectacle that called to mind another archbishop's martyrdom twenty years earlier. John called an assembly of barons and bishops in association with the commune of London, to a meeting in October 1191 for 'great and arduous business of the king and the kingdom'.[29] The arrogant chancellor was excommunicated and removed from office, despite his attempts to bribe Count John; and he soon fled England ignominiously. Walter of Coutances then took the justiciarship, forestalling any steps John might take to assume power as *summus rector regni*; yet the barons seem to have taken an oath of fealty to the count, recognizing his right to succeed Richard as their king.

Aside from his selection of William Longchamp, the Lionheart showed sound sense in naming his agents in England, usually relying on men who had proven their ability through service to his father. Outstanding examples are the knight William Marshal, one of the *appares* left behind on the king's departure for the Holy Land, and a clerk, Hubert Walter, who accompanied him on the crusade. Hubert, trained in the household of his uncle, the justiciar Ranulf de Glanvill, returned to England in 1193; he led efforts to raise the king's ransom and won promotion to the justiciarship and the archbishopric of Canterbury in 1194. The government of England was largely in Hubert Walter's hands during the last five years of the Lionheart's reign; he proved a natural administrator, bringing new efficiency and effectiveness to the central government and enabling the exchequer to raise the enormous sums needed for Richard's ransom and continental wars.

The count of Mortain remained powerful after Long-champ's fall, and he did not stop scheming to draw all royal castles under his control. In the spring of

29. Ralph Diceto. Stubbs (1876) vol. 2, p. 98.

1192, Richard learned about John's plotting; and he also heard rumours of the count's conspiring with the Capetian monarch, who had returned early from the Holy Land. Apparently Richard's failure to meet death in the Holy Land made John impatient for the succession, and Philip Augustus had no scruples against participating in plots with him as the crusader king made his way home. John nearly accepted an offer from Philip to discuss his taking all the Angevin continental possessions in return for marrying a Capetian princess, former fiancée of Richard. His mother, Eleanor, rushed to England in time to stop his sailing from Southampton, however. Later that spring, Longchamp sought to regain a foothold in England and return to office through purchase of John's support. Another baronial assembly prevented this, but the barons had to outbid Longchamp's bribe to John with more money and with another oath of fealty recognizing him as Richard's heir.

Richard sailed back to Europe in October 1192. Fears of John's and Philip Augustus's plotting caused him to avoid landing at Marseilles, and instead, he sailed up the Adriatic and was shipwrecked near Venice. After crossing the Alps, he was captured by the duke of Austria's men and turned over to Henry VI, the German emperor, who demanded a huge ransom of 150,000 silver marks. Richard Lionheart's capture in Germany appeared to end Count John's fears about the succession; it seemed to position him for usurping the English throne in his brother's absence. As soon as he learned of the Lionheart's imprisonment, he rushed to the Continent, proceeding to Paris, when the Norman nobility refused to transfer their fealty from Richard to him. He did homage to Philip for his brother's continental possessions, and he agreed to set aside Isabelle of Gloucester and marry Philip's sister. The French king invaded Normandy and collected forces in Flanders for an invasion of England to aid his new ally. John returned to England with a mercenary force, announced his brother's death, and demanded recognition as king, but Richard's committee of associate justiciars refused it. Then in April 1193 news arrived from Germany that the king was alive.

Count John's 1193–94 revolt in England had little

success. The justiciars, rallied by the queen-mother, remained loyal to the king and besieged John's castles. They hesitated to push him too far, however, fearing that if Richard should fail to recover his freedom and return to England, his brother might well become their king. Then, in July, word arrived of the emperor's acceptance of terms for the Lionheart's release from captivity. John's erstwhile ally Philip II made a truce with the king's representatives at Nantes which forestalled departure of the French invasion fleet for England, although it cost Richard 20,000 marks. Philip and John's plans for bribing the emperor to detain Richard in captivity collapsed. By January 1194, Count John was desperate, and he tried to buy continued Capetian support by making concessions that would have dangerously weakened Angevin power on the Continent. He agreed to cede most castles guarding the Norman frontier with the French kingdom and all of Normandy northeast of the Seine with the exception of Rouen; in the Loire valley, he agreed to surrender Tours and other castles protecting the Touraine. The count's complicity in plots against his brother led a council of English bishops and barons to excommunicate him and to order his lands seized and his castles besieged.

Richard was freed on 4 February 1194, and he landed in England on 13 March. He quickly took the castles of Tickhill and Nottingham, which were holding out for Count John, and he seized the lands of his brother and his supporters. John was once again 'Lackland', deprived of counties and castles. He refused to cross to England to obey a great council's summons to trial at the end of March; instead, he waited until his brother returned to Normandy to approach him there. Richard received his tearful and repentant brother in May 1194 'with good-humoured contempt',[30] allegedly explaining to John, 'You are a child. You have had bad companions.'[31] Richard's

30. Barlow, F. (1988) *The Feudal Kingdom of England 1042–1216*, 4th edn, Longman, p. 362..
31. Meyer, P. (ed.) (1891–1901) *Histoire de Guillaume le Maréchal* (3 vols), vol. 2, Société de L'Histoire de France, Paris p. 10, lines 10363–419; translation, Powicke, F.M. (1960) *The Loss of Normandy*, 2nd edn, Manchester UP, p. 100.

excuse for John, dismissing a twenty-seven-year-old as a child and refusing to take him seriously, must have been deeply humiliating. His former allies had to purchase restoration of their lands and Richard's goodwill with large fines; the bishop of Coventry, for example, offered 2000 marks.

Richard was a realist, aware that a disgruntled heir might bolt to the French court as he himself had done during his father's reign. John was also realistic, recognizing that his brother's goodwill could mean not only restoration of his lands and castles, but also recognition as heir in place of Arthur of Brittany. He joined the king's household, and his own elaborate establishment merged with Richard's *curia regis*. Eventually, his military services to the Lionheart in Normandy seemed to indicate that he had reformed. By autumn 1195 the king restored to him his English honors of Eye and Gloucester and Mortain in Normandy, and in addition, an annual allowance of 8000 *1. Angevin.* These grants enabled him to reconstitute a small household of his own, several of whose members would continue to serve him as king. As a precaution, however, John's castles were still withheld from him, as were the six shires he had held. His resources for making mischief were much reduced from their pre-1194 levels.

Meanwhile, Philip Augustus was pressing into the Angevins' continental lands, especially Normandy, overrunning the Vexin and almost taking Rouen. Richard returned to the Continent in May 1194 after two months in England to spend his remaining years, 1194–99, struggling to defend his empire and to recover land lost while he was held captive. The Count of Mortain served his brother energetically as a soldier during those five years, demonstrating none of the sloth or indecision later attributed to him. By the time of Richard's death at the siege of a rebel vassal's castle in the Limousin, he had regained with John's help most of what had been lost to the Capetians during his captivity and he was well disposed toward his brother. In 1196, the Bretons had refused to give custody of young Arthur of Brittany to Richard and instead handed him over to the French king's care. This likely brought the count of Mortain tacit acknowledgement as his brother's heir by the next year. Yet nothing could erase John's reputation for treachery that his earlier plots with the Angevins' greatest enemy had earned him.

Philip Augustus saw that by pushing into Berry and Poitou he could attack the Angevins' Loire valley lands from the south. The French threat from this direction could sever links between Aquitaine and Normandy, threatening the Angevin empire's unity. While Richard concentrated on this threat, defending Touraine and Poitou from Philip's thrusts, Count John contested the French for control of castles in the Seine valley above Rouen. During his brother's final five years, John served capably enough as a soldier, gaining experience. Soon after the two brother's reconciliation, John rushed to Evreux with a band of knights, taking the town after only a day's siege and slaughtering its garrison, apparently achieving success by trickery since Evreux's defenders were unaware that he had abandoned Philip's side. Striking success came to John again in spring 1197, when he and Mercadier, a mercenary captain, attacked Beauvais and captured the warrior-bishop, Philip of Dreux, cousin to the French king. Before Richard I died of an arrow's wound on 7 April 1199, he seemed to have accepted Count John's reform and to have taken steps to acknowledge his brother as heir.

. . .

JOHN'S SUCCESSION TO THE THRONE

After Richard died in April 1199, John had to fight for his continental inheritance, for he had a rival in Arthur of Brittany; the nobles of Brittany, Anjou, Maine, and Touraine recognized his twelve year-old nephew as Richard's heir. John also had the opposition of Philip Augustus, the Angevins' great rival, who had custody of young Arthur. The disputed succession gave the French monarch an opportunity to practise his skill in pitting one member of the Plantagenet family against another. The existence of a rival claim to the Angevin empire doubtless exacerbated John's sense of insecurity, experienced since childhood. His uncertainty eventually pushed him to acts of cruelty, first the murder of his nephew and then of

Matilda de Braose and her son, starved to death because she spoke too openly about Arthur's death.

Arthur of Brittany, as representative of his father Geoffrey, an elder son of Henry II, could claim at least a share in a partition of the Angevin lands; and some Anglo-Norman magnates, alarmed at the prospect of John as their lord, might support Arthur as heir to the entire patrimony. This question – succession of a cadet or younger son (John) versus succession by his nephew (Arthur), representative of a deceased elder son (Geoffrey of Brittany) – came to tbe called the *casus regis* in England. It caused uncertainty about rules of succession in similar cases until the mid-thirteenth century.

Feudal rules of succession afforded few guidelines on Richard I's death without an heir of his body. At the end of the twelfth century within the Angevin territories, two patterns of succession were available to be applied to the lands of Henry II's family. One pattern, strict male primogeniture, would prevail in England; while *parage*, or partition among sons, lingered in Anjou and Normandy.[32] Richard Lionheart had accepted this latter principle at Messina in 1191, in a treaty with Philip Augustus, arranging the succession of his continental lands held as fiefs of the Capetian king. At that time Richard, although not yet married, assumed optimistically that he would leave more than one son; and it was arranged that the eldest would hold his continental lands in-chief of the French monarch. A potential second son should also hold his share directly of the French king; whether Normandy, Anjou and Maine, or Poitou and Aquitaine was unspecified.

Philip Augustus could be counted upon to support Arthur's claim to a portion of the Angevin legacy in the hope of splitting the resources of this powerful rival house standing in the way of expansion of French royal power. Richard Lionheart's treaty with the French king at Messina in 1191 had created a wedge for future Capetian interventions in Angevin-held provinces. By that agreement, applying the principle of *parage* to his

---

32. See Chapter 3, pages 63–65 for a discussion of this.

anticipated offspring, he had recognized the French royal court's jurisdiction over his continental possessions.

Factors other than feudal law would play their part in determining the succession to Richard; they include the wishes of the late king and of the great men of the Angevin domains. The dying Richard most likely designated John as his heir; even if he had not, his mother and the men around his deathbed would have spread the story of such a designation. Eleanor evidently had little love for her grandson's mother, Constance of Brittany, who was filled with anti-Angevin prejudices. In any case, members of the royal household soon joined John and swore fealty to him. Among the English and Norman nobility, little opposition to John's succession manifested itself. Administrators in the Anglo-Norman realm knew John from the time of Richard's absence on crusade, and although his actions then had given them little reason to trust him, they had less reason to favour Arthur, a lad dwelling at the French court, reared by a pro-Capetian mother.

William Marshal apparently voiced majority opinion when he spoke against the archbishop of Canterbury's suggestion that Arthur be accepted as Richard's successor. The Marshal replied, 'Ah, sire, that would be a bad thing . . . Arthur has bad councillors, and he is proud and passionate. If we put him at our head we will cause trouble for he has no love for the English.' He added in support of Count John's claim an apparent paraphrase of the Norman *coutumier*, 'The son is nearer the land of his father than the nephew is.'[33] The rule in England was less clear, as the lawbook *Glanvill's* expression of doubt about the son's or the nephew's right shows. Hubert Walter was won to John's cause, but in his coronation sermon, he cited the elective principle to justify John's succession, stating that the community of the realm (*universitas regni*) had a right to elect 'one from the dead king's stock who is more outstanding than the others'.[34]

33. *Guillaume le Maréchal*. Meyer (1891–1901) vol. 2, pp. 63–4, lines 11877–908; translation Powicke (1960) p. 131.
34. Matthew Paris. Luard, H.R. (ed.) (1872–84) *Matthaei Parisiensis Chronica Majora* (7 vols), Rolls Series, vol. 2, p. 455.

The archbishop, the justiciar Geoffrey fitz Peter, and William Marshal met with some wavering English barons at Northampton to win them over to acceptance of John. These magnates – Ranulf, earl of Chester, Richard de Clare, earl of Hertford, William de Ferrers, earl of Derby, Roger de Lacy, and William de Mowbray – had claims to castles, lands, or other possessions that they felt to be rightfully theirs and wrongfully withheld from them by Henry II or Richard I. They were persuaded to support John with his promise, conveyed by the justiciar and William Marshal, that he would 'render to each of them his rights',[35] and they swore fealty to him. While some had their claims recognized shortly after John's coronation on 27 May 1199, others waited in vain for redress. In June John sought to ingratiate himself with his English subjects by issuing a 'constitution' or charter, supposedly abolishing his brother's evil customs, but actually doing no more than rolling back Richard's exorbitant rates for sealing chancery documents.

Eleanor of Aquitaine, although in her seventies, roused herself to action after Richard's death to protect Aquitaine from Philip Augustus. While she may have had some doubts about John's capacity for rule, they were offset by her mistrust of her Breton daughter-in-law and grandson, and she was concerned to prevent Philip from asserting authority over her patrimony. Her youngest son, unlike Richard, was not duke of Aquitaine at the time of his accession to the English throne, and the possibility of some French intervention made it necessary that Eleanor reassert her authority. She hastened to Poitou to take the homage of her subjects, and then she did homage to her Capetian overlord in mid-July. Soon afterwards, Eleanor and John issued charters in which she ceded Poitou (and cession of Aquitaine also is implied) to her son, and he returned the province to his mother to rule as *domina* during her lifetime. While her authority over Aquitaine was genuine, shown by the charters she issued, John named seneschals in Poitou and Gascony who carried

---

35. Howden, *Chronica*, Stubbs (1868–71) vol. 4, p. 88; translation Norgate (1902) p. 65.

out his commands. The arrangement was 'a diplomatic masterstroke',[36] for it cemented the duchy's links to the English crown, guaranteed continued Angevin authority over southwestern France, and denied Philip Augustus any excuse for intervention on Eleanor's death in 1204.

Although the Anglo-Norman realm embraced John's claim, and Eleanor made Aquitaine secure for him, nobles of Brittany, Anjou and Maine, and Touraine inclined towards Arthur's cause. The uncertainty of John's claim against his nephew provided a pretext for Philip Augustus as the Angevins' feudal overlord and the boy's guardian to intervene in the disputed succession, cut off Normandy from Aquitaine, and sow discord. William des Roches, the most powerful Angevin lord, supported Arthur and accepted the seneschalcy of Anjou from Philip. The possibility of the Angevin domains splitting into three separate entities presented itself to John: the Anglo-Norman realm, his mother's patrimony in southwestern France, with Brittany and greater Anjou under Arthur separating the other two.

John moved energetically in taking possession of Richard's lands and in confronting the French threat. On learning of the Lionheart's death, he quickly made his way from Brittany, where he had been visiting his nephew, to the Loire valley to secure the strategic castles of Chinon and Loches; after seizing the treasury at Chinon, a combination of Breton and Angevin troops forced him to withdraw from the Angevin heartland. He turned north to Normandy to be consecrated as duke on 25 April, and from Rouen he rushed to Le Mans to punish the city for its acceptance of Arthur as lord, razing the castle and city walls. He then crossed to England to be crowned king on 27 May. Once John held England and Normandy, he was able to give full attention to the Loire region.

In August 1199, a meeting between the two kings on the Norman frontier resulted in no agreement about succession to the Angevin lands. Philip Augustus complained that John's taking possession of Normandy with-

---

36. Holt, J.C. (1986) 'Aliénor d'Aquitaine, Jean sans Terre et la succession de 1199', *Cahiers de Civilisation médiévale*, 29, p. 97.

out first obtaining his lord's recognition as rightful claimant justified his making war on him. That September John headed from Normandy to Anjou and Maine, surprising Philip as he was besieging Lavardin and driving him out of Maine. Luckily for John, the French king managed to alienate William des Roches and other Angevin barons. John occupied Le Mans, where he made peace with William, with his young rival, Arthur, and the boy's mother Constance of Brittany in early autumn. Sometime later in the year, however, Philip Augustus would regain custody of Arthur, keeping him as 'a weapon to be held in reserve'.[37]

The reconciliation of John and Arthur forced Philip to agree to a truce, which became a supposedly permanent peace settlement at Le Goulet, 22 May 1200. John won recognition as Richard's lawful heir, and the French king's court found for John as rightful lord of Anjou and of Brittany, which Arthur would hold in fee of him. John agreed that Arthur, although his vassal, could not have his rights altered unless by the Capetian court's judgment. John's confirmation of the French royal court's jurisdiction, already acknowledged by his brother, would come back to haunt him. The legalism that had been growing throughout the twelfth century was everywhere turning feudal custom into law. Philip intended that the Angevins' homage, which had formerly simply expressed friendship, should denote definite obligations, especially subjection to the judgments of the Capetian *curia regis*. Just as Henry II had increased his authority by encouraging under-tenants to appeal against their immediate lords to their overlord's court, the English *curia regis*, so Philip was soliciting appeals from John's continental subjects to the French royal court at Paris.

Philip II, in addition to securing his court's jurisdiction, won other advantages from his recognition of John as ruler of all the Angevin lands. Perhaps his most visible gain was John's acknowledgement of his vassal status by payment of 20,000 marks as relief. Also John abandoned alliances with Philip's vassals, the counts of

37. Powicke (1960), p. 138.

Flanders and Boulogne, cemented by Richard I. John agreed to a French strengthening of the Norman frontier with adjustments in the Vexin and ceding the county of Evreux. To seal the treaty, Philip's son Louis was to wed John's niece Blanche of Castile, to whom John assigned dower lands in the border region of Berry. Overall, however, John had done well. He gained his goal by threatening force without seriously using it; and the settlement with Philip II bought him two years of peace, during which he could consolidate his power over his continental possessions. He seemed to be establishing control over his continental lands from the English Channel to the Pyrenees.

John inherited from his brother an able group of administrators, capable of operating government smoothly in the king's absence. Since his own comital household had been quite small after 1195, he had little difficulty merging his late brother's and his own households. Key personalities in John's government in England were the three men who had persuaded the barons to accept John as king over his nephew: William Marshal, a paragon of chivalry who had been one of the *appares* governing England while Richard I was away on crusade and had fought alongside the late king in France; Geoffrey fitz Peter, a longtime royal servant whom Richard had promoted to the justiciarship in 1198, replacing Hubert Walter; and Geoffrey's predecessor, the Archbishop of Canterbury, an administrative genius chiefly responsible for England's efficient government in the five years before Richard's death. John promptly rewarded these three. At his coronation, he belted the two laymen as earls: the marshal, previously married to the Giffard heiress, now acquired the title of earl of Pembroke: and Geoffrey fitz Peter, already holding the Mandeville inheritance through his wife, gained the title of earl of Essex. Also on his coronation day, John appointed Hubert Walter to another secular office, this time to head the chancery.

All three remained highly visible in King John's counsels. While the earl of Pembroke was not so much an administrator as royal companion, counsellor and military commander, the earl of Essex headed

England's administration in his post as justiciar until his death in October 1213. Hubert, the former justiciar, would remain John's chancellor and continued to work closely with Geoffrey fitz Peter until his death in 1205. Their co-operation can largely account for England's tranquillity during John's early years; doubtless their work in the royal administration restrained some of his more autocratic tendencies. Another of Richard's chief officials, the treasurer William of Ely, remained at his post until civil war led to the exchequer's closing in the spring of 1215. A fourth great official of Richard's, Hugh de Neville, remained in his office of chief forester. Hugh became one of John's close companions, often gambling with him, and his wife may have been even closer to the king. All four of John's great officers of state, then, were holdovers from his brother's government: justiciar, chancellor, treasurer, and chief forester.

Four men present at Richard's deathbed would enjoy John's favour, possibly because they influenced the dying king to name his brother as his heir. William de Braose, a baron of the Welsh marches, quickly became a royal intimate and took advantage of the king's friendship to increase his English and Welsh holdings and to purchase Limerick, an Irish lordship. His position came to equal that of an earl, but he would lose John's favour in 1208, and the king's cruel pursuit of him and his family would form a tragic epilogue to his career. Thomas Basset served John as sheriff of Oxfordshire, and royal favour brought him valuable grants. In 1203 he rose to baronial rank, when John granted him Headington, Oxfordshire; and two years later, he received custody of the heir to the earldom of Warwick with the right to marry his daughter to the boy. Another of those present at Richard's deathbed. Gerard de Furnival, succeeded in marrying his son to a claimant to a Yorkshire honor and securing her recognition as heiress by 1207. The fourth, Peter of Stoke, became one of the seneschals of John's household.

Since so many of the late king's men stayed on in John's service, continuity was maintained in the government of England. Two of Richard's servants, whom he had named associate justiciars in 1190 along with William Marshal and Geoffrey fitz Peter, would be influential in King John's government. William Briwerre, noted for his financial expertise, served John throughout his reign as a baron of the exchequer, a royal justice, and multi-purpose royal official. He took shameless advantage of his friendship with the king to increase his profit and power, his acquisition of lands a splendid example of royal officials' calculating greed. The other associate justiciar, Hugh Bardolf, continued until his death in 1203 to serve John at the exchequer and bench and in other posts, as he had Henry II and Richard I.

Others of the Lionheart's servants remained in the new king's service. Warin fitz Gerold, a member of his military household in 1198–99, was hereditary chamberlain of the exchequer; and he frequently attended King John, witnessing his charters. William de Sainte-Mère-Église, *protonotarius* or chief chamber clerk to Richard, won election to the bishopric of London just before his master's death. He served John as a baron of the exchequer until the Canterbury succession crisis caused him to distance himself from the royal government. Simon of Wells, or Simon fitz Robert, was another of Richard's chamber clerks, who shared custody of King John's seal with John de Gray in 1199. He remained a royal clerk, 'most closely and continuously occupied about the king's business'.[38] until his election as bishop of Chichester in 1207. His relatives, Hugh and Jocelin of Wells, followed him into King John's chancery and also won bishoprics. John de Brancaster, vice-chancellor in Richard I's household, became a senior chancery clerk early in John's reign. Of all Richard's clerks, the one who rose to greatest prominence under his successor was Peter des Roches. This Poitevin knight turned cleric had served the Lionheart as receiver of his chamber and he quickly became John's chamberlain, in fact if not in title; then in 1214 before the king sailed for Poitou, he assumed the justiciarship. He was a financial expert to whom John showed great favour, acting 'with savage vigor'

38. Stenton, D.M. (general ed.) (1933–64) *Great Roll of the Pipe, 1–17 John*, Pipe Roll Society, new ser. 14, p. xv [Pipe Roll 3 John].

to secure his election to the rich bishopric of Winchester, 1204–05.[39]

Three members of John's comital *familia* in the years just before his accession to the throne would remain close to the king, absorbed into the royal household. John de Gray, a clerk who had served as household chancellor, acted as royal vice-chancellor or keeper of the seal, although without formal title, before he was elected bishop of Norwich in 1200. He remained close to the king, 'probably the only man whom John trusted absolutely and without reservation for the entire period of their association';[40] and he would be the royal nominee for the archbishopric of Canterbury following Hubert Walter's death in 1205 and later for the see of Durham, 1213–14. His nephew, Walter de Gray, purchased the office of chancellor on Hubert Walter's death in 1205, and he secured election to the bishopric of Worcester in 1213–14 and translation to the archbishopric of York in 1215, after allegedly spending £10,000 at the papal *curia*. Hubert de Burgh, Count John's chamberlain, held the title until 1205, when he fell out of favour for a time on account of his inability to defend Chinon Castle from the French. In any case, he was too busy with military responsibilities to spend much time in the royal household. William de Cantilupe had served as steward or seneschal of Count John's household, and he continued as seneschal of the royal household throughout John's reign, earning a barony in 1205.

Some of John's associates in his abortive rebellion of 1193 returned to prominence once he ascended the English throne. Henry of London, archdeacon of Stafford, who had offered a £200-fine for Richard I's goodwill in 1195, took on financial and diplomatic tasks for John as early as 1200. By 1205, he was an officer of the chamber and his services to the king, especially during the quarrel with Pope Innocent III, won him John's trust and generosity. In 1213, he became archbishop of Dublin

39. Painter, S. (1949) *The Reign of King John*, Johns Hopkins UP, Baltimore, p. 160.
40. Painter (1949) p. 79.

and for a time he united in himself spiritual and secular supremacy in Ireland, serving as John's justiciar there. Another supporter of John during his rebellion was Gerard de Camville, who had been one of his men since 1191. His support for John's rebellion had cost him his hereditary custody of Lincoln Castle plus a 2000-mark fine to purchase Richard's goodwill; once John took the throne, however, he regained the castle and the shrievalty of Lincolnshire, 1199–1205. Another knight who had aided Count John was Philip of Oldcotes, a minor tenant of northern honors in the king's hand; he fought for the king on the Continent and was captured at Chinon Castle in 1206. After his return to England, John named him one of the custodians of the vacant bishopric of Durham, a profitable post and strategically important to John in controlling the North.

The new king had a corps of capable assistants, then, most of whom would serve him loyally throughout their lives. Typically, they were either new men who had risen in rank through their service to the Plantagenets, or else they came from families with a tradition of service in the royal administration. In their zeal to safeguard the king's and their own interest, enriching themselves and their families in the process, such men would fuel the discontent of John's barons.

Chapter 3

THE ANGEVIN DOMAINS ON JOHN'S ACCESSION

THE NATURE OF THE ANGEVIN 'EMPIRE'

When John succeeded his brother in April 1199, he fell heir to his father's Angevin patrimony, the Anglo-Norman realm, and the possessions of his mother, Eleanor of Aquitaine. We must remember that John, Henry II, and Richard I were not simply kings of England but lords of wide domains in western France from the English Channel to the Pyrenees. They did not regard England as their homeland, and possibly they did not even regard it as the most important of their possessions. John may well have viewed Anjou as the heartland of his empire; certainly some of his trusted agents came from there and from Poitou. John, like his father and brother, valued the Anglo-Norman realm for the wealth that its strong government enabled him to tap easily; the Plantagenets took its resources for their endless wars on the Continent to resist their overlord, the Capetian monarch, and to subdue rebellious vassals.

The Angevins' lands formed 'an elegant geographical bloc stretching from Northumberland to the Pyrenees'.[1] England's unity, of course, was assured by geography and history before its conquest by John's Norman ancestors. In the continental possessions, cities lying on the banks of great rivers had possibilities for economic integration, with their ready access to the sea; and old Roman roads running north and south still connected them with

1. Hallam, E. (1980) *Capetian France 987–1328*, Longman, p. 180.

one another, affording easy communication between Rouen and Bordeaux. The Loire River, flowing across greater Anjou – Anjou, Maine and Touraine – linked the Anglo-Norman realm with Aquitaine, a recruiting ground for mercenaries. Yet the Loire valley also provided a ready route for French forces, offering them a path for invasion from Berry and Poitou to split apart the Angevin domains.

Significant differences in political development divided the Plantagenet domains. They fall into three political zones stretching from north to south. First was England and Normandy, which some scholars see after the Conquest as 'in many respects two parts of a single political unit';[2] there the king/duke held strong powers approaching sovereignty. Below Normandy lay Anjou, Maine, and Touraine, an intermediate zone, where a powerful baronage, grown accustomed to the counts' ineffectual feudal lordship since the late eleventh century, contested re-imposition of public authority by early twelfth-century counts. Farther south was the patrimony of Eleanor of Aquitaine, where the continental feudal tradition was hardly challenged and few central institutions existed to enforce ducal authority over a turbulent nobility.

One authority recently wrote, 'The notion of an "Angevin empire" is nothing more than a convenient invention of modern historians.'[3] Historians tend to reject the possibility of the Plantagenets' collection of lands achieving permanence and political stability, seeing them merely 'as the lucky acquisition of a quarrelsome family and not as an institution'.[4] Although these lands are lumped together under the convenient term, Angevin or Plantagenet 'empire', few see much evidence for any Angevin concept of imperial doctrine or permanent union. In the Middle Ages the only true empire was the Roman Empire's

---

2. Hollister, C.W. (1986) *Monarchy, Magnates and Institutions in the Anglo-Norman World*, Hambledon Press, p. 24; reprint of 'Normandy, France and the Anglo-Norman *Regnum*' (1976), *Speculum*, p. 51.
3. Hollister (1986) p. 56.
4. Clanchy, M.T. (1983) *England and its Rulers 1066–1272*, Fontana, p. 112.

successors in East and West. Richard I and John's seals bore the inscription *Rex Anglorum, Dux Normannorum et Aquitanorum et comes Andegavorum;* they had no name for the bloc of lands assembled by their father. Nonetheless, John, like his brother, concentrated his energy and resources on preserving his nameless empire, fighting to protect it from the Capetian king. This largely accidental assemblage of territories was no less stable than the Capetian kingdom in the twelfth century.

Henry II and his sons' concept of their 'empire' and its permanence proves a difficult question; no concrete notion of unity for this 'empire' seems to have taken shape. Despite centralizing tendencies in England and Normandy, the Angevin monarchs made no attempt to impose a uniform administration on their other continental territories. While Norman and English law and administration under Henry II followed closely parallel lines, he followed his father's advice in his other domains, avoiding imposing uniform laws or institutions and ruling according to their different laws and customs. It is impossible to know exactly what notion John had of his inheritance other than a bloc of family possessions and feudal rights, source of his family's wealth and political power. Many of his subjects, however, were coming to see the Plantagenets' congeries of lands as 'a curious anachronism'.[5]

The little evidence in existence for the Angevins' view of their domains consists mainly of Henry II's changing plans for the succession. Richard Lionheart left no direct heir, and John's two legitimate sons were too young at the time of his death for him to have made plans for their inheritances. Although the trend among feudal princes was away from the old Carolingian tradition of dividing territories among heirs in favour of primogeniture, Henry II sought some land from his own and from his wife's domains for all his sons. As noted in Chapter 2, he first indicated this in 1169, when he gave his adolescent elder sons – Young Henry, Richard, and Geoffrey – territorial titles. John, born in 1167, had no part in this

5. Warren, W.L. (1973) *Henry II*, California UP, Berkeley, Ca./Eyre Methuen p. 627.

tripartite division; and Henry II's attempts to make some provision for him increased tensions with his older sons. Evidently, Henry reserved the right to switch his sons around from one territory to another as circumstances changed; his new schemes for partition angered Young Henry, Richard, and Geoffrey, making them jealous of each other and of little 'John Lackland'. Henry insisted on maintaining an overall superiority, while his elder sons resented his refusal to give them adequate authority or estates that would have provided them independent resources, pushing them toward rebellion.

It is difficult to know what goals Henry II had in applying his partition schemes. Did he have any vision of the Angevin and Aquitainian domains as a unity, or did he view them as 'a family assemblage' to be used to provide for his offspring?[6] It seems unlikely that Henry had any ambition of cementing his diverse lands together in a tightly integrated state on the Anglo-Norman model. Not even his almost perpetual motion could maintain sufficient contact with the great men of his scattered territories to mold them together. Yet he did not envisage them as simply personal possessions to be carved up on his death, with no measure of political or family unity surviving.

Henry II's Angevin patrimony has been aptly described by a modern scholar as a group of diverse lands and liberties acquired through marriage, inheritance, or conquest 'for the purpose of enhancing the political interests of a family and directed by the head of that family'.[7] It was bound together by a loose family unity that had proven more capable of coping with lack of heirs, premature deaths, or quarrels among heirs than the more structured Anglo-Norman realm. Except for a time in the late eleventh century, members of the house of Anjou had worked together harmoniously for the family interest with each generation preserving its acquisitions for the next.

6. Le Patourel, J. (1965) 'The Plantagenet dominions', *History*, 50, p. 301. Reprinted in Le Patourel (1984) *Feudal Empires, Norman and Plantagenet*, Hambledon Press.
7. Bachrach, B. (1978) 'The idea of Angevin Empire', *Albion*, 10, pp. 298–9. See also Bachrach (1984) 'Henry II and the Angevin tradition of family hostility', *Albion*, 16, pp. 126, 129–30.

This Angevin tradition was one that Henry knew well through his family's concern for chronicles and histories; his Angevin great-grandfather had authored a chronicle himself. Doubtless, Henry hoped that as his sons grew up they could share in this tradition of a 'broadly based and flexible' network of family ties,[8] acting as viceroys in outlying regions and enabling him to withdraw from day-to-day activity. If that was his hope, then he would be deeply disappointed.

One scholar whose work consistently stresses England's ties with the Continent, John Le Patourel, argued that Henry II's succession schemes reflect this tradition among the counts of Anjou of seeking to keep their territories intact, each generation preserving its acquisitions for the next. Modern historians of medieval England have tended to view the Angevin empire and Henry's notion of it only from an English perspective. Looking at it from the Angevin counts' viewpoint provides a different perspective, however. It permits a vision of a permanent Angevin empire incorporating greater Anjou and the Anglo-Norman realm. The Angevins had earlier expanded their possessions through marriages, and the union of Henry II's parents, the Anglo-Norman heiress Matilda and young Geoffrey Plantagenet, continued that expansion, as did Henry's own marriage to Eleanor, heiress to Aquitaine, in 1152.

Feudal custom offered Henry the only guidelines governing descent of his lands. Unfortunately, custom was not yet fixed in the late eleventh and twelfth centuries; rules of succession were changing from partition among sons to a pattern of strict lineal descent to the eldest son. Within a single province feudal inheritance patterns could vary greatly. In northwestern France and the Low Countries, and most fully developed in Normandy, the custom of *parage* prevailed over the strict primogeniture usually associated with feudal law, maintaining a lineage's cohesion despite partitions. *Parage* has been aptly described as 'a kind of partible inheritance under the chairmanship of one son'.[9] The deceased tenant's sons made an agree-

8. Bachrach (1978) p. 299.
9. Searle, E. (1988) *Predatory Kinship and the Creation of Norman Power 840–1066* California UP, Berkeley, Ca. p. 143.

ment providing for partition of the fief among themselves, while some semblance of family unity was maintained by the eldest son alone doing homage for the *caput* or chief castle. From the lord's point of view, the feudal holding was not divided; younger brothers would hold of their eldest brother and assist him in fulfilling the required feudal services.

Henry II seems to have followed the principle of *parage*, with the Anglo-Norman realm and greater Anjou going to his eldest son and outlying acquisitions – Brittany and Aquitaine – going to younger sons, holding of their elder brother by fealty. In other words, appanages. Henry's practical concern that Aquitaine and Brittany demanded the full attention of resident rulers, and that Young Henry would have had his hands full ruling the Anglo-Norman realm and greater Anjou may also have inclined him toward such a solution. As Le Patourel put it, 'the periphery was expendable',[10] but Angevin tradition would not sanction total separation. Henry's insistence that Richard and Geoffrey perform homage to their elder brother shows that he sought some unity for the Angevin dominions after his death, with the appanages subject under feudal law to Young Henry.

Another factor influencing Henry was *parage* custom in the Anglo-Norman realm. There inherited estates passed intact to the eldest son; once a father had provided for his first-born, however, he could then divide his own acquisitions or 'conquests' among younger sons as he wished. This rule seems to have been operative as early as 1087, on William the Conqueror's deathbed division of his domains, granting the duchy of Normandy to his eldest son and his newly conquered kingdom of England to his second son. Certainly Henry II's conferral of the lordship of Ireland on his youngest son, John, conforms to this tradition. Henry had both Angevin and Anglo-Norman precedent, then, for arrangements other than strict male primogeniture. *Parage*, customary in both Anjou and Normandy, afforded Henry a means by which his younger sons could share in the succession while preserving some continued cohesion for his territories.

10. Le Patourel (1984) p. 10 (article IX).

The drawback was that it demanded a strong family bond among the brothers.

Eleventh-century experience with appanages among the Angevin and Norman ruling families had cast doubt on their usefulness for strengthening the lineage, however. Such early appanage arrangements failed to solve succession problems and often promoted violence, giving cadets a territorial base within the succeeding senior male's lands from which to challenge his right. Although the chances of mortality meant that lands given to cadets often reverted to the senior line, the Angevin provisions lacked the special features of the later Capetian appanages or the late medieval English barons' fee tail that were devised to encourage reversions by limiting descent of fiefs to legitimate male offspring only.

Nonetheless, Henry II expected that his sons would maintain an alliance with ties of vassalage providing some cohesion, with periodic consultation among the brothers on common concerns. As Henry's biographer, W. L. Warren states, 'He conceived the future of the Angevin dominions not as an *empire* but as a *federation*.'[11] Most scholars, then, agree that Henry II had only a primitive concept of the state, viewing his 'empire' as private family property. His Capetian rivals had no more advanced notion of the state, not yet viewing their holdings as a unitary royal domain. They never imposed administrative unity on provinces incorporated into the royal domain, promoting instead a sense of national identity centred on the French royal family. If Henry had no idea of molding his diverse lands into a single state, however, he did assume – wrongly – that continuing family ties would preserve some semblance of family unity for his possessions. Evidently Richard Lionheart shared a similar view. Although he recognized his brother John as lord of Ireland, he exercised an overlordship over the island; and John was also Richard's vassal for the county of Mortain and the earldom of Gloucester.

Complicating matters was the status of Henry's continental lands as fiefs of the Capetian monarch. The Norman kings' homage for their duchy to their Capetian

11. Warren (1973) pp. 561–2, 627, 'a dynastic federation'.

overlords, done on the borders of Normandy and Ile de France, had signified no more than 'a tenuous non-aggression pact'.[12] After the accession of the Angevin kings, however, the Capetians were no longer content with the vague overlordship acknowledged by the new dukes of Normandy; instead, they were seeking to clarify their Angevin vassals' subordinate status, demanding that they perform homage at Paris. Philip Augustus would use the Angevins' feudal obligations as fief-holders to cloak with legitimacy his efforts to take their lands by force.

Henry II never solved satisfactorily the problem of disposition of his inheritance, and it led to his downfall. His sons' fealty to the French crown for constituent parts of the Angevin empire enabled their French overlords to cultivate their friendship and tempted the Capetians to support them against their father. Like many feudal fathers, Henry could not accept strict linear succession that would have left younger sons landless. He clearly had a soft spot in his heart for John, his youngest, and sought a larger legacy for him than the lastborn son in a feudal family could reasonably expect. Yet the price of providing for John was his elder brothers' resentment and rebellion. Apparently Henry believed, despite evidence to the contrary, that his sons could co-operate. This problem of preserving the family interest while still providing land for younger sons would confront the later Capetians, who solved it more successfully with their appanage policy; and it would also face the late medieval English baronage, who sought to achieve the same end through legal devices that facilitated return of cadets' estates to the senior line.

Perhaps nothing could have held the Plantagenet possessions together. Henry II had joined them together in a personal union; and he intended, even after partitioning among his sons, to preserve some connection as a family entity just as his Angevin predecessors had earlier for their smaller fiefs. Mutual mistrust among father and mother, sons and siblings, exacerbated by Capetian meddling, however, would have doomed Henry's hope for per-

---

12. Strayer, J.R., 'Fief'. Strayer, J.R. (general ed.) (1982–9) *Dictionary of the Middle Ages* (13 vols), Scribners, New York, NY, vol. 5, p. 59.

manence and at least loose family unity for his domains. The fierce hostility within his immediate family, probably fanned by his wife Eleanor's bitterness toward him, only failed to tear apart the Angevin empire because Young Henry and Richard Lionheart died without direct heirs. The pattern of *parage*, which provided a model for Henry to apportion his domains among his sons, depended upon feelings of family solidarity that his offspring lacked. A 'family firm' could not prosper amid family members' constant quarrels.[13]

Nineteenth-century nationalist historians looked for grander explanations than family enmity for Henry's failure to create a lasting political unit. They are joined by more recent historians, who describe the Angevin domains as 'heterogeneous and unwieldy', the result of 'an unholy combination of princely greed and genealogical accident'.[14] Scholars note too that the Angevin monarchs provided no unifying principle, no common culture that could bind their Anglo-Norman, Angevin, and Aquitainian subjects together. Their 'empire' was a new creation, and Henry only began to construct administrative machinery in its constituent parts after the 1173–4 rebellion. Philip II saw to it that Richard I and John would not have time to complete construction of a political structure, a cosmopolitan ruling class, or patterns of commerce that might have fostered a sense of unity.

To hold all these far-flung lands together was a difficult task. The diversity of peoples living in the wide expanse of lands meant that personal, itinerant rule could never be as effective as in the more compact and homogeneous Anglo-Norman realm. Although the commercial classes of the port cities saw some benefits in incorporation into a maritime Angevin empire, other groups could see no great advantage. Indeed, considerable hostility marked

13. Gillingham, J. (1984) *The Angevin Empire*, Holmes & Meier, New York, NY/Edward Arnold. p. 31.
14. Hollister, C.W. (1976) 'Normandy, France, and the Anglo-Norman *Regnum*', *Speculum*, 51. Reprinted in (1986) *Monarchy, Magnates and Institutions*, p. 50; Holt, J.C. (1975) 'The end of the Anglo-Norman realm', *Proceedings of the British Academy*, 61, reprinted in Holt (1985) *Magna Carta and Medieval Government*, Hambledon Press, p. 40.

relations between the nobility of the Anglo-Norman realm and lords of lands to the south. From the view point of the Angevins' subjects in Langue d'oc, England and Normandy were far distant provinces with which they had few ties. They saw no reason to contribute to the defence of Normandy, except as mercenaries fighting for profit. The nobility of Anjou had grown apathetic toward Plantagenet rule, seeing little advantage to being part of their empire, and they resignedly accepted their seneschal's defection to Philip II in 1203. Ties binding the inhabitants of Anjou, Poitou, and Gascony together would never be as tight as those connecting England and Normandy, where barons holding lands on both sides of the Channel formed a single aristocratic society. Anglo-Norman lords did not acquire landholdings in Anjou or Aquitaine to cement tenurial ties; neither did they intermarry with southerners in any significant numbers. English barons often showed little concern for nearby Normandy and less for Angevin possessions further south, and some were resisting their obligation to perform military service on the Continent.

Perhaps more serious was the overlordship of the Capetian kings of France. Of course, this afforded the Capetians a wedge of feudal rights by which they could force their way into these lands' internal affairs, claiming to regulate relations between their Angevin vassals and their subvassals. Many Loire valley nobles would decide that 'the intermediate lordship of the king of England offered few compensations for the complications it caused them with their ultimate lord, King Philip'.[15] Capetian overlordship also enabled the Angevins' subjects to play off one lord against another. Philip Augustus's condemnation of John and confiscation of Normandy followed an appeal by Hugh de Lusignan, one of John's Poitevin vassals, for justice against him in the French royal court. In the midst of Angevin-held lands, the Capetian kings had direct rights over lands and churches that supplied another wedge for influence and feudal claims; for example, at Tours, the abbey of St. Martin and the

15. Stacy, R. (1987) *Politics, Policy and Finance under Henry III, 1216–1245*, Oxford UP, p. 160.

archbishopric were under French royal protection. Many Norman nobles were being attracted to the Capetians by their reputation for good lordship and by the cultural prestige of Paris; also the royal court and monks at Saint Denis were beginning to create a myth of French national unity under the crown that their Plantagenet vassals could not counteract.

We must remember that because of the ill-will within Henry II's family only accidents of mortality among his sons kept the Angevin lands under a single ruler down to 1204. It must also be recalled, however, that Richard I spent his last years struggling to defend those domains; and the empire's survival of the stresses of his reign is testimony to the strength of its institutions. Then King John made recovery of lost portions his priority after 1204; many of the troubles that so blacken John's reputation stem from his zeal in carrying out that task. Clearly, he saw his empire as more than merely a chance collection of scattered territories.

. . .

THE ANGLO-NORMAN REALM

The Anglo-Norman realm was the most strongly governed of the Angevin dominions, with a legacy of effective government from the Norman king/dukes. King John inherited from Richard Lionheart in 1199 a complex administration in England and Normandy capable of functioning in his absence and of raising much revenue, and he had the good sense to keep in his service several of his brother's appointees who had proven administrative ability. First Henry I and then his grandson, Henry II, had set in motion a process of applying reason to government, centralizing authority, and creating offices that conducted business through written documents – a proto-bureaucracy. All this resulted in what some historians call 'administrative kingship' in England and Normandy.[16]

John's reign marks a watershed in this progress towards

16. Hollister, C.W., Baldwin, J.W. (1978) 'The rise of administrative Kingship: Henry I and Philip Augustus', pp. 867–905. Reprinted in Hollister (1986) *Monarchy, Magnates and Institutions*.

administrative monarchy with much more systematic record-keeping. It is doubtful that the king himself deserves much credit beyond his giving consent; it was most likely due to his chancellor, Hubert Walter, archbishop of Canterbury. He had a long and distinguished career as a royal servant, taking the chancellorship on John's accession after having served as Richard I's justiciar. While justiciar, he had introduced the practice of making three copies of final concords or agreements made before royal justices to settle lawsuits by compromise, one for each of the contending parties and one to be deposited at the treasury as a permanent record. Then, on taking office as John's chancellor, he began the practice of enrolling on separate rolls copies of all royal charters, letters close and letters patent.

With the Angevins, royal or ducal government came to deal directly and frequently with the mass of their subjects. The Anglo-Norman realm was no longer, if it ever had been, a 'feudal monarchy', governed indirectly through great lords. The Angevins took direct management of much of the work of governing that had been left to localities and landlords under the Norman kings. In both England and Normandy, doctrines of royal or ducal power permitted frequent interventions in the fiefs of tenants-in-chief, 'overturning the principles and the functioning of a feudal regime of the classic type'.[17] Most obvious is the growth in the royal and ducal courts' jurisdiction due to Henry II's reclaiming responsibility for serious criminal offences, pleas of the sword in Normandy, pleas of the crown and breaches of the king's peace in England. Just as important were the possessory assizes and the grand assize, which removed suits concerning possession of feudal tenures from baronial honor courts and brought them into the king/duke's courts. Furthermore, financial machinery – the exchequer – made possible more effective exploitation of rights of feudal overlordship for raising revenues.

Central government in England was becoming more

17. Boussard, J. (1963) 'Aspects particuliers de la féodalité dans l'empire Plantegenêt' *Bulletin de la Société des Antiquaires de l'Ouest*, 4th ser., 7, p. 34, my own translation.

intrusive with assizes regulating prices of ale and wine or setting standards for weights and measures. Such assizes were enforced by itinerant justices, who periodically left the centre of government at Westminster to make circuits about the counties. A characteristic of Anglo-Norman government since William the Conqueror had been the supervision of English sheriffs, Norman *baillis*, and other local officials by such itinerant commissioners sent from the royal court. The chief constitutional issue was no longer strengthening royal power against a feudal baronage to prevent the kingdom's disintegration, but now it was how the monarchy would use the power it had acquired. Would the new machinery of government operate for the king's personal interest, or for the public good, the *utilitas reipublicae*?

A commonplace of modern thought about growth of administration or bureaucratic government is that it brings 'routinization', reducing the monarch's freedom of action, making him simply the state's chief functionary. The old days when kings could rule through their domestic households and infrequent councils of bishops and barons had ended. The scope of activity for royal government had grown so greatly since Henry II's reforms that the itinerant royal household could no longer handle all the routine work. Yet the king remained the centre of government, resisting becoming tangled in the red tape of a civil service responsible to him. John certainly was capable of mastering the machinery of his government and imposing his personal stamp on it.

With John resident in England almost continuously by 1204, much government would function through the king directly; he played an active role in the work of his courts and in finances. While surviving plea rolls show the king tirelessly at work overseeing justice, fine rolls and pipe rolls depict him concentrating royal finances in his own hands, as he engaged in a desperate search to raise funds for warfare. As Sir James Holt writes, 'John was not just the power behind the administrative machine. He was often the machine itself.'[18] This has

18. Holt, J.C., *The Northerners: A study in the reign of King John*, Oxford UP (1961) p. 145.

won John the admiration of some scholars, who see him making decisions for every department of state. Holt warns, however, 'To be an efficient civil servant or an inventive administrator was only part of the job of being a great king. These standards are essentially those of the twentieth rather than the thirteenth century.'[19] Such a picture may be a distortion, due in part simply to the survival of many more records from John's reign and in part to his enforced residence in England for far longer periods than his predecessors.

Yet there can be no doubt that John was a very active ruler in Normandy before his withdrawal at the end of 1203 and afterwards in England, constantly travelling, passing through regions that had rarely experienced a royal visit, meeting his subjects and learning of conditions. As the king moved about, his court expanded or contracted as local dignitaries, officials from Westminster, others on royal business, and petitioners came and went. Because of the king's constant movement, he required two groups of government servants: his household staff accompanying him, and another group stationary at some convenient centre, Westminster for England and Rouen or Caen for Normandy. A royal viceroy, the justiciar in England or seneschal in Normandy, supervised this second group, and exchequer clerks and other staff were as much those officers' servants as they were the king's.

Like other rulers, John sometimes found the great offices of state at Westminster that had withdrawn from the itinerant royal court less responsive to his will, and he turned to household officials for counsel and to carry out his commands. John showed great flexibility, reshaping his household offices and giving them new functions. The situation has a modern parallel in the United States government today, where the president often finds the great departments of state stifled by bureaucratic routine and prefers to rely upon members of his White House staff for initiatives. John's concentration of authority in his own hands stems in part from his suspicious personality, but perhaps in larger part from a

19. Holt, J.C. (1963) 'King John', Historical Association (General Studies 53). Reprinted in Holt (1985) *Magna Carta and Medieval Government*, p. 95.

militarization of financial administration that had begun during Richard I's campaigns in France. John applied to civil administration men and methods he had first used while fighting in Normandy.

Innovations under the Angevins required increased numbers of royal servants capable of operating the new machinery of government. Ambitious knights and clerks, often younger sons of minor knightly families, sought to join the king's itinerant household or the exchequer at Westminster in search of advancement. A group of a dozen or so companions travelled about with the king, some holding household offices, others without specific posts. To link the itinerant court and the sedentary offices at Westminster, John relied upon this small number of all-purpose royal servants, holding multiple offices, performing myriad tasks. These royal confidants moved back and forth constantly between the shires, Westminster, and the king's household. The precarious military situation in Normandy before 1204 required John to rely on an even smaller number of trusted agents there.

Attestations to royal charters reveal the names of many of the royal *familiares*; about fifty-four appear frequently as witnesses to John's charters. Among them were eleven earls, three of whom might be classed as new men who had won their titles through marriage, and one of whom was the king's illegitimate half-brother, William Longsword, earl of Salisbury. Eleven bishops attested frequently, all former royal clerks and some of whom continued to hold offices in the royal administration. The remaining thirty-two include officials such as Hugh de Neville, chief forester, Warin fitz Gerold, hereditary chamberlain of the exchequer, Simon of Pattishall, senior royal justice, or Robert of Turnham (or Thornham), seneschal of Poitou; household officers such as two stewards, William de Cantilupe and Peter of Stoke; and multi-purpose royal servants, such as William Briwerre or Robert de Vipont.

While a few members of the old aristocracy, such as Earl Ranulf III of Chester or William de Ferrers, earl of Derby, were nearly always included in this group of royal intimates, they were present more in the capacity of counsellors than office-holders. Another element that was growing more significant under John consisted of mercenary captains, simple knights, and clerks, whose counsel he sought on day-to-day work of war and government and sometimes on great matters of state as well. Because John more often sought counsel from such men and from a few friends of higher rank – the *privata familia regis* – than from a formally summoned council of the baronage, suspicions would arise that his oppressive policies resulted from the advice of low-born or foreign-born *curiales*.

Some contemporary writers, jealous of the growing influence of these *familiares regis*, were contemptuous of them, criticizing them as ambitious new men. In moralizing or satirical works, they lumped them together as *familiares regis* or *curiales*. The term *familiaris regis* means literally a member of the king's household, while *curialis* might be translated as 'courtier'; the latter term usually implies a seeker of favour – usually a government post – through cultivating a patron. To their critics, *curiales* were new men of obscure birth, cultivating patrons through flattery, weaving networks of friendships, in order to obtain office, influence and wealth. John's household officials – stewards or seneschals, constables, and chamberlains – were often knights of obscure origins who demonstrated competence at varied tasks and won his confidence; conservative upholders of a static social structure accused them of taking places among the king's counsellors that rightly belonged to members of baronial families, exemplars of traditional feudal values. In John's view, the new men he chose for his service were competent, hardworking, more devoted to his interests and deserving of their rewards than barons of old families.

The royal household had three different aspects. The first was domestic, seeing to the feeding, clothing, and sheltering of the king and his companions; it included the *pincerna* or butler and such lowly servants as washerwomen and bathmen. The second aspect, closely connected to this one, was financial, the king's personal financial offices – chamber and wardrobe – covering the household's daily expenses. The third function of the royal household was protection of the king's person by household knights and serjeants, the king's bodyguards. In time of war, they could form an important nucleus of leadership in the royal army.

Head of the royal household was the steward or seneschal; the post grew in significance under John, vying for a place in the government alongside the great officers of state. Throughout the reign, William de Cantilupe had the title, although from time to time other *familiares* such as Peter of Stoke or Brien de Insula were also called seneschals. A domestic officer of growing importance was the chamberlain of London, who acted as chief purchasing agent for the royal court. During much of John's reign, this official was Reginald of Cornhill, also sheriff of Kent, who died in 1210. The Cornhills were one of London's great mercantile families, and their wealth won them baronial status. Reginald illustrates the multiplicity of tasks that John's *familiares* might assume; one scholar writes, 'It would be but a slight exaggeration to call Reginald de Cornhill John's business manager.'[20] He was active as one of the 'keepers of the ports', organizing along with a royal clerk, William of Wrotham, a fledgling English navy, fleets of galleys after 1203 that protected England's coasts and transported forces abroad.

The two household offices for finances – chamber and wardrobe – took on new importance during John's reign. The chamber had once been the office caring for the king's personal belongings; but it became a sort of travelling treasury department, the king's personal treasury, apart from the treasury at Winchester. In the almost continual warfare after Richard I's return from captivity, much money had flowed directly into the king's chamber without passing through the Norman exchequer. Under John, the chamber had significance as a secretarial office as well; it had charge of the king's privy seal, his personal seal, authenticating commands to the chancellor to issue documents bearing the great seal. Probably it was the seal John had used as count of Mortain, an antique gem set into a ring with the legend SECRETUM IOHANNIS.[21] The chamber was headed by two or three

20. Painter, S. (1949) *The Reign of King John*, Johns Hopkins UP, Baltimore, p. 137.
21. Jones, M.P. (1949) 'A collection of the Acta of John Lord of Ireland and Count of Mortain', Unpublished M.A. Thesis,

chamberlains and a staff of clerks. Some of the men who bore the title of chamberlain were often absent from the king's household assigned to other duties, for example, Hubert de Burgh, who had more important work as a military commander.

The wardrobe had been, until John's reign, little more than the chamber's strong-room, charged with receiving and storing money and treasure. During John's many military campaigns, however, it almost swallowed up its parent, the chamber; by 1209–10 it had become a kind of war office, supervising spending on men, weapons, and other resources for warfare. In theory, all moneys spent by the wardrobe passed through the exchequer, but in fact, money could be dispatched by sheriffs or crown debtors directly to it without being accounted for at the exchequer. The king himself or chamber clerks such as Peter des Roches or Richard Marsh often negotiated fines or terms for debt payments. By 1207 John devised a system of provincial treasuries at key castles to resupply promptly his household with coin transferred from Westminster or Winchester. By John's last years, the wardrobe was the key household office for finance and administration. In 1213, four new chests had to be bought to store its archives of rolls and charters.

Beyond the circle of royal intimates surrounding the king was a second, larger group of over a hundred royal servants at Westminster or in the counties, serving as sheriffs, constables of castles, custodians of royal lands, coroners, and foresters. These two groups could occasionally merge to some extent, for such secondary servants might join the king's household when he visited Westminster or their counties. Also some of John's intimates always held local offices in addition to their places at court. The key local officials in Normandy were the *vicomtes* or later *baillis*, each of whom occupied a ducal castle as his base. In England, of course, their counterparts were the sheriffs, who were now burdened with routine responsibilities, no longer semi-independent governors

21. Cont'd.
     University of Manchester, pp. 35–6. Also Tout, T.F.T. (1920–33) *Chapters in the Administrative History of Medieval England* (6 vols), Manchester UP, vol. 5, pp. 133–34.

of their shires. The Angevin kings often named their *familiares* as sheriffs, sometimes over blocs of shires; for example, William Briwerre, first a sheriff under Richard I, held multiple shrievalties under John. Such curial sheriffs left the routine work of the shire to undersheriffs. This system seemed to the Angevins a means of strengthening the ties between the central administration, the royal household, and the outlying provinces. In 1204, however, John began experimenting with appointments of lesser men who could be counted on to increase royal income from the counties.

Henry II, after crushing the rebellion of 1173–74, sought in each of his domains a single official to act as his viceroy in his absence. The justiciarship already existed in England to supervise the sheriffs and other officials, and the seneschal came to act as ducal deputy in Normandy for Henry and his sons. The justiciar and the seneschal concentrated in their hands administrative, financial, and judicial activities, giving the kingdom and the duchy effective government during the king's absences. King John inherited his justiciar, Geoffrey fitz Peter, earl of Essex, from Richard I; after Geoffrey's death in 1213, John promoted one of his closest friends, Peter des Roches, bishop of Winchester, to the justiciarship. John inherited his first Norman seneschal, William fitz Ralph, who held the post from 1177 until his death in 1200; then others followed in quick succession: Guerin de Glapion for a few months, then Ralph Tesson, who held the post from late 1201 to August 1203, and William Crassus (*le Gros*), John's last seneschal, 1203–04, left behind when he fled the duchy.

The English exchequer, over which the justiciar presided, came to be the centre of most routine business of royal government, and much of its everyday work was conducted through written documents, requiring employment of a number of clerks. The justiciar presided at the exchequer when the sheriffs presented their accounts for audits, recorded on the pipe rolls. In Normandy, the seneschal's responsibilities paralleled the justiciar's; he presided over an exchequer at Caen, which audited the *baillis'* accounts and kept its own pipe rolls. Of course, endemic warfare from Richard I's last years until 1204 sapped Normandy's resources and reduced the seneschal's ability to collect revenues.

The justiciar and the seneschal also took responsibility for justice. They organized periodic circuits of royal justices that carried the king's justice to the shires or *bailliages*, creating a new link between central government and the localities. Geoffrey fitz Peter organized three general eyres for England, searching investigations by justices into all aspects of local officials' activities. In addition, he sat at the head of a bench of justices at Westminster that had separated from the barons of the exchequer in 1194 to concentrate on hearing pleas. Since Henry II's assizes, these royal tribunals were providing alternatives to the honorial courts of feudal lords, protecting freeholders' tenures. Most of John's justices owed their selection to the justiciar and were as much Geoffrey fitz Peter's servants as the king's. Under John, however, a new tribunal accompanied the royal household – the *curia regis coram rege* – co-existing with the bench at Westminster until 1209, when the bench was closed temporarily.

The second of the great officers of state, the chancellor, was still associated with the royal household in the early thirteenth century. As keeper of the great seal, he had to be someone in the king's confidence. John had three chancellors: first Archbishop Hubert Walter who died in 1205; then Walter de Gray, nephew of John de Gray, one of John's greatest favourites, who purchased the office for 5000 marks; and in 1214 Richard Marsh, who had been senior chancery clerk in charge of the royal seal, 1206–13. Although the chancellor sometimes joined the king's household, he was often away from court supervising clerks at Westminster or performing other tasks. Because of this, John employed senior chancery clerks in his household such as the brothers Hugh and Jocelin of Wells, 1203–06, and then Richard Marsh for several years; they had the duties of vice-chancellor, although they rarely had the title.

The work of the treasurer was largely routine, and members of the same family had held the office since Henry I's time. William of Ely, who took the post under Richard I, was a relative of his predecessor, and he held the treasury for almost John's entire reign. His responsibilities covered all routine aspects of the financial administration, including collection and disbursement of royal moneys, transporting treasure, and sitting at the exchequer sessions, supervising the transcribing of pipe rolls.

The chief forester had charge of the royal forests, vast stretches of England set aside for the protection of the game that the king loved to hunt. Those regions – whether uninhabited woodlands or settled agricultural lands – lay under a special forest law, harsher and more arbitrary than the customary law of shire and hundred or the common law of Westminster. The chief forester's administration paralleled that of the justiciar; he had his own forest justices, who held forest eyres, and his own exchequer; he may have exercised almost as much power as the justiciar. John inherited his chief forester, Hugh de Neville, from Richard I, but he soon gained the new king's confidence.

The loss of Normandy in 1204 marks a watershed in England's government because the king would become an almost permanent resident. Since government offices had begun to multiply in Henry II's middle years, administration in the king's prolonged absences from the realm had been largely in the hands of the justiciar and other royal servants, who became accustomed to little royal intervention. John viewed such a situation as an aberration, and he intended to involve himself personally in the daily work of governing England. Seeking to mobilize men and money for the struggle to regain his lost continental lands, he gave particular attention to financial matters. John's seeking to concentrate power in his own hands and to act as his own first minister made the office of justiciar something of an anachronism. His subjects saw his involvement as a nuisance, and they would hold the king personally responsible for his government's acts of oppression and injustice.

. . .

GREATER ANJOU AND AQUITAINE

South of Normandy in the Loire valley lands of Anjou, Maine, and Touraine, public authority was less con-

centrated in the count's hands; something closer to
the 'classical' feudal regime of the textbooks prevailed,
with performance of public functions – judicial and
police powers – exercised by nobility who tolerated little
interference from their overlords. Farther south in the
duchy of Aquitaine, nobles showed an independent spirit,
even a tendency toward anarchy that proved an obstacle
to the centralizing tendencies of Angevin rule in the
Anglo-Norman realm. Despite the turbulent tradition of
Poitou, it took on new importance after John's withdrawal
from the Continent at the end of 1203 as a base for attacks
on Philip Augustus, aimed at recovering Normandy.

The Plantagenet overlords' authority ranged from 'the
intensive and authoritative' in the Anglo-Norman realm
to 'the diffused and occasional' in the domains that
fell to them through the marriage of Henry II and
Eleanor of Aquitaine.[22] South of Normandy and Brittany,
the Angevin overlords had not succeeded in imposing
obligations of fixed quotas of knights on tenants-in-chief
as the king/duke had on his Anglo-Norman barons. The
Angevins never made themselves keepers of the peace,
responsible for suppression of crime in the lands south
of the Loire. Neither did they have a pattern of local
public administration paralleling the nobles' seignorial
organization as they had in the Anglo-Norman realm;
instead, central authority was 'patchy' at best,[23] effective
only within their own estates.

The degree of comital authority in greater Anjou falls
between two extremes, less effective than in Normandy
or England, but stronger than in Aquitaine. Tenth- and
eleventh-century Anjou had been one of the strongest
of the small states rising on the ruins of the Carolingian
Empire. While Anjou is usually seen as the model of a
successful small feudal state, the counts had considered
themselves heirs of Carolingian officials; and they pre-
served some authority from Roman and Frankish times.
Even in the eleventh century, some sense of 'the public

22. Davies, R.R. (1990) *Domination and Conquest: The Experience of Ireland, Scotland and Wales 1100–1300*, Cambridge UP, p. 46.
23. Gillingham (1984) p. 35.

role of the state' is expressed in the counts' charters.[24] They sought to prevent their vassals from usurping all their prerogatives as public officials, from collecting taxes and undermining the comital court's overall responsibility for justice. Above all, the counts of Anjou kept control over strategic castles and their castellans, but they also controlled nominations to the see of Angers and to most abbeys in their county.

During the years 1060–1106, the same time that William of Normandy was asserting his supremacy over the nobles of his duchy, the power of the counts of Anjou was weakening. Castellans in Angevin territory took advantage of civil war caused by uncertainty over the succession to usurp castles, to replace local comital authority, to reject jurisdiction of the count's court, and to control offices in his household. Castles, the source of the counts' power, became the hereditary property of the castellans' families. By the early twelfth century, Fulk V and his son Geoffrey Plantagenet, Henry II's father, were trying to reverse this trend; but their power came chiefly from the castles remaining under their direct control, lying on comital demesne lands. The only local officials over whom they had effective control were the *prévôts*, in charge of their own estates. While Henry I of England was constructing an administrative monarchy, Anjou's administrative system remained rudimentary. Yet the Plantagenets did reassert their rights as feudal overlords, insisting that their vassals fulfil their obligations of loyalty and services.

The counts of Anjou had worked to increase their landholdings, conquering the county of Touraine in the mid-eleventh century, and acquiring the small county of Vendôme and the larger one of Maine by marriage. The most brilliant of their matches, however, was the marriage of Geoffrey Plantagenet to Matilda, the widowed German empress, daughter and heir of the Anglo-Norman king, Henry I, in 1128. Following Henry I's death, her husband claimed Normandy on her behalf and occupied it by 1144,

24. Bachrach, B. (1988) 'The Angevin economy, 960–1060: ancient or feudal?', *Studies in Medieval and Renaissance History*, new ser., 10, p. 32.

while she struggled to secure England. Their son, Henry II, brought Brittany into the Angevin orbit by an invasion in 1166 and marriage of its heiress to his son.

Some of Henry II's administrative principles may well owe as much to his Angevin ancestors as to his Norman ones. The counts' keen interest in history resulted in considerable literature circulating at their court to record his ancestors' exploits. Henry, like his Angevin ancestors, claimed overall responsibility for justice, ready 'to take cognizance of cases without any legal theory of appeals from his vassals' courts'.[25] He felt entitled to disregard social distinctions in selecting his counsellors, looking beyond his barons to trusted companions, *familiares comitis*. He saw clearly the importance of the castle and its castellan, both militarily and for purposes of administration. Henry worked 'prudently and patiently' to continue the work of his predecessors,[26] taking back lands, castles, and privileges granted away or usurped; and he laboured to construct an administration that could carry out comital authority in his absence. The Anglo-Norman realm provided financial resources for strengthening his control over greater Anjou, and in the years just after his sons' rebellion of 1173–74, he largely succeeded in regaining effective power there. His financial and military resources from England and Normandy far outstripped those of any of his vassals, and after 1174 they did not dare revolt.

The marriage of Henry Plantagenet to Eleanor of Aquitaine in 1152 was the most brilliant of all the Angevins' matches. It achieved a long-sought goal of the counts of Anjou, bringing into their orbit the possessions of the counts of Poitou. This was a confusing collection of lordships including the duchy of Aquitaine or Guyenne and the county of Poitou, and since the mid-eleventh century, the duchy of Gascony further south. The duke/count was one of the great lords of France, the Capetians' vassal for Poitou and Guyenne, but not for Gascony, which was an allod free of any attachment to the

25. Powicke, F.M. (1906) 'The Angevin administration of Normandy', *English Historical Review*, vol. 21, p. 648.
26. Powicke (1906) vol. 22, p. 36.

French monarchy. The great size of Gascony alone, a sort of federation of thirteen counties, made it difficult to govern. The duke/counts never attempted to create any central organs of government for Aquitaine; they ruled their two domains, the county of Poitou and the duchy of Gascony, separately, summoning their vassals to meet with them in two separate councils. Poitou and Gascony had little in common, not even language, for one province spoke northern French and the other Provençal dialect. Each had a port important for wine exports – La Rochelle and Bordeaux – and their economic competition was more a cause of conflict than of common interests.

Unfortunately, Poitou had a number of great lords by the late twelfth century who were building regional lordships of their own, forming an intermediate seignorial level between the count and lords of modest holdings. Such large lordships containing a number of castles could act as a check on the count's authority, much as in eleventh-century Normandy before William the Bastard imposed order on it. For example, Aimery, viscount of Thouars, was the most important noble in Poitou with over a dozen castles to dominate the county; close behind him in resources were the lords of Parthenay, Talmond, and Lusignan. At the same time that these regional lords were bringing more castles under their control, the number in the count's hand or those of his own *prévôts* was decreasing. Richard I had controlled fourteen castellanies in Poitou, but the number in John's hands dropped to five; and the count/duke had hardly any in neighbouring territories such as Périgord, the Limousin, or Angoumois. As the number of Poitevin castellanies under comital control steadily declined during John's early years, he sought to buy his nobles' loyalty with money-fiefs.

In Gascony, the ducal domain had never been large, and even less of it survived by the beginning of the thirteenth century; the counts and *vicomtes* were regional lords practically independent of ducal authority. Their power prevented the English kings from asserting control over castles, private warfare, oversight of baronial courts, and other rights of overlordship that they enforced effectively in the Anglo-Norman realm, and to some extent in greater Anjou. From 1199, the power of ducal government declined steadily in both Poitou and Gascony. After 1204, these territories had value for John chiefly as bases for land attacks on the French from the south, part of his grand strategy for recovering Normandy, and as recruiting grounds for mercenaries. He brought a Poitevin force to England under Savaric de Mauléon, a great Gascon noble, for support against rebel barons in 1215–16. John struck what bargains he could with his southern vassals to secure their military support, seeking to purchase their loyalty by granting to them his comital or ducal powers and privileges, while they were always tempted to seek greater advantage from Philip Augustus, the feudal overlord of Poitou.

Henry II learned a lesson from the 1173–74 rebellion that led to administrative changes. He could not enforce his will over such a disparate empire by 'hard riding',[27] rushing about from one region to another; and beginning about 1176, he gave each of its constituent parts a regional governor as its administrator. He already had such an official in England, the justiciar, who had proved his value during the war. The English justiciar plus the seneschal (sometimes also called justiciar) of Normandy and the seneschal of Anjou would be 'veritable viceroys' in each territory,[28] authorized to act in his name, with the local royal officials – sheriffs, *baillis, vicomtes*, or *prévôts* – serving under them. Each royal deputy would be his representative, responsible to the king and removable at his will. Henry would make his sons, Geoffrey and Richard, rulers of two provinces, Brittany and Poitou.

Richard I and John introduced this pattern of viceroys to their mother Eleanor's lands, sometimes with a single seneschal for all Aquitaine, sometimes with separate ones for Poitou and Gascony. In 1200, John named as seneschal for Poitou and Gascony Geoffrey de la Celle, who had previously served Richard; then came several in rapid succession: Robert of Turnham, an English knight, in Poitou; Martin Algais, a mercenary soldier, as seneschal of Gascony and Périgord; and later other English knights, Hubert de Burgh and Geoffrey de Neville. Only one

27. Clanchy (1983) p. 114.
28. Boussard (1963) p. 46, my translation.

native Poitevin, Savaric de Mauléon, held the post for John. The Plantagenets had a cosmopolitan outlook in appointments to offices, then, with John sending Anglo-Normans to Aquitaine as seneschals and naming Poitevins to prominent posts in England. Over time, such a policy may have eventually knit together a single ruling class, but in the short run, it fostered resentment of 'foreigners' among his English subjects. John's first seneschal of Anjou and Maine in 1199 was Robert of Turnham, who had served his father and brother there. He replaced him with William des Roches, a powerful Angevin baron, who was won over from support of Arthur of Brittany. William presided over a slightly more advanced administrative and judicial system than did his Poitevin counterpart, and he had charge of treasuries at Chinon and Loches.

Yet none of the provincial seneschals outside Normandy had much administrative machinery to aid in asserting authority over local officials, the *prévôts*, or over former comital castles that had fallen to hereditary castellans. Unfortunately, Henry II and his sons tended to rely more on military solutions to the problem of power in greater Anjou and Aquitaine than on governmental ones. Their endless military campaigns, employing large numbers of mercenaries, aimed at confiscation or destruction of castles in private hands. Such preoccupation with warfare did little for political stability, preventing more permanent administrative innovations and contributing to a political vacuum that local lords rushed to fill, consolidating regional power blocs.

Evidence for revenues from Anjou and Aquitaine is fragmentary. Earliest records survive only from the Capetian occupation – 1221 for Anjou and 1238 for Poitou – and they show revenues of only about £1500 sterling from each of the two territories. Nothing suggests that an advanced financial system similar to the English and Norman exchequers took shape in either territory, although treasuries at the castles of Chinon and Loches supplied funds for the fighting in the region. Poitou and Gascony were fertile lands with fruitful vineyards and an expanding wine trade. Yet the Angevin kings enjoyed only modest income, mainly feudal dues from their few direct tenants and duties on exports and imports from the ports. John was prodigal in granting away even the customs revenues to communes – surrendering to the La Rochelle merchants in 1200 all the town's royal revenues for a year and in 1214 exempting Bordeaux merchants from paying duties – whereas his father had sought to preserve his income from towns. While such grants won John the towns' loyalty and support of their militias, he still would have to depend upon England's wealth to pay for his Poitevin campaigns of 1206 and 1214, just as he had earlier for his failed defence of Normandy. Shortly after John's death, his son's seneschal was poorer than the barons he was supposed to rule; the only comital income collected from Poitou under Henry III was an insignificant sum paid at the ports.

Chapter 4

CRISES OF JOHN'S REIGN: CONTINUING FINANCIAL PROBLEMS

. . .

THE ANGEVIN FINANCIAL CRISIS, C. 1180–1220

A continuing financial crisis exacerbated all other conflicts of King John's reign. A financial burden that had borne heavily on Henry II and Richard I because of costs of almost constant warfare, repressing rebellions or fighting the French kings, continued to press on John. Conflict on the Continent had become endemic shortly after Philip Augustus's accession to the French throne in 1180; in addition, Richard Lionheart had the costs of his crusade and his ransom. Under John, conflict continued with a campaign at the beginning of his reign against Angevin supporters of Arthur of Brittany, his failed defence of Normandy 1202–04, a 1206 expedition to Poitou, campaigns against the Welsh and Scots and an expedition to Ireland, and the final 1214 continental expedition. Costs of warfare grew in the course of the twelfth century with the need for a force in the field over long periods pushing the Angevins into hiring mercenaries, and with improvements in military science requiring recruitment of such specialists as crossbowmen or siege engineers. Within England, the Angevin kings' greatest regular expense was castle construction and repair with costs averaging about £1000 annually under King John.

In effect, John was following his brother in organizing a 'war economy', and their financial policies appear unclear unless we notice the 'strong military colour' of their rule.[1]

---

1. First phrase, Prestwich, J.O. (1954) 'War and finance in the Anglo-Norman realm', *Transactions of the Royal Historical Society*,

John or his household clerks took over negotiation of fines for favours (roughly equivalent to bribes in today's language), and more and more moneys went from crown debtors or custodians of royal lands directly into the chamber. John's system of castle treasuries is indicative of this militarization of government. His need to put money quickly into the hands of fighting forces in Normandy led him to create provincial treasuries, convenient for receiving cash shipped across the Channel and avoiding the Norman exchequer at Caen. John adopted a similar decentralized treasury system in England by 1207, dispersing his moneys from the old treasuries at Winchester and Westminster to various castles in charge of constables who had served him on the Continent. This made funds immediately available to the itinerant royal household, circumventing the slow and methodical exchequer procedures.

Noticed less often than military expenditures, but also a growing financial burden for the Angevins, was maintenance of an impressive standard of living at court. Henry II generally had given little heed to ceremony or luxury, but he sometimes saw a need for display to enhance the royal dignity. On his daughter Joan's marriage to the king of Sicily, he presented her with gold and silver plate and other gifts, including a robe valued at almost £115. Such an expenditure, when many knights had incomes of barely £20 a year, stands out as conspicuous consumption. All the Angevin monarchs were builders of castles, most notably Richard I with his enormous expenditure of £11,500 on Château Gaillard, but they also constructed or renovated royal residences and hunting lodges without military importance. Much of the work John ordered on royal castles went to embellish his residential quarters, making them more palatial. John favoured splendid trappings of monarchy that his father had eschewed, observing feastdays with ceremony and

1. Cont'd.
5th ser., 4, p. 20; second, Jolliffe, J.E.A. (1948) 'The chamber and castle treasuries under King John' in Hunt, R.W., Pantin, W.A., Southern, R.W. (eds) *Studies in Medieval History presented to F.M. Powicke*, Oxford UP, p. 118.

costly banquets. Records of his purchases of expensive jewels, plate, and fur-trimmed robes for himself and his household attest to his love of splendour. John spent £700 on robes for his 1205 Christmas feast, more than the entire cost of his eldest brother's coronation in 1170.

At the same time that spending on larger and better equipped armies and on luxuries at court was rising, inflation was pushing costs even higher. Because concrete information is so scarce, economic historians have difficulty explaining this English inflation *c.* 1180–1220. Some scholars offer a demographic explanation, while others base price rises on increased currency supply; in fact, the causes were multiple. The monetary explanation rests on exceptional supplies of silver in England, noticeable even early in the twelfth century. Silver became widely available from new mines in eastern Germany and the metal reached England through a favourable balance of trade with Germany and the Low Countries from increasing wool and grain exports.

The demographic argument is that population growth pushed up grain prices and land values without true economic growth. Although population was growing throughout the twelfth and thirteenth centuries, agricultural methods, despite some improvements, remained too primitive to increase crop yields much without increasing the acreages under cultivation. England's economy remained backward compared to Flanders or northern Italy, where a commercial revolution was underway. Since English exports were agricultural products, wool and grain, little surplus could be saved for capital investment, and supplies of food and other goods did not grow as fast as population. Whatever the cause, the twelfth century saw a long cycle of inflation, reaching 100–200 per cent by the last two decades. Manorial lords coped with rising prices by switching from letting their estates at fixed farms, collecting traditional dues and services from their peasant tenants, to demesne farming, direct exploitation of their estates by hired bailiffs.

While large landholders could keep up with inflation because surplus population kept wages low, the royal government experienced a crisis. Because of political and administrative limitations, the king could not follow his barons' example and exploit his royal demesne directly. He was not benefiting from the increasing prosperity of his greatest subjects. His costs kept climbing, as soldiers' pay rose, as the luxury of court life increased, and as more officials were recruited to collect additional revenues, but income remained static. Since Domesday Book, the royal demesne had diminished through grants to relatives, retainers, and the Church. In an economy with limited growth, traditional sources of royal income simply were not keeping pace with costs of government; and the Angevin monarchs had to be predators if they were to secure their share of the kingdom's wealth. The *Dialogus de Scaccario*, written by Henry II's treasurer, states baldly that the wealth of kings 'is not invariably theirs by strict process of law . . . but sometimes from the secret desires of their own hearts and sometimes even from their mere arbitrary power'.[2]

The barons, like taxpayers in every age, resented paying more, convinced that traditional royal sources of income should be sufficient. Knights also fell victim to Angevin thirst for money. Many of them were crown tenants, holding at least one fee directly of the king, or tenants of escheated honors and other estates temporarily in royal custody. To the feudal classes and conservative monks, the king's growing corps of officials appeared as the Stuart royal court did to seventeenth-century country gentry: parasites, not public servants. The barons particularly resented funding projects which appeared of no benefit to them, and many were seeing less and less need for expeditions to protect Plantagenet possessions across the sea. As royal financial measures grew ever more extortionate, especially after 1204, much of the English baronage lost all interest in the fate of Normandy, where only a handful had lost large holdings; and Poitou held even less attraction for them. Sir Richard Southern wrote, 'There is a direct connection between the over-great financial and military burden of this Continental policy and the failure of the English kings to create any warmth

2. Johnson, C. (ed. and trans.) (1950) *Dialogus de Scaccario*, Oxford UP (Oxford Medieval Texts), p. 1.

of sentiment operating in their favour among the most powerful classes of society.'[3]

A key to understanding the financial crisis facing Richard I and John is the increased cost of countering the French threat to their continental empire. It seems clear that financial strains again increased after 1194 and also after 1204, as John sought to fill a vast war chest for recovery of his lost possessions. Recent studies suggest that their Capetian rival Philip Augustus was increasing his revenues, tipping the balance, so that the Angevins no longer enjoyed the great financial advantage they had held in Louis VII's time. Several scholars stress financial strains that the contrast between the Angevins' precarious finances and the Capetians' growing wealth was placing on England and Normandy. In short, Philip II could afford to wage larger and longer wars.

Medieval financial records are notoriously incomplete, and the earliest surviving French royal accounts date from 1202–03. Despite a continuous run of pipe rolls from Henry II's early years, the record also is incomplete for England. Not all royal revenues passed through the exchequer; the chamber handled much receipt and expenditure, and moneys passing through it often left no mark on the pipe rolls. For example, John's chief forester had his own exchequer at Marlborough Castle and transferred funds directly to the chamber. Furthermore, the *Rotuli de Oblatis et finibus*, rolls of offerings for favours kept by the chancery and often paid directly to the chamber, only date from 1199. Few Norman pipe rolls survive, for John's reign only a partial 1203 roll, and no financial records at all survive from the Angevins' southwestern territories. Such gaps enable some scholars to argue that the financial balance was tipping in favour of the Capetians and others that it stood in the Angevins' favour.

Recent research indicates that the French government had grown more efficient in the 1190s and that new lands coming into the royal domain in 1191 made Philip

---

3. Southern, R.W. (1970) 'England's first entry into Europe' in Southern (1970) *Medieval Humanism and Other Studies*, Harper & Row, New York, NY/Blackwell, Oxford. p. 152.

Augustus much richer than his predecessors. Whereas they had been too poor to hire mercenaries to fight Henry II, Philip could hire a permanent force of some 2500 troops for use against Henry's sons. Analysis of the earliest surviving French royal accounts, 1202–03, reveals ordinary income of roughly 141,500–197,000 *l. parisis* (£51,000–72,000 sterling), including such windfalls as feudal reliefs and a special war tax, the *prisée des sergents* (26,000 *l. parisis*). When Sir James Holt compares Capetian and Angevin resources, he finds that John had no more than 74 per cent and possibly as little as 41 per cent of Philip's funds. John W. Baldwin, latest biographer of Philip Augustus, concludes, 'The accounts of 1202/03 . . . convey the distinct impression that Philip's finances were indeed in order and adequate to his political designs against the Angevin lands on the Continent.'[4]

Holt has made the most searching study of the Angevin kings' income, and he concludes that England was being drained by the costs of defending Normandy. He calculates from the pipe rolls that English revenues after Henry II's accession rarely equalled those of Henry I in 1130; only John's harsh measures in his middle years moved royal revenues ahead of early twelfth-century levels. When a century of inflation is taken into account, this means that the Angevins' income before the loss of Normandy could not have equalled that of their Norman predecessors. Holt estimates English royal income for 1203 to have been little more than £34,500. He argues, further, that because of inadequate revenues from Normandy, only a flow of funds from England paid for the duchy's defence. It had produced almost as much annual revenue for Richard I as England, but as Sir Maurice Powicke pointed out long ago in his authoritative *Loss of Normandy*, the duchy was saddled by 1194 with debts from Richard's crusade and ransom. Enormous expenditures on construction of Château Gaillard added to that debt. By 1203, if not earlier, the Norman treasury was empty, and money had to be found in England for its defence.

4. Baldwin, J.W. (1986) *The Government of Philip Augustus*, California UP, Berkeley, Ca., p. 174.

Richard Lionheart's biographer, John Gillingham, firmly rejects these estimates showing Angevin resources inferior to the Capetians'. He maintains that the French figures for 1202–03 may be inflated by borrowed funds or a reserve from earlier years. He further argues that £34,500 is too low a figure for English revenues. In addition, Gillingham counts some £1500 John was receiving from Ireland in 1202–03 and sets a figure between £20,000 and £34,000 as John's income from Normandy. Such numbers represent pure guesswork, based on the last complete surviving Norman pipe rolls for 1195 and 1198. Clearly, John was receiving some income from Normandy; but in the confused conditions of French invasion wide areas escaped paying taxes, and yields cannot have been great. When Gillingham adds all these numbers, he arrives at an income of £63,000 to £77,000 for John, comparable to Philip II's £51,000–72,000 income.

Sir James Holt also calculated Norman revenues, using the 1195 and 1198 Norman pipe roll figures for comparison with Capetian income in 1202–03; and he rejects Gillingham's optimistic estimates. Holt makes a telling point that the Angevin monarchs' total revenues are irrelevant, that the figures which count are the sums shipped across the Channel to Normandy. He compares the flow of funds from England for the duchy's defence to sixteenth- and seventeenth-century Spanish treasure fleets crossing the Atlantic to finance Habsburg wars. Financial records document a steady outflow from the English treasury to the king in Normandy even before the outbreak of war in 1202, for example, 3000 marks in October 1201. Once war was underway, amounts increased dramatically. The 1203 liberate roll records almost £15,000 received from England, and the patent roll for the next year notes that 3500 marks had been sent from the chief forester to the king at Rouen.

Gillingham turned to Richard I's and John's south-western territories, seeking other sources of income for the struggle against the Capetians. Admitting the absence of any record evidence from greater Anjou or Aquitaine, he argues nonetheless that they were rich lands, capable of adding much wealth to the Angevins' treasury. He points to indirect evidence for a functioning financial system in Anjou, with its treasury at Chinon Castle, and for profits from Poitevin wines exported from La Rochelle. Gillingham rejects the earliest record evidence, surviving from the Capetian occupation, which shows Anjou, Touraine, and Poitou producing little income. He argues that the Capetians gave away many seignorial rights that had produced revenues for the Angevins. Despite an absence of supporting evidence, Gillingham concludes, 'If John was no match for Philip Augustus, it was not because he had inherited inadequate financial resources; it was because he did not know how to rule.'[5]

Gillingham over-estimates these southern lands' potential for producing revenues. Except for England and Normandy, the Angevin possessions lacked administrative machinery to exploit their wealth. Since many lords of those territories were in revolt, John could have collected little for his war chest. Even Gillingham has to admit that in Anjou and Aquitaine King John's authority was spotty. Because increasing numbers of lordships lay outside the control of comital or ducal agents, John's seneschal of Poitou had almost no regular income. In 1219, young Henry III's seneschal wrote that 'we ... because of our poverty are unable either to defend the land or subjugate [the Poitevin barons], nor do they value me any more than a little boy.'[6] Again Holt's studies find no evidence that Anjou and Gascony sent any funds for Normandy's defence; in fact, cash was flowing in the opposite direction from the English treasury to Anjou and Gascony. After the loss of Normandy, defence of Poitou demanded large sums from England. A chronicler supplies a figure of 28,000 marks sent to Poitou in 1204, and royal writs show that John received 14,000 marks in shipments from England on his 1206 expedition. Nothing indicates Angevin ability to exploit the southwestern provinces' wealth effectively; neither is there evidence for excess revenues from them contributing to Normandy's defence.

5. Gillingham, J. (1978) *Richard the Lionheart*, Weidenfeld & Nicolson, p. 304.
6. Chaplais, P. (ed.) (1964) *Diplomatic Documents*, vol. 1, *1101–1272*, HMSO, 1964, p. 42, doc. no. 43.

Almost continuous warfare from Richard I's return from captivity until 1204, then, left England to shoulder alone the burden of defending the Angevins' continental possessions and King John's attempted recovery of Normandy. Gerald of Wales wrote that John, his father, and his brother remained wealthy despite heavy expenditures on war; he explained that 'although their regular revenues were much smaller than their predecessors', they took care to make good the amount from exceptional sources, relying more upon occasional profits than upon steady income'.[7] In the eyes of many modern historians as well, Magna Carta and baronial rebellion against King John were simply the result of exploitative policies in place since Henry II. Sir James Holt wrote, 'Henry II was the architect both of the fortunes and failings of his house . . . John consummated what Henry II had begun.'[8] He finds financial demands − amercements, reliefs, fines for favours − becoming markedly more burdensome in Henry's last years. Sidney Painter also concluded that John was more greedy in his financial demands than his predecessors, but saw John's extortions as 'a question of degree not of nature'; he found John generally remaining 'within the framework of custom set by his predecessors even though he strained it at the edges'.[9]

Unlike John, Henry seems to have convinced most of his subjects that his demands lay within established custom; and even when he did demand large sums, he offered easy terms of payment stretched over long periods. William of Newburgh saw Henry II's financial exactions only 'somewhat immoderate',[10] compared to

7. Gerald of Wales. Brewer, J.S., Dimock, J.F., Warner, G.F. (eds) (1861–91) *Giraldi Cambrensis Opera* (8 vols), Rolls Series, vol. 8, p. 316.
8. Holt, J.C. (1992) *Magna Carta*, 2nd edn, Cambridge UP, pp. 40–1.
9. Painter, S. (1949) *The Reign of King John*, Johns Hopkins UP, Baltimore, p. 223.
10. William of Newburgh. Howlett, R. (1885–90) *Historia Rerum Anglicarum of William of Newburgh*. In *Chronicles, Stephen, Henry II and Richard I* (4 vols), Rolls Series, vol. 1, p. 280; translation, Douglas, D.C., Greenaway, G.W. (eds) (1968) *English Historical Documents*, vol. 2, *1042–1189*, Eyre & Spottiswoode, Cambridge, p. 371.

Richard Lionheart's. Some recent studies support the Augustinian canon's view, suggesting that 'the idea of the burdensome nature of early Angevin monarchy' needs rethinking. Some suggest that Henry II did not increase royal revenues over the level of his grandfather's collections, and that only John's harsh measures actually pushed Angevin income ahead of the Norman kings'. One study denies that Henry followed extortionate policies in relation to his barons; it states, 'He wanted their loyalty and their service, not their money.'[11] Yet Richard I and his brother both required more money than their father because of warfare and rising prices, which they could not raise by traditional means, forcing them to exploit feudal privileges more rigorously. Certainly the Lionheart had a reputation for great greed; one contemporary stated, 'Surely you are aware . . . that the lord king thirsts for money like a dropsical man for water.'[12]

Questions arise about the extent to which John's financial policy deviated from his predecessors'. Did his policy differ only in degree from Henry II's and Richard I's, and was he simply reaping accumulated grievances against all the Angevins? Or did royal financial demands differ in substance as well as in degree? The pipe rolls for John's reign spell out his quickening rate both of raising and spending money. By his middle years, he had increased considerably his English revenues over those of his father and brother. To raise revenues to match the French monarch's enhanced resources required new financial policies, and John introduced a number of innovations. The English king had to resort to measures that pushed his magnates' feudal obligations beyond what they thought were acceptable bounds. The result was that many barons and knights came to resent his money-raising measures as unjustified novelties, tyrannical demands

11. Quotations. Keefe, T.K. (1983) *Feudal Assessments and the Political Community under Henry II and his Sons*, California UP, Berkeley, Ca., p. 113; also Keefe, T.K. (1981) 'Henry II and the earls: the Pipe Roll evidence', *Albion*, 13, p. 203.
12. Douie, D.L., Farmer, H. (eds and trans.) (1961–2) *The Life of St Hugh of Lincoln* (2 vols), Thomas Nelson (Medieval Texts), Walton-on-Thames, vol. 2, p. 124.

tending towards absolute monarchy. Clearly, his greater financial need pressed him to harsh expedients beyond his father's and brother's policies, and his exploitation of the kingdom appeared so burdensome that it pushed his tenants-in-chief into rebellion.

A glance at the poverty of the government of little Henry III during the years just after his father's death affords a new viewpoint on John's financial exigency and his furious search for revenues. It points to the necessity for his iron-fisted rule in the face of hostile economic conditions. Of course, physical devastation and impoverishment caused by the 1215–17 baronial rebellion contributed to the English government's poverty during the Minority, but more important was the weakening of its control over the countryside, its inability to collect traditional dues and services owed to the king. The scutage of 1217–18 to pay an indemnity to the invading Prince Louis of France produced less than 40 per cent of the sums assessed; even members of the ruling council proved reluctant to pay. Estimated average income for 1218 and 1219 was about £8175, less than a quarter of John's income in 1203, and by the time of the Easter Exchequer 1220, the royal treasury was empty. Across the Channel, French financial accounts for 1221 show Philip Augustus's treasury filling with a surplus of some 25,000 *l. parisis*, as income outran expenditures by a third.

. . .

KING JOHN'S FINANCIAL INNOVATIONS

John's first year saw new demands on a country that had already raised revenues on an unprecedented scale during the decade of Richard I's rule. John proved even readier than his brother to sell new privileges, licences, and exemptions, or confirmations of old ones; the city of London offered 3000 marks for confirmation of its liberties, and the Jews bought confirmation of their royal charters for 4000 marks. In 1200, John followed his brother in trying the carucage, a revival of the Anglo-Saxon geld assessed on the carucate (plowland), a measure of land, probably producing as much as £7500. The 1202–04 conflict over Normandy was consuming money as fast as it could be raised. Much money flowed directly from crown debtors or royal agents into the chamber overseas without taking time to travel to the exchequer.

John's financial demands grew even more oppressive after the loss of Normandy in 1204, as he sought to build up a huge war chest for a campaign of recovery. He spent at least £5000 in 1205 on military and naval preparations for an expedition to the Continent that baronial opposition prevented from ever leaving port. Lady Stenton's study of the pipe rolls for John's middle years left her with an impression that 'the king was seeking by every means to extract more and more money from his subjects'.[13] Before 1204, John had been willing to sell privileges, pardons, properties and offices for quick cash. This afforded 'political safety valves',[14] since purchasers could see themselves gaining something in return for their payments. After 1204, however, as he concentrated on careful husbanding of resources for renewed war on the Continent, he was unwilling to part with privileges. His quest for money seemed more arbitrary, more tyrannical because there was no longer any *quid pro quo*, and people were more conscious of exploitation. The pipe rolls for 1209–11 reveal increasing numbers of fines for the king's benevolence and for release from prison. John's 1210 tallage of the Bristol Jews, outstanding for its savagery, indicates the tendency toward tyranny. A chronicler, seeking to accent the king's cruelty, wrote that resistance by a Jew of Bristol to his 10,000-mark tallage caused John to order a tooth a day extracted until after losing seven teeth, he agreed to pay.

By introducing a percentage levy on his subjects' wealth and by other new measures, King John in his middle years succeeded in filling up a large war chest. After 1209, during the interdict, the king enjoyed the wealth of ecclesiastical property in his hand, perhaps £50,000 added income. Even his justices in the common law courts felt

13. Stenton, D.M. (general ed.) (1933–64) *Great Roll of the Pipe, 1–17 John*, Pipe Roll Society, new ser. 28, p.xxxiii [Pipe Roll 13 John].
14. The view of Holt, J.C. (1961) *The Northerners: A Study in the Reign of King John*, Oxford UP, pp. 148–50.

pressures to increase royal revenues. After 1207 oblations for departures from standard judicial procedures appear more frequently, apparently peaking about 1210–12. The king and his judges accepted offers of money, horses, or hawks for favours to hasten or smooth the course of justice. Also royal justices were readier to impose amercements on litigants and erring or absent jurors.

In the period preceding John's 1214 continental campaign, the connection between his military plans and his financial oppression became transparent. Because barons were less willing to follow the king on campaigns with their full quotas of knights, John had to scramble to secure the needed numbers of fighting men. He began to remit debts of crown debtors who would agree to supply knights for service in Poitou. Robert of Berkeley in 1213 agreed to send ten knights overseas for a year in return for forgiveness of a 500-mark debt, and the following year, another baron had respite from debts to the Jews while two of his knights were in Poitou. By 1214 just as King John's expenses for his continental campaign were mounting, he suffered setbacks in finances. He lost his ecclesiastical revenues; indeed, he had to levy a tallage to repay the Church for damages it had suffered during the interdict. Widening discontent since the summer of 1212 was causing discontinuation of some of his harsh policies in an attempt to placate potential enemies. Although John may have had a war chest of nearly 200,000 marks at the beginning of his great 1214 expedition, by autumn that money was fast disappearing. Costs of his campaign in Poitou plus subsidies paid to his Flemish and German allies quickly consumed this surplus. The king's predicament drove him to new expedients, launching a forest eyre in hope of imposing amercements and soliciting fines, and even selling surplus supplies of wine and other goods. Fines negotiated with barons for feudal incidents were growing more exorbitant, reaching shocking figures by 1214.

Lacking a steady, reliable source of public revenues, the Angevin kings showed a tendency to turn to opportunistic expedients, exploiting aggressively their feudal rights over their tenants-in-chief, keeping them barely within the bounds of custom. This exploitation grew more ruthless under King John, eventually arousing opposition that culminated in baronial rebellion. Aspects of the feudal bond between lord and man – or king and tenants-in-chief – that had been peripheral were growing more important than the formerly central aspects of personal loyalty and military service. As a result, the feudal relationship between king and baronage was less and less about personal military or court service and more and more about finances, approaching the later Tudor 'fiscal feudalism', as many magnates were falling deeply in debt to their lord.

The king's position as feudal overlord gave him financial advantages that exploited carefully and sometimes cruelly could increase royal income. Any lord had a right to require his tenants to pay a 'gracious aid' on three occasions: the knighting of his eldest son, the marriage of his eldest daughter, and his ransoming if he should be captured. Also in a time of emergency, he could ask for extra financial help. The lord could only collect such an aid after taking counsel with his tenants, however; he could not arbitrarily collect it, as he could a tallage from his peasants. Perhaps because of this element of consent, John never sought a gracious aid, but relied on the feudal incidents.

Of course, the basis of the feudal arrangements between lord and tenant was the obligation of military service, a lord's feudal levy of knights holding land of him. By the time of the Angevins' wars with Philip Augustus, however, a money payment used to hire professional soldiers was more important than actual performance of knight service. During the years since the barons' quotas of knight service had been first set by William the Conqueror, they had enfeoffed more knights than required for the royal host. Henry II's attempts to increase knight service to include the additional knights his magnates had enfeoffed aroused too much oppostion, however; and by 1187 he had settled for service only from knights of 'the old enfeoffment', those enfeoffed before 1135. Even so, some barons in Richard I's and John's reigns continued to protest their assessments; for example, Roger Bigod offered a fine in 1213 to reduce his quota from $125\frac{1}{4}$ to 60 knights.

Richard and John in fact rarely summoned the full feudal levy, resulting in *de facto* reductions in quotas of knights that would become the rule in Henry III's reign. For the endemic warfare in France, the Plantagenets needed a small, skilled force that could remain in the field for long periods. They preferred to collect scutage from their barons and then hire mercenaries, soldiers with better training and willing to fight beyond the obligatory forty days. Since scutage was a substitute for a military obligation owed to the king, he did not need to obtain consent before levying it. Always some barons escaped scutage, either because they performed personal military service with their reduced contingents of knights or because of royal pardons. John continued his brother's practice of allowing some barons to offer fines or lump-sums for exemption from service. These payments frequently totalled more than actual scutage would have, gaining him an average of almost £2500 additional revenue.

With time, scutage came to be levied so often that it resembled a tax, but only the feudal classes were liable for it. Henry II levied a total of seven and his successor three scutages, although Richard I preferred to accept fines from his barons, who then could recoup their fine by collecting scutage from their own tenants. Since such payments depended on bargaining with the king, some lords obviously could negotiate better terms than others. John's first scutage was at two marks to the knight's fee, up from Richard's highest rate of twenty shillings, and his scutage policy after 1204 indicates a shift toward more arbitrary demands, with a rate at two and a half marks per fee levied in 1204. The amount actually collected in that year's scutage was larger because all sorts of tenants were assessed, whether they owed knight service or not. John levied eleven scutages in sixteen years, raising an average of £2020 from each, and his last scutage in 1213–14 was at a rate of three marks (£2 6d) per fee, arousing such strong protests that Sir James Holt sees it as a *casus belli*. In fact, even at such high rates, the king was not meeting his costs. If he had actually hired substitutes for the forty days' service of knights paying scutage, he would have spent four pounds, for knights' daily wages had risen from eight pence under Henry II to two shillings (40 days × 2 s. = £4). John gradually abandoned any pretence that his scutages were for purposes of warfare, collecting them in 1204, 1205, and 1209 for campaigns that never took place. Demands for scutage payments for non-existent military campaigns proved galling to the barons, who saw this as a departure from accepted feudal practice. Their demands for consent to scutages would form part of their reform proposals in 1214–15.

The feudal incidents included relief, rights to wardship of minors and their marriage, and rights of escheat and forfeiture, opening opportunities for periodic royal exploitation of tenants-in-chiefs' lands. The Angevin kings regarded these payments as negotiable, not figures fixed by custom. Relief was a payment made when the tenant died and his son succeeded him as holder of the fief, harking back to the days before fiefs had become hereditary. The lawbook *Glanvill* stated that the customary relief for a knight's fee was 100 shillings, but that relief for tenants-in-chief of the king was 'at his mercy and pleasure'; neither did the *Dialogus de Scaccario* note any fixed figure, but stated that a baronial heir must 'make what terms he can'.[15] The barons came to feel that custom limited their relief to £100, however, although the Angevins sometimes charged enormous sums, especially when an heir's legal status was shaky. Demands by John for ever higher reliefs, especially for inheritances that heirs felt were rightfully theirs anyway, embittered them. Like the privileged in any society, barons felt that their superior status entitled them to special privileges, including moderate relief payments.

It can be argued that demands for higher reliefs from the barons were justified. Since magnates enjoyed exemptions from many other dues, their payment of relief was the one occasion when the king could collect a substantial sum from them. In one scholar's view, the barons had an obligation to pay for 'the privilege,

15. Glanvill. Hall, G.D.G. (ed. and trans.) (1965) *Tractatus de Legibus et Consuetudinibus Regni Anglie qui Glanvilla vocatur*, Thomas Nelson (Medieval Texts), Walton-on-Thames, p. 108; *Dialogue of the Exchequer*. Johnson (1950) p. 96.

power, social positions, their estates afforded them'.[16] As a portion of the total value of inheritances, reliefs were no more unreasonable than death duties or inheritance taxes. Furthermore, many heirs to baronies had their debts pardoned and others rarely paid in full, or paid only in small interest-free instalments spread over many years. Until John's time, exchequer officials had applied little pressure for prompt payment of crown debts; one authority examining baronial debt found 'either great leniency or great slovenliness in the work of the officials'.[17]

John extorted payments for succession to baronies far in excess of the £100 that the barons considered customary relief. In 1210, the king demanded a 10,000-mark fine from Reginald of Cornhill on his father's death, the same figure from William fitz Alan for his father's Shropshire barony, and 7000 marks in 1213 from John de Lacy for his father's honor of Pontefract. It should not be surprising to find these three among the rebel ranks in 1215. A total of some 60 sons succeeded to their fathers' baronies during John's reign, and their fines or reliefs range from only 40 marks to 10,000 marks, with an average of about 600 marks. John was especially likely to demand a fine when lack of legitimate offspring designated a collateral heir as successor. Brothers who inherited baronies rarely escaped with £100 offerings; their average approached 2000 marks, and more distant kin could expect to pay more. Painter concluded that while John charged exorbitant reliefs throughout his reign, 'some of those imposed in 1213 and 1214 can only be described as fantastic'.[18]

The king always had many estates in his hand as feudal custodies or escheats, and besides taking their income, he acquired minor heirs and widows with the right to grant them in custody and to arrange their marriages. While custodies of baronial landholdings in the royal hand could be sold, they were useful not simply as financial

16. Keefe (1983) pp. 128–9.
17. Poole, A.L. (1946) *The Obligations of Society in the 12th and 13th Centuries*, Oxford UP, p. 107.
18. Painter (1949) p. 221.

resources. They provided patronage, rewards to *curiales* in place of money payments, and wardship of barons' widows, daughters, or minor sons was a major resource for rewarding loyal servants. William Briwerre, for example, one of John's intimates, purchased a half-dozen wardships at prices from 10 to 10,000 marks. Escheated baronies or those passing to female heirs also provided a means of providing for members of the royal family, such as William Longsword, John's bastard half-brother, who acquired the earldom of Salisbury through marriage.

Rights of wardship and marriage were so valuable that the itinerant justices' instructions included inquiring into wards and widows in the king's gift. When a tenant died without leaving an heir of age, the lord could take custody of minor children or the widow, keeping the fief in his hands and taking all its profits, until the heir came of age. King John was more guilty than his brother of profiting from his feudal privilege of wardship and marriage. A recent study of the Angevin kings' policies concerning custodies concludes that Henry II raised relatively modest revenues from fines for wardships, with revenues increasing under both Richard and John. The fines became so frequent and heavy under John, however, that they can be termed extortionate. Average fines for wardships and consent to marry pinpoint the increase under John: for Henry II 101 marks, 174 marks under Richard I, and a rise to 314 marks under John. Some offerings to John for marriages to heiresses were as fantastic as reliefs demanded late in his reign. The fine of Peter de Maulay, one of his alien administrators, for 7000 marks to marry a Yorkshire heiress in 1214 is surpassed by the 20,000-mark fine offered that year by a young baron out of royal favour, Geoffrey de Mandeville, for marriage to the king's ex-wife, heiress to the honor of Gloucester.

In the cases of widows and heiresses, the lord had the right to arrange their marriages, in practice, selling them off to the highest bidder, since men would pay well to marry a woman who brought with her a great estate. Widows of royal tenants-in-chief could avoid forced remarriages by offering fines for the right to remarry or not, as they pleased. Evidence of royal revenues from consent to widows' remarriages or consent to remain unmarried also reveals increases under Henry II's sons; amounts offered by widows increased under John, from an average fine of 110 marks under Henry to 278 marks. Fifty-nine widows thought it prudent to pay King John. Among them was the countess of Aumale, heiress to northern lordships; already widowed three times, she offered 5000 marks in 1212 to avoid taking a fourth husband. If widows remarried without the king's consent and did not offer a fine, they could expect to pay an amercement. The Angevin kings also demanded fines somewhat comparable to relief from widows for the right to enter into their inheritances, *maritagia*, or dowers.

John sought to modify feudal custom in order to increase further his income from wardships. Traditionally, minors who came of age and took possession of their fiefs did not pay relief, since their lord had already enjoyed the income from their lands for some time. According to *Glanvill*, this demand for relief from minors coming of age was contrary to custom; but the *Dialogus de Scaccario* stated that relief was owed unless their land had been in custody for several years. John frequently insisted that minors offer fines on coming of age, in lieu of relief, regardless of how long their estates had been in royal custody. With John fines for royal assent to marriages of male heirs in royal custody became common, although feudal lords had not traditionally exercised such control over male wards' marriages. John also instituted a practice known as prerogative wardship, whereby he took custody of all lands of a deceased tenant-in-chief of the crown, including those tenements held of intermediate lords. This meant that even if a minor held only one fee directly of the king, all his/her estates fell into royal custody, cheating barons of a profitable feudal incident. With a quarter or more tenants of baronial honors also tenants-in-chief of the king, prerogative wardship brought much land temporarily into the king's hand.

Similar to custody of minors was the regalian right to ecclesiastical lands vacant due to a bishop's or abbot's death. John prospered from this right during the interdict, 1209–13, when such properties were taken into his hand due to his bishops' flight. By the spring of 1213, seven bishoprics and over a dozen abbacies were in the king's hand, any one of which might yield an income of several hundred pounds a year. He increased profits by tallaging at least once estates of vacant bishoprics in his hand, whether or not he levied a tallage of the royal demesne. In addition, King John used the excuse of the interdict to take into his hands many other clerics' possessions. An indication of what he gained is his promise, as a price for ending his long quarrel with the Church, to pay the English clergy 100,000 marks for its losses.

Not only did the sums John demanded of his barons rise, but John insisted on prompt repayment, ending the leniency about crown debts that had prevailed earlier. He took steps to tighten the law of the exchequer, making it a potent instrument of oppression. At a 1201 council, John decreed that baronial stewards, who appeared before the exchequer as their lords' agents, must be able to pay any amercement that might be imposed on them. This meant that they must be men of substance whose imprisonment by the king would cause their masters concern. As an added means of debt collection, the king might require some unfortunate subject owing relief or a fine for some other feudal privilege to make a *conventio*, a charter scheduling payments that could be enforced at the exchequer. A new pipe roll entry became common by 1207, consolidating all an individual's debts which had been scattered about the roll under different headings and in different shire accounts. These consolidated entries make plain the exchequer clerks' special effort to search out debts that might otherwise have been overlooked. Changes such as this indicate 'the increasingly searching and demanding interest of the King in the individual baronial debtor'.[19]

At the same time, John decreed that men who offered fines for recognition of their right to land, or some other privilege could have their estates seized for failure to keep up payments. He was shaping distraint of lands, a feudal remedy for lords' enforcement of tenants' obligations, into

19. Holt (1961) p. 171.

a potent new weapon. By 1207, John was pressing for prompt payment of debts to Jews, using distraint of land as a means of collection, a measure affecting numbers of knights. By moving directly to disseizin of lands, he was ignoring distraint of chattels, the traditional first step in enforcement of obligations. Debtors forced to offer fines for family lands that they felt to be rightfully theirs anyway were doubly distressed if they defaulted and found their lands taken into the king's hand. Previously, an older view had separated relief payments from fines, offers freely made for some favour; now John's decree equating relief payments with fines meant that possession of inheritances remained precarious until the relief was fully paid.

John's feudal tenants soon learned that he would not only disseize them, he might also imprison them for failing to pay crown debts. The law of the exchequer was becoming an instrument of political discipline as well as a financial one. Once a royal subject fell into the king's debt, the threat of a demand for repayment, followed by distraint of land or imprisonment, was enough to keep him obedient and docile. Even John's barons, whose debt burden was mounting, began to experience fear of personal ruin through the exchequer's operations.

Thomas of Moulton's misadventures illustrate what could happen to unlucky crown debtors. In 1205 Thomas purchased the office of sheriff of Lincolnshire for a proffer of 500 marks and five palfreys, and an annual increment of 300 marks over the ancient farm of the shire. The next year he paid a quarter of his fine, but expected profits from his shrievalty did not materialize, and he soon fell behind on his payments. At the Easter exchequer of 1208, he was removed from office, imprisoned in Rochester Castle, and amerced 1000 marks; King John demanded that Thomas's imprisonment continue until he paid 'to the last penny' all that he owed.[20] In 1207, Thomas was amerced an additional 200 marks for incorrect statements he had made before the *curia*

20. Hardy, T.D. (ed.) (1835) *Rotuli Litterarum Patentium 1201–1216*, Record Commission, p. 85b, [*Rot. Lit. Pat.*].

regis. He had ties to other Lincolnshire gentry who had also fallen into debt to the crown, among them Simon of Kyme, who owed over £850 principal plus over £400 interest to the Jews by 1211–12. Simon compounded with the king to pay £1000 over a 3-year period, but it was an impossible sum for him to pay. It is not surprising that both Thomas of Moulton and Simon of Kyme would be found in the rebel ranks, 1215–16.

John's pressure upon crown debtors sent many of them to Jewish money-lenders, the chief providers of credit in Angevin England, and their level of indebtedness was rising. The Jews were an important financial resource to the Angevin kings, tolerated in the kingdom only on the king's sufferance. Because they carried on their money-lending activities with royal protection, and all that they had technically belonged to the king, debts to them were indirectly owed to the crown, and the royal government ensured that all debts to the Jews were collected. Debts to Aaron, a Jew of Lincoln who had died in 1186, amounted to so much that Henry II took over their collection, establishing a special office at the exchequer that had grown into the Exchequer of the Jews by Richard I's time. The tense situation following a failed conspiracy in 1212, however, led John to moderate his policy on repayment of Jewish debts.

John's urgent need forced him to exploit to the limit traditional non-feudal revenues. As greatest landlord in England, the king could demand a tallage (*tallagium, taille*) or *commune auxilium, donum* from the tenants of his demesne, just as any manorial lord might take such a payment periodically from his peasants, free and unfree. John extended to Ireland tallages of the royal domain, that is, tenants of crown manors and royal boroughs and also lands in temporary royal custody. This cash revenue became more important than traditional manorial income. Tallages usually were assessed along with feudal levies, such as scutages or gracious aids, in order to raise some revenues from the non-feudal classes. Most profitable was tallage collected from royal boroughs, for the commercial class of the towns was beginning to possess significant wealth. Similar to tallages were the *dona* that King John demanded on occasion from the English Church.

Because of its seignorial origin, tallage was arbitrary, not requiring consent from those on whom it was imposed. In principle, royal agents assessed the tallage on individuals, but in practice boroughs and manors often negotiated with the king's men, paying a lump sum. Because of such bargaining, it varied from one town or manor to another; the city of Lincoln in 1206 negotiated a payment of £400, payable in two instalments. Although the reign of John reveals more aggressive tallaging of the royal boroughs, tallages did not produce outstanding yields. His tallages mostly yielded figures no higher than Henry II's average of £4000–5000, although John's 1210 tallage produced 'an unprecedented sum' of almost 15,000 marks.[21] After that, other sources of revenue seem to have led him to turn away from tallages of the royal demesne and he took only one more, in 1214.

An important experiment by John was his attempt to reap greater resources from his sheriffs. The most ancient and regular royal revenues were included in the sheriffs' 'farm of the county', a figure fixed by Henry II in the 1160s at about £10,000 and changing little until the late Middle Ages. Under the Norman kings, shire farms had consisted chiefly of income from royal demesne manors but as more and more royal estates were alienated, the proportion of non-manorial income from the counties increased. Profits of justice, various local levies, and feudal custodies and escheats became more significant. Sheriffs also had responsibility for collecting some revenues that did not form part of the county farm. They collected private debts owed to the king, for petitioners purchased all sorts of favours: offices, custodies of estates, special judicial proceedings, even his goodwill or remission of his wrath.

The sheriff spent what he needed in carrying out the king's business in the shire, then paid the balance of the farm into the treasury. Whatever he collected beyond his fixed farm went into his own purse as profit. Naturally, the post of sheriff was very profitable, for the twelfth-

21. Mitchell, S.K. (1914) *Studies in Taxation under John and Henry III*, Yale UP, New Haven, Conn., p. 948.

century inflation meant that he could increase income from royal manors, while his farm remained fixed. One of John's sheriffs offered him 1000 marks in 1208 to escape an investigation into exactions he had made while in office.

Ambitious men were willing to purchase shrievalties, convinced that profits would be greater than their proffers. Besides selling the office, the Angevin monarchs tried two means of increasing their share of shires' income beyond the sheriffs' fixed farms. One was Richard I's demand that sheriffs pay a fixed annual sum, an *incrementum* in addition to the traditional farm, first imposed in 1194 on his return from captivity. John continued this policy of imposing increments on new sheriffs. People in the counties, from whom the sheriffs squeezed their increments, viewed them as unpleasant novelties. By early 1213, John was reversing his policy of pressing for increments, renouncing them two years before Magna Carta would require it. Doubtless this was due to a policy of conciliation that the king adopted following the abortive rebellion of 1212 and before his 1214 expedition.

Another innovation was John's device of 'custodian-sheriffs' in 1204, turning over counties to sheriffs who were salaried officials rather than farmers, accounting in detail to the exchequer for all 'profit', revenues beyond traditional fixed farms and increments. *Curiales* in about half the shires were removed and replaced as sheriffs with lesser men, often their under-sheriffs. The new system was an 'overall success',[22] but by 1207–09 it required some adjustment. Several curial sheriffs had regained their offices from the custodians, although the experiment continued in other shires. The reasons for its abandonment in some counties appear more administrative than political; the custodian system required more complex accounting procedures than the exchequer could carry out. Possibly a deteriorating political situation convinced John that he needed strong and reliable supporters in charge of certain counties. Nonetheless,

22. Harris, B.E. (1964) 'King John and the sheriffs' farms', *English Historical Review*, 79, p. 537; correcting Painter (1949) p. 122.

replacement of a custodian-sheriff by a traditional farmer-sheriff always resulted in imposition of a new and higher increment. John's experiments with increments and with custodian-sheriffs enabled him to increase his income from the shire farms by some fifty per cent.

Another way John had of increasing revenues was to remove a borough or manor farm from the sheriff's control and to grant it to someone else for a higher payment. Inhabitants of towns were willing to offer the king more money for freedom from the sheriff's control, and both John and his predecessor eagerly sold them charters of self-government, while their father had opposed urban liberties. Painter estimates that John's new profits from custodian sheriffs and from boroughs and manors removed from shrieval custody increased his revenues by £3500. Sale of charters to continental towns gives John's reign significance for growth and municipal liberties in his French territories. Some seventeen cities had purchased communal status in Normandy before its loss, and Bordeaux and other Gascon towns also won recognition for their communes. This policy contributed to the towns' consistent support of King John.

The royal forests were not under sheriffs' control, but under a separate administration. They were a source of valuable resources, providing venison for feasts and firewood for royal residences or timber for repairs to them. John's foresters also collected payments for permits to feed pigs in the forest, pasturage for other livestock, for assarts or licensing the clearing of forest land for crops, and for other privileges. Henry II had vastly extended the forests in area, but Richard I and John sought income by selling extensive rights to deforestation. In 1204, the men of Essex paid 500 marks for deforesting a portion of the royal forest in their shire; men of Cornwall paid King John 2200 marks and 200 palfreys for freeing their county from restraints on assarting, and Devonshire men paid 5000 marks. Remaining royal forests produced significant funds. In 1208 the chief forester, Hugh de Neville, accounted for returns of over £15,000 covering a six and a half year period.

Forest law was more arbitrary than the custom of the shire courts or the common law of the royal courts, and eyres to enforce it produced amercements and fines for infractions against the king's beasts and for assarts. Forest eyres produced impressive sums in amercements that fell on barons, knights, and villagers alike; apparently the pipe rolls underestimate income from John's 1207 and 1212 eyres, making his forest policy appear less harsh than his father's. Yet figures for forest amercements were large, £1300 in 1207 and £1250 in 1212 from Yorkshire alone. The forest system fell especially heavily on the North of England, a source of northern barons' resentment of John.

John looked beyond simply increasing traditional revenues to novel ways of tapping his realm's resources. He needed a dependable, regular source of royal revenue that would tap the resources of the whole kingdom, not simply his own feudal dependants, the royal demesne, or landed wealth. The Angevins had little experience with regular, general taxation, however; Henry II had done nothing to introduce new, non-feudal taxes until the Church's search for funds for the crusades provided an excuse for an exceptional tax on wealth. In 1188, in preparation for the Third Crusade, Henry levied the Saladin Tithe, a percentage of the income and personal property of those who did not take the cross. It was an extraordinary levy for the rescue of Jerusalem, sanctioned by a great council, not a precedent for general taxation for ordinary governmental expenditures.

John tried the carucage in 1200, a land tax collected by Richard I in 1198, but no records of it survive to reveal how much he raised, and it likely proved too difficult to collect in relation to yield. A new general levy was needed, one that tapped more than landed wealth. Both Richard and John remembered the handsome sums that the Saladin Tithe had yielded. They continued the percentage levy on incomes and personal property inspired by papal crusade levies, turning it to secular ends. In 1193, officers ruling in Richard's absence demanded the incredibly high figure of a quarter of all the movable wealth in the kingdom to raise his ransom. John seems to have followed this precedent with a seventh in 1203, a percentage levy on movable goods possibly paid only by barons and bishops. Since no records survive, it is not at all certain how much revenue it raised, but an estimate of £7000 seems reasonable.

Most important for marking the transition to general taxation is John's levy of a thirteenth (actually a shilling of every mark) on incomes and movables in 1207. It produced £60,000, an amount ten times larger than traditional scutages and tallages.[23] The thirteenth was not levied for a specific military campaign, as were feudal aids or scutages, or to meet some emergency, as were Henry's and Richard's percentage levies; it was collected on property of all classes, lay and clerical, feudal and non-feudal, and the methods of assessment were national, with individual property-holders swearing to their goods' value before special justices sent out to the shires. Perhaps most significant, because it was an extraordinary levy, John sought authority by 'the common counsel and assent of our council',[24] a powerful precedent for baronial approval. The thirteenth inspired considerable opposition, however, and the instability of John's later years meant that he never dared collect such a profitable tax again. Nonetheless, a precedent had been set for later parliamentary subsidies.

Other financial innovations during John's reign include the introduction of import and export duties, another non-feudal source of revenue. Before his reign, customs duties had gone to local authorities at the ports, who might pay a farm to the king for the privilege. In 1202, King John instituted customs duties at a rate of one-fifteenth of the value of cargoes imported or exported, and he provided machinery for collection, appointing three chief custodians. Possibly it was first aimed at merchants from enemy lands, mainly Flemish wool merchants, but by 1204, it had become a general levy on imports and exports paid by both native and foreign merchants. Although it was producing well, with the four busiest ports each

23. Stenton (1933–64) new ser. 22, p.xxi [Pipe Roll 9 John]: £57,431 paid in; £2615 outstanding. This does not include money raised from the thirteenth in Ireland.
24. Stubbs, W. (ed.) (1913) *Select Charters and Other Illustrations of English Constitutional History*, 9th edn, Clarendon Press, Oxford, p. 278.

paying over £650, it had to be abandoned in 1206, when John's truce with Philip Augustus mandated free trade between England and France. John made up for some of the loss by imposing a tax on wine imported from his own continental possessions, which proved profitable, and he seems to have partially reinstituted export duties in 1210 with a levy on woad. Also John sought to increase his income from the wine trade by rigorous enforcement in England of an assize regulating wine prices. The itinerant justices in 1206 imposed so many amercements for selling wine contrary to the assize that this practically amounted to a new levy on vintners. Such measures show how widely John was casting his net in seeking new moneys.

King John raised vast sums, but when he returned to England in October 1214 after failing to recover his continental possessions, he was not only defeated but much poorer. Possibly the barons' awareness of his awkward financial situation emboldened them. John's own recognition of his lack of funds probably explains some of his uncertainty in dealing with the barons and his attempts at compromise in the months before Magna Carta. John's inability to replenish his treasury before the outbreak of civil war left him dangerously weakened. Only the plunder of rebels' confiscated estates provided funds for continuing the war, and he spent the last months of his life living from hand to mouth on the countryside. By June 1216 the king was melting down his plate to pay his troops.

Chapter 5

CRISES OF JOHN'S REIGN: THE LOSS OF NORMANDY AND FAILURE TO RECOVER IT

. . .

THE CAMPAIGN OF 1202–04

John's failure to defend Normandy, 1202–04, his loss of all the Angevins' continental lands except Aquitaine, and his inability to recover his French empire in 1214 defined his entire reign. Nearly all his energy went into the effort to recover Normandy, and his failure almost fatally undermined his prestige. Had John returned to England victorious in 1214, it is unlikely that he would have had to contend with a baronial rebellion. An essential measure for judging medieval kings, applied by their contemporaries, was bravery in battle. War was the profession of the feudal nobles, and no king who failed to prove himself a valiant warrior would earn their respect. Warfare is recognized as Richard Lionheart's chief concern, yet John was also at war or planning for war throughout his reign. Although recent scholarship has preferred to concentrate on John's administration, the energy he expended on government only makes sense if placed against a background of war finance; it was mainly aimed at raising funds for military campaigns.

Contemporaries lacked the perspective to see the loss of Normandy as simply the culmination of a long process begun once Philip Augustus consolidated his power, and they could not avoid comparing John's defeat with his brother Richard's military prowess, overlooking Richard's cessions of land to the Capetian king. While John did not measure up to his predecessor as a general, he hardly deserves the reputation for 'military incapacity and incredible lethargy' and for 'the indolence of the self-indulgent' that still clings to him in textbooks.[1]

Clearly, King John was a failure as a general in his defence of Normandy, yet some condemnations of his military competence are due to misunderstanding the nature of medieval warfare. Anachronistic notions of the chivalric quest for glory stand in the way of an awareness of how war actually was waged. An example of such a mistaken view is H.G. Richardson and G.O. Sayles's 1963 comment that early thirteenth-century warfare 'called for little strategy, for little military science', and that it consisted chiefly of 'small bodies of knights and serjeants engaged in cavalry charges where tactics and personal prowess were the only things that mattered.'[2] Others also have failed to see any strategic planning in John's campaigns, dismissing accounts of castles besieged and countryside ravaged as dreary reading. Yet John, like any capable general, had a sense of geography and an ability to plan a strategy to gain ground. The victor in a medieval war was not the impetuous hero eager to meet a hostile army head-on in a pitched battle, but one who plundered the enemy's resources and besieged his castles, laying waste his land and impoverishing his people. As John Gillingham has observed from the *Histoire de Guillaume le Maréchal*, 'pillage and robbery' were basic elements of chivalric warfare.[3] This characteristic of medieval warfare accounts for some criticisms of John's lack of boldness; his rival Philip Augustus was no bolder in offering battle.

Philip was as eager to weaken John as he had been his father and his brother. The peace settlement at Le Goulet, 22 May 1200, opened the way for the French

---

1. First phrase, Lyon, B. 'John, King of England'. In Strayer, J.R. (general ed.) (1982–9) *Dictionary of the Middle Ages* (13 vols), vol. 7, Scribners, New York, NY, p. 130; second phrase, Powicke, F.M. (1929) 'England: Richard I and John'. In Tanner, J.R., Prévite-Orton, C.W., Brooke, Z.N. (eds) *Cambridge Medieval History*, vol. 6, Cambridge UP, p. 220.
2. Richardson, H.G., Sayles, G.O. (1963) *The Governance of Mediaeval England*, p. 366.
3. Gillingham, J. (1987) 'War and Chivalry in the *History of William the Marshal*'. In Coss, P.R., Lloyd, S.D. (eds) (1987) *Thirteenth Century England II*, Boydell & Brewer, Woodbridge.

royal court's jurisdiction within John's territories. The English king's marriage to Isabelle of Angoulême soon gave Philip an opportunity to assert his court's authority over him as a vassal of the French monarch. John set aside his first wife, Isabelle of Gloucester, to marry in August 1200 another Isabelle, daughter and heiress of Count Ademar of Angoulême. His first marriage had produced no offspring, and since Isabelle of Gloucester and John were cousins who had never received the Church's dispensation to marry, nothing stood in the way of an annulment. A complication was his new bride's betrothal to Hugh le Brun, a Poitevin vassal of John, lord of Lusignan and brother to the count of Eu, Normandy.

Contemporaries were at a loss to explain John's action in offending the Lusignan family, important lords in lower Poitou. They attributed his marriage to 'a mad infatuation with a beautiful princess, already the prize of another'. A strange passion it was, since she was all of twelve years old. While some modern writers continue to accept this romantic version of the marriage, others see it as 'calculated and passionless'.[4] The new marriage seemed an astute diplomatic move, for the Angoumois was a rich territory strategically located astride roads connecting Poitou and Gascony. To bring the castles threatening the Angevin king's passage to Bordeaux under his direct control was a *coup*. Preventing Isabelle's marriage to Hugh le Brun was an added consideration. The counts of Angoulême and the Lusignan family had long contested control of the county of La Marche, and the betrothal was expected to bring peace between them. John's marriage would both prevent the two warring houses from making peace and stop an extension of Lusignan power into La Marche.

Probably John could have appeased the Lusignans by compensating them for his denying them their county of La Marche; instead, he treated them with contempt, answering their appeals to his court with a challenge to trial by battle with champions. Their revolt prompted John to make war on them, moving to seize the Norman

4. Richardson, Sayles (1963) p. 366.

possessions of Hugh's brother. By autumn 1201, the Lusignans had appealed to the court of John's overlord, Philip Augustus, who summoned John to appear before his court at Paris shortly after Easter 1202. John refused on grounds that as duke of Normandy he was only obliged to come before his overlord on the borders of the duchy. Philip's court rejected John's argument, since he was summoned as count of Poitou; and it condemned him to be deprived of all lands held of the French crown, not for particular acts in Poitou, but for his and his predecessors' refusal to offer a vassal's obedience. Philip, having secured a formal judgment to legalize a war he was eager to prosecute, promptly launched an attack on Normandy and accepted Arthur's homage for his uncle's lands.

John's failure to defend Normandy following the French royal court's condemnation in April 1202 damaged his military reputation beyond repair. John had lost some of the advantages his brother Richard had enjoyed in the late 1190s or that he had before 1202. Old alliances with Flemish princes which could have forced Philip to fight on more than one front had collapsed; and farther south, the count of Toulouse had switched sides. The advantage ought to have lain with John, nonetheless, a defender who could simply wait out the invading French, for his frontier castles should have denied the enemy freedom to roam about the Angevin domain and live off its resources. Since no territory could be secured without taking control of its fortifications, military campaigns in the Middle Ages often settled into lengthy sieges. Because well-stocked castles could resist most seiges, the Angevin kings knew their importance, and John must be recognized as both a skilled builder and besieger of castles. John had the disadvantage of a long frontier stretching all the way from the Seine to the Garonne, however; this required him to spread thinly his resources among many fortresses. Philip Augustus had the advantage of interior lines of communication, a compact centre in the Ile de France from which to advance, enabling him to concentrate all his forces on attacks down the Seine or Loire valleys.

Medieval warfare required careful planning and provision for men and their supplies. Especially difficult was keeping an army in the field more than a few weeks; and this meant hiring costly mercenaries, since English knights were less and less willing to serve on long campaigns abroad. John sought out siege engineers, crossbowmen, and Welsh longbowmen, while also hiring common soldiers, foreigners known as *Brabançons* regardless of actual origin. A successful general needed administrative skill, capacity for raising and spending large sums to pay for extended campaigns; even John's harshest critics acknowledge his capability in administration, especially at raising revenues. While the St Albans chroniclers depict him doing nothing to defend Normandy in 1202, administrative records picture him busy mobilizing resources, active in all phases of government.

In the spring of 1202 the situation resembled that of 1199 with Philip Augustus launching a series of frontier raids against castles of eastern Normandy, and Arthur and his Bretons joining with dissident Angevins and Poitevins to attack south of the Loire. King John adopted the usual defensive strategy, avoiding immediate action and remaining behind his ring of Norman castles. He lost patience, however, and began 'flitting ceaselessly about',[5] allowing several eastern frontier fortresses to fall, yet rarely making contact with the French. The one time the two forces did meet, at Radepont near Rouen in early July, Philip withdrew quickly, but John failed to give chase. Once John had recruited a mobile force of mercenaries, he turned south toward Anjou and Maine, heartland of the Angevin realm. At Le Mans on 30 July, he learned that his mother Eleanor of Aquitaine was under siege by forces of Arthur and the Lusignans at Mirebeau Castle.

The danger to the dowager queen roused John to the most decisive military action of his career, an action so bold that it still confounds his critics. He marched swiftly from Le Mans, covering eighty miles in forty-eight hours, to reach by 1 August Mirebeau, where his mother and her defenders had been driven into the keep. With William des Roches, his seneschal of Anjou, he surprised the besiegers before they had breakfasted, making them

5. Norgate, K. (1902) *John Lackland*, Macmillan, p. 85.

the besieged. Like many who tangled with John, they underrated his capability and found themselves quickly defeated. John took an impressive number of prisoners, whom he marched off weighted with chains to a harsh imprisonment. He had caught all the prominent rebels at once, including young Arthur and the Lusignan brothers, leaving them leaderless. News of John's victory forced Philip Augustus to give up his assault on the northeastern frontiers of Normandy, abandoning his siege of Arques to march south into the Touraine.

With Mirebeau, fortune seemed to be smiling upon King John. The heartland of the Angevin empire, linking Normandy and Aquitaine, was securely in his hands. His lack of proportion, his tendency to push things too far, spoiled his success, however. His arrogance after the battle, his refusal to take counsel with William des Roches, his cruelty to the captives, all cost him any advantage. Twenty-two prisoners died from harsh conditions, and rumours eventually spread of the murder of his nephew, Arthur. The defection of William des Roches brought defections by other Angevin and Poitevin nobles, leading to the loss of the vital Loire valley by spring of 1203. Arthur's rumoured death spread rebellion to the Bretons, meaning that John's enemies could attack Normandy from three directions: Bretons from the west, William des Roches and his allies from the south, and Philip II from the east.

By the beginning of 1203, John's nerve was failing him. In mid-January he learned that his queen, Isabelle of Angoulême, was in danger of capture at Chinon. He set out south from Normandy to her rescue, stopping on the way as a guest of the count of Alençon; no sooner had he departed than he learned of the count's defection to the French. John found the roads to his wife blocked, and he took refuge at Le Mans until a force of mercenaries could rescue her and they could return together to Normandy. More and more betrayals by his Norman and Angevin vassals during late 1202 and early 1203 were demoralizing enough to him; and they can explain the inaction and indecision which Roger of Wendover blames on his young queen. His expectation that papal intervention would secure him a truce as a breathing space may also account for his paralysis. Innocent III did send envoys to Philip in May 1203, but the French king rebuffed them, denying any papal right to intervene in a feudal dispute between lord and vassal.

John's fears of treachery drove him to an action in 1203 that would cost him more support. After discussions with his closest counsellors, he decided to eliminate his nephew, Arthur of Brittany, a possible focus for opposition to him. Just before Easter, the boy disappeared from the tower at Rouen, victim of a premeditated political murder either by his uncle's own hand or at his order. According to one chronicler, John had earlier aimed at mutilating Arthur – either blinding or castrating him – to make him incapable of exercising power; but the boy's gaoler, Hubert de Burgh, refused to carry out such a cruel command. After Arthur was out of sight about a year, rumours of the boy's death spread by the spring of 1204; and they drastically damaged John's moral authority, especially with those nobles whose sons he held hostage. In the Middle Ages, even the most brutal baron had a strong family feeling that made him incapable of condoning parricide. Yet young Arthur was a traitor to his sworn lord, captured while fighting against him, who could lawfully have been condemned to death; and Pope Innocent III was not much upset when he learned later that John had killed him. Nonetheless, the boy's murder was an error in political judgment as well as a criminal act, offsetting everything that John had won at Mirebeau.

King John's removal of his rival seems to have restored his confidence, and by late August 1203 he had overcome his lethargy. He made an attempt to retake Alençon, but withdrew when rumours spread that Philip was approaching. Soon John had to turn to the defence of Château Gaillard. This fortress, built by Richard I at great cost, incorporating the latest military science, stood as an obstacle to French advance down the Seine valley to Rouen. By the end of August John had devised a bold plan for running the French blockade and resupplying the castle. Kate Norgate commended his plan for the relief of Château Gaillard as 'a masterpiece of ingenuity', showing 'how mistaken are the charges of sloth and incapacity ... brought against "John Softsword"'.[6] The plan, requiring close co-ordination of forces arriving by land and by water, failed because of a miscalculation in timing. The slow progress of boats moving up-river against the current prevented a planned rendezvous with troops marching overland for a simultaneous assault, enabling Philip's forces to rout the two forces one at a time. This is not the only time that John devised an imaginative plan that was impossible to carry out.

Leaving the defenders of the great castle to hold out as best they could, John, in September 1203 marched toward the Breton border, a region relatively untouched by war and with castles recently repaired and resupplied. Probably he aimed to draw Philip Augustus from his siege of Château Gaillard, as his earlier plunge to Mirebeau had diverted the French from Arques. John proceeded to invade Brittany, his last serious military effort before abandoning the Continent on 5 December 1203, but the campaign ended in failure. The cruelty and destruction wrought by John's mercenaries only embittered the Bretons.

John's secret flight in December 1203 did not mean abandonment of Normandy's defence. Early in 1204, he sought to prepare a defence of lower Normandy – Caen and the Cotentin – while Philip Augustus was occupied to the east with the sieges of Château Gaillard and Rouen. This western territory was protected by castles to the south, and John organized a defensive line to its east along the Touques River; such a move made some strategic sense, although it meant abandoning the defenders of Château Gaillard to their own devices. On 6 March 1204, the Lionheart's great fortress was taken by storm just as John was planning a return to the Continent; and less than a month later, Eleanor of Aquitaine died (1 April 1204). This double blow to John may have left him emotionally immobile, incapable of coping with military matters for a time. In May Philip overran the duchy, by-passing Rouen, the only remaining Angevin stronghold on the Seine. Turning to the south, he executed 'a brilliant left-hook',[7] avoiding the Touques

6. Norgate (1902) p. 96.
7. Warren, W.L., (1961) *King John*, California UP, Berkeley, Ca./Eyre Methuen, p. 97.

defensive line. Argentin, Falaise, and Caen fell easily, and Rouen surrendered without a struggle on 24 June. Once Normandy had fallen, Philip Augustus moved to secure submission of the Loire valley lords. He marched south in August 1204 easily establishing his authority over Anjou, although two fortresses – Chinon and Loches – held out until spring 1205. Since Eleanor, lady of Poitou, was dead, no niceties of feudal law prevented Philip from pushing into Poitou, much of which he overran.

Treason by the Norman baronage, or at least their indifference to their lord's struggle against the French, was a factor in the loss of Normandy. Indeed, Sidney Painter saw the basic cause as 'the unenthusiastic if not actually treasonable behavior of the Anglo-Norman baronage'.[8] The count of Alençon's defection in January 1203 was followed in late spring by the defection of other important Norman barons, whose castles protected the way into lower Normandy. Later in the year others defected; even John's onetime seneschal for Normandy, Guerin de Glapion, deserted him and accepted appointment as Philip's seneschal in 1204.

Also in the spring of 1203 John grew suspicious of English barons, such as the earl of Chester, who had substantial Norman holdings. The desertion of Earl Ranulf's brother-in-law, the lord of Fougères, Brittany, may have sharpened John's suspicions, but he quickly regained confidence in Ranulf. In July 1203 two English barons, Robert fitz Walter and Saher de Quency, surrendered the castle of Vaudreuil to Philip Augustus without offering any resistance. Even the French king viewed them as cowards and traitors, although John later took responsibility on himself, mysteriously making a statement that they had surrendered on his orders. Perhaps he meant to hide the truth about their disobedience, or perhaps he calculated that purchasing their future loyalty in England was more important than punishing their present betrayal in Normandy. Whatever his thinking, their later careers as rebel leaders show that his excuses for their treachery failed to win them over.

8. Painter, S. (1949) *The Reign of King John*, Johns Hopkins UP, Baltimore, p. 27.

In autumn 1203, according to William Marshal's biographer, the earl marshal warned the king that his position in Normandy was untenable, stating, 'Sire, you have not enough friends.' He chided him that 'you have not been careful to avoid irritating people. If you had, it would have been better for us all.'[9] It should be no surprise that in the face of so much treason John scarcely knew what to do. Kate Norgate explained King John's 'restless movements, his unaccountable wanderings, his habit of journeying through bye-ways, his constant changes of plan' by his fear of treachery, his inability to trust anyone.[10]

Since the Normans made little effort to defend themselves, John had to rely upon a few faithful English barons and foreign mercenaries. Norman nobles were willing to come to terms with Philip Augustus, and once they surrendered their castles to him, defence of the duchy was hopeless. With John across the Channel by the end of 1203, barons openly made truces with the Capetian king, and towns had little option except to open their gates to the French. Even leading English barons sought a solution of dual fealty, disingenuously asserting that they could hold their Norman lands of Philip and their English lands of his bitter enemy without conflict of interest. William Marshal, while visiting Paris to negotiate on John's behalf in 1204, used the occasion to make such an accommodation. Neither could John feel secure on his southern flank, where Loire valley lords had begun treating with Philip Augustus by March 1203. Farther south, he had to contend with the legendary faithlessness and fickleness of the Poitevin nobles and in 1205–06 an invasion by his brother-in-law, the king of Castile.

The Norman bishops showed no more enthusiasm for John's cause than did the barons. While accustomed to close ducal control, many Norman clerics resented John's brazen financial exploitation and brutal interference in episcopal elections. Philip Augustus, in contrast, cultivated

9. Meyer, P. (ed.) (1891–1901) *Histoire de Guillaume le Maréchal* (3 vols), Société de l'Histoire de France, Paris, vol. 2, pp. 93–4, lines 12721–42; translation, Norgate (1902), p. 98.
10. Norgate (1902) p. 100.

an image of benevolence towards the Church before 1204, using the bishopric of Evreux, his possession since 1200, to demonstrate his policies of free elections and renunciation of regalian rights. The Norman clergy lost all patience with the Angevin cause. Not even Walter of Coutances, archbishop of Rouen, showed much concern for the fate of John's rule over Normandy, even though he belonged to a family of Angevin royal servants who owed their good fortune to Henry II and his sons. Norman bishops saw no advantage in resisting Philip's takeover of the duchy, concluding that only direct French rule could assure peace, security for church property, and possibility for free episcopal elections.

Such widespread desertions raise the question: Why did the Normans so readily abandon their Plantagenet duke for the Capetian king? This is a matter larger than merely John's military skill, raising the issue not only of his character, but also of the nature of Angevin rule over Normandy. Gerald of Wales saw the extension to the Normans of 'the violent domination and insular tyranny' with which the king/dukes had oppressed the English as an explanation for their flagging resistance to Philip.[11] Comparison of Angevin and Capetian policy towards their vassals' castles illustrates the authoritarian tendencies of Henry II and his sons. Part of their programme for centralized power was to reduce the number of baronial fortresses by confiscating or razing them, often without regard to right or custom. Philip Augustus's fortress policy, in contrast, appeared less despotic. He was willing to grant away Norman castles as rewards for loyal vassals, although guaranteeing his right to occupy them in case of emergency.

The Capetians benefited from a reputation for good lordship that contrasted with Angevin tyranny, and especially with John's behaviour. John's abandonment by so many of his subjects may have been his own fault; his suspicion of them contributed to their distrust of him.

11. Gerald of Wales. Brewer, J.S., Dimock, J.F., Warner, G.F. (eds) (1861–91) *Giraldi Cambrensis Opera* (8 vols), Rolls Series, vol. 8, p. 258.

A vicious circle whirled: John's jealousy and suspicion undermined his nobles' loyalty and moved them to desert him, while their disloyalty and desertions fed his suspicions. By autumn 1203, he could even believe that his barons were plotting to take him prisoner and present him to Philip Augustus, leading to his hasty departure from the duchy in December.

John's mistrust of the Normans made him more and more rely on foreign mercenaries for a fighting force; and their employment created another vicious circle, heightening his barons' mistrust. Although the nobility considered mercenary captains socially unacceptable, John trusted them more and enjoyed their company more than he did his barons. Not only did he rely upon them as military commanders, but he began to appoint them to posts in the Norman administration. Their brutality, rapacity, and destructiveness alarmed many of the Angevin king's subjects and turned them toward acceptance of French rule, if that promised peace and order. William Marshal's verse biographer complained that one captain mistreated the Norman non-combatants and plundered them with as much abandon as if they were hired soldiers. A quarter-century later some Normans still judged the rapacity of John's mercenaries and the hatred they aroused as the chief cause for his loss of the duchy. The expense of maintaining mercenary armies points to John's ever harsher financial demands that doubtless added to the Normans' disillusionment. As seen in Chapter 4, several scholars stress the strain that military expenditures were placing on England and Normandy after 1194, contrasting the Angevins' precarious finances with the Capetians' growing wealth.

The Barnwell chronicler, one of the more balanced contemporaries treating King John's reign, believed the loss of Normandy to have been inevitable. While some modern scholars disagree, arguing for military and political contingencies, others argue that Normandy was not John's to lose, that its absorption by the French monarchy was simply part of an inevitable separation from England. In the opinion of a scholar writing in Normandy today, 'The old equilibrium between England and Normandy had reversed itself completely, in favour of England.'[12] Native Normans saw most of the benefits from belonging to an Anglo-Norman realm going to their by-now distant English cousins. Family and tenurial ties no longer bound the Norman and English nobility together, since no more than two dozen English earls and barons any longer had significant lands in Normandy and fewer major Norman lords held large estates in England. Many knights on each side of the Channel, however, forced to choose between the English or French kings as overlord, lost small cross-Channel holdings. Certainly the Norman bishops were drawn toward Paris, not only because they concluded that French rule alone could end the constant warfare but also on account of the attraction of the schools and spiritual centres. Norman towns, however, profiting from trade with England and Aquitaine and from privileges of self-government, proved loyal to John almost to the end.

If Normandy and England were drifting apart, it is plausible to see the entire Plantagenet holdings on the point of collapse. As noted in Chapter 3, the Angevins' central administration was too short-lived to create an economy bound together by maritime commerce, a cosmopolitan class of civil servants, or a common nobility with ties of land and family in several provinces. The Angevin monarchs supplied no sense of unity, no shared culture to bind their English, Norman, Angevin, and Gascon subjects together. They could not compete with the myth of French national unity under the royal crown that the Capetians and their propagandists were constructing.

. . .

JOHN'S ATTEMPTS TO RECOVER HIS CONTINENTAL POSSESSIONS

King John did not accept the separation of Normandy from England as permanent. He recognized that he could not win back the duchy from Philip Augustus by a naval campaign from England, but would need a secure land

---

12. Musset, L. (1982) 'Quelques problèmes posés par l'annexion de la Normandie au domaine royal français'. In Bautier, R.-H. (ed.) (1982) *La France de Philippe Auguste, le temps de mutations*, Paris (Colloques internationaux du CNRS 602), p. 292.

base in the Loire region, with its points of contact with Brittany, Normandy, and France proper. After 1204, he turned his attention to his remaining lands south of the River Loire. Poitou offered protection for the roads that Philip might follow from Tours towards Bordeaux, a spring-board for an English expedition into Anjou, and a recruiting ground for mercenary soldiers. Furthermore, John felt at home among Poitevin mercenaries; for him, the captains whom the Anglo-Normans so resented were not aliens but old friends.

The loss of Normandy meant that the sea now provided the only secure link between England and the duchy of Aquitaine. More important, the English Channel was no longer an internal waterway for an Anglo-Norman realm but a boundary with the hostile French; a navy was needed to protect the kingdom's coasts. John set about organizing fleets for coastal defences and for attacking French territory. It might almost be said that the history of the British navy begins with King John. He had to fuse ships from three different groups into a fighting fleet: his own galleys, ships of the Cinque Ports, and merchant vessels impressed into the royal service. By 1204 John had about fifty galleys and the next year began construction of more. William of Wrotham, a royal clerk active in many aspects of administration, played a prominent part as 'keeper of ports' or 'keeper of galleys', titles which are rough medieval equivalents for First Lord of the Admiralty. Familiar with finances, a wardrobe clerk and collector of the fifteenth on goods at the ports of England, he was active in naval activity from the time of an aborted expedition planned for 1205.

By January 1205, John was so anxious about a potential invasion of England that he seemed close to panic. Philip Augustus was encouraging Flemish princes whose wives had claims to English estates to assert their right with military force, promising that he would follow with a French invasion. John introduced drastic military measures for the defence of the kingdom. The whole realm was constituted a commune, or sworn association for the defence of the realm and the preservation of peace, and all males over the age of twelve took an oath to oppose foreigners and other troublemakers. Each shire was to have a chief constable appointed, who in turn would appoint constables for the hundreds and vills, to muster local levies. Even though this enactment seems to have been soon forgotten, it represents a reiteration of Henry II's Assize of Arms, an imposition on all Englishmen of a national obligation to bear arms, an attempt to organize a non-feudal fighting force.

John saw that England's post-Conquest pattern of feudal quotas of knight service was completely out of date, and that a small permanent force of knights was needed for his almost continuous fighting on the Continent. John's innovative solution came later in 1205, when he was preparing a Poitevin expedition. He and his great men agreed on a new means for raising a force of knights; each shire should send one of every ten knights to his army with the other nine paying two shillings a day, the expenses of this tenth knight, who would go wherever ordered and serve as long as needed.

When the threatened French invasion of England failed to materialize, John planned two separate campaigns against Philip Augustus for summer 1205. He proposed a pincer movement against Philip that foreshadows his 1214 plan: a land force proceeding from Poitou under his illegitimate son, Geoffrey, and a naval force under the king's own command departing for Normandy. A large fighting force and fleet assembled at Portsmouth and Dartmouth in May, probably the most elaborate expeditionary force ever seen in England except for Richard's crusading host. Despite the soldiers' and sailors' eagerness to follow their king across the sea, the main force never sailed, disbanded chiefly due to opposition voiced at a council of barons. It stemmed in part from baronial resistance to overseas service in principle and probably in larger measure from their exasperation with John's money-raising methods. William Marshal, who had reached agreement with Philip for keeping his Norman lands, was one of the opponents, leading John to smell a conspiracy. His barons' lack of enthusiasm for these projects pushed him toward reliance upon the counsel of his aliens. Eventually, a smaller force under the king's bastard son and William Longsword, his bastard brother, did set sail for Poitou.

John did not succeed in leading his own expedition to Poitou until summer of 1206, when he reverted to customary means of financing. His aim now was not recovery of Normandy, but checking a threat from Alfonso III of Castile to his mother's inheritance. Alfonso had marched on Gascony, claiming it as the inheritance of his wife, John's sister Eleanor, but he met resistance from Bordeaux and other cities. John landed at La Rochelle in early summer and made a series of raids through Saintonge deep into Gascony to besiege Montauban. He showed his skill as a castle-breaker, and the supposedly impregnable fortress fell to him on 1 August. This victory ended the threat to John's southern possessions and forced the Spanish prince to return across the Pyrenees. John turned from Montauban to northern Poitou to launch a raid into Anjou, occupying Angers. This ended his advance, for Philip Augustus approached with an army, and the Poitevins hesitated to meet their overlord in battle in person.

King John achieved his limited goal of reasserting his lordship in Gascony with the 1206 expedition, and he concluded from his success that his larger goal of recovering his lost possessions in northern France was practicable, but would require far greater resources. Consolidation of control over his southern lands was necessary before he could contemplate any attack on Philip II. In October 1206, the two monarchs made a two-year truce at Thouars; the result was that John succeeded in securing his position from Poitou to the Pyrenees. He set to work between 1206 and 1214 to exploit huge sums of money from England for purchasing allies and professional fighters for a military campaign on an unprecedented scale. He needed to bring Angevin royal revenues up to the Capetian king's spending level, a more difficult task now that Philip possessed Normandy and its resources. The connection between John's great financial needs for his military projects on the Continent and his alienation of the English baronage becomes clear. It is this, not the mere fact of his enforced residence in England, that explains his energetic supervision of the kingdom that led his subjects to see him as an oppressor or tyrant.

John's preparations for the 1214 campaign show a capacity for planning on a grand scale, the largest military operation ever devised by an English or French monarch, perhaps too grand given the limited means medieval communications and intelligence had for co-ordinating such a plan. He worked to construct a pattern of alliances against Philip Augustus that would permit a combined operation in southwestern France and to the northeast, requiring the Capetian king to fight on two fronts. The construction of a coalition became easier because many continental princes were growing fearful of the increase in Capetian power after 1204. French conquest of Normandy had alarmed nobles in the Low Countries. By 1212, Philip's 'brutal opportunism' in seizing territory had alienated two princes, Renaud of Dammartin, count of Boulogne, and Ferrand of Portugal, count of Flanders.[13] Their fear of the French plus generous English subsidies led them to join John, and they brought with them other lords in the Low Countries. Another ally to Philip's east was John's nephew, Otto of Brunswick, the Guelf contender for the imperial crown who had grown up at the court of his grandfather Henry II. On a 1207 visit to England, he and his uncle cemented an alliance, and John began negotiating with major German magnates as well. The English king was aiming at a grand alliance with the Low Countries and Germany against the French, and he spent much treasure purchasing allies.

The English king had first planned his expedition for 1212, then 1213, but baronial opposition to service in Poitou and other problems caused postponements. In the spring of 1213, Philip Augustus commissioned his son Prince Louis to lead an invasion of England, and the French overran Flanders to gather an invasion force along the Flemish coast. John then had to thwart this projected invasion of his kingdom. He and his Flemish allies launched a fleet of 500 ships against the French at Damme, 30 May 1213, under joint command of John's half-brother, William Longsword, Renaud of Boulogne, and the count of Holland. The English fleet found the

13. Baldwin, J.W. (1986) *The Government of Philip Augustus*, California UP, Berkeley, Ca., p. 204.

French invasion force unguarded in the harbour of Damme, the port for Bruges, and captured or destroyed most of the ships; then Philip had to set on fire his remaining ships to keep them from falling to the enemy. This proved one of the earliest victories for the fledgling English navy, perhaps due to luck as much as to planning. Philip II had to acknowledge that no invasion of England was now possible, and he withdrew his forces from Flanders.

John hoped to turn the force he had collected for the defence of England into an invasion force for France in 1213. A number of northern barons refused to follow him, however, citing the excuse of his excommunicate status. The delay of his expedition until 1214 deepened royal resentment of the barons. When John landed at La Rochelle on 15 February 1214, his plan was not a frontal assault on Normandy. Instead, he sought a decisive victory elsewhere in France that would convince the Norman nobility of Capetian weakness and persuade them to return to Angevin allegiance. John aimed to march northwards, forcing Philip Augustus to divide his forces between Poitou and the allied armies pushing towards Paris from the Low Countries. With the allies in Flanders was John's bastard brother, the earl of Salisbury. It is impossible to estimate the size of the English force in the southwest; the chronicler Ralph of Coggeshall states that he sailed with 'few earls, but with an infinite multitude of knights of lesser fortune'.[14] Actually a good number of his nobility accompanied the king to Poitou, including some who would join in rebelling against him by the next spring.

John reasserted his lordship over the Aquitainian nobility, marching about Poitou, across the Angoumois and Limousin, and as far south as La Réole below Bordeaux. He had some success in regaining support from the southwestern nobles; at Limoges on 3 April, the viscount of the Limousin did homage to him. Kate Norgate notes a double purpose to the king's wanderings: 'to baffle Philip, and to ascertain the extent of his own resources in the south'.[15] In Poitou John once again

14. Ralph of Coggeshall. Stevenson, J. (ed.) (1875) *Radulphi de Goggeshall Chronicon Anglicanum*, Rolls Series, p. 168.
15. Norgate (1902) p. 198.

proved his ability as a besieger of castles shortly after his arrival, taking the castle of Milecu after a siege of only three days (2 March). He also made rapid assaults in mid-May on two Lusignan strongholds, Mervent and Vouvant in the Vendée; their fall persuaded the Lusignan brothers to return to John's fealty. He wrote back to England, 'And now, by God's grace there is given us an opportunity to carry our attack upon our chief enemy, the king of France, beyond the limits of Poitou.'[16] John swept towards the Loire in a move of great boldness, marching rapidly on Nantes on 13 June, where his army defeated the French garrison. He took prisoner Robert, eldest son of the count of Dreux, cousin to the French king and brother of Peter, count of Brittany. The victory at Nantes led William des Roches to withdraw from Angers, allowing John to enter his ancestors' chief city on 17 June without a struggle.

John set to work besieging castles in the area around Angers. A few miles west of the city, William des Roches had built a new castle, La Roche-au-Moine, which King John invested on 19 June and spent two weeks besieging. Meanwhile Philip Augustus with his son Louis moved southwards, proceeding as far as Châteauroux on the frontier between Berry and Poitou. The French realized that they had to stop the English advance or risk the Loire valley lords returning to John's allegiance. Some time late in April, Philip II returned to the Flemish front, leaving his son to march to La Roche-au-Moine's relief. Prince Louis arrived at the castle on 2 July with some 800 knights. Scouts brought John word that he had clear superiority in numbers, and he was eager for a pitched battle; but his Poitevin barons refused to fight, either because of fears that they were outnumbered or because of refusal to attack openly Louis, their overlord's heir. John had to abandon his planned push northwards and retreat south of the Loire; by mid-July he was at La Rochelle seeking reinforcements to replace the feckless Poitevins.

16. Roger of Wendover. Hewlett, H.G. (ed.) (1886–9) *Chronica Rogeri de Wendover . . . Flores Historiarum* (3 vols), Rolls Series, vol. 2, p. 100.

A recent study of Philip Augustus charges John with cowardice at Roche-au-Moine: '. . . as so often throughout his military career, John was struck with panic. Believing himself to be hopelessly outnumbered, whether rightly or wrongly, he fled the scene with amazing alacrity.'[17] Contemporary chroniclers, however, tell a different story. Not even Roger of Wendover, who repeated with relish any story that blackened John's reputation, accused John of cowardly conduct. He depicts John as eager for battle, but betrayed by the Poitevins, who 'disdaining to follow the king, said that they were not prepared for a pitched battle'.[18] Guillaume le Breton, French royal chronicler, blamed Aimery de Thouars' treachery; he has the viscount hinting mockingly that John's eagerness for battle was mere boasting, and that the king would never actually confront the French force. In any case, Aimery's withdrawal with his men then made it impossible for John to risk engaging Louis' army.

Three weeks separated John's return to La Rochelle and the rallying of his allies in the Netherlands for their assault on the French. The earl of Salisbury, the counts of Boulogne and Flanders, and their English-paid Flemish mercenaries had to await the arrival of Otto of Brunswick and German Rhineland princes. This delay gave Philip Augustus time to summon his feudal host, militias of townsmen, and whatever other troops he could raise, without worrying about an attack by John's force to the rear. The allies were confident of victory when they met Philip's force at the bridge of Bouvines on Sunday, 27 July, but they were disappointed. Philip too felt himself ready for that rarity in medieval warfare, a pitched battle. At Bouvines, he risked his whole kingdom's fate on the outcome of battle, a massive trial by combat. It was a decisive victory for the French monarchy with capture of most of the enemy leadership, and it dealt a death-blow to John's strategy for a dual strike against the Capetians.

Once again, John had failed in implementing a strategy that was sound in concept. Poitevin undependability

17. Baldwin (1986) p. 213.
18. Wendover. Hewlett (1886–9) vol. 2, p. 105.

at La Roche-au-Moine and delays in arrival of Otto's German forces in Flanders undermined it. As at Château Gaillard earlier, inability to co-ordinate precisely troop concentrations meant failure; it enabled Philip Augustus to defeat one army at a time. Yet it should not be forgotten how close King John had come to succeeding in his great gamble; as Painter commented, 'if Bouvines had been won, John would have been the dominant power in Europe.'[19]

John's position in Poitou was now vulnerable, as Philip's army marched south to join Prince Louis, and he sent for 300 Welsh soldiers. Since some leading Poitevins with their usual undependability deserted John for the French king, he could not offer battle. In September he agreed to a truce with Philip Augustus, and he sailed to England in October. Bouvines meant that all John's furious fund-raising efforts in England had been in vain, and on his return in autumn 1214, he had to face the probability of revolt by discontented barons. His harsh measures, even more extortionate than his father's and brother's, had caused much of the English baronage to lose all interest in the recovery of Normandy and the Angevin lands in France.

. . .

JOHN AND THE BRITISH ISLES

After King John's loss of Normandy in 1204, he turned his attention to his Celtic neighbours in his island kingdom, whom his predecessors had tended to neglect in favour of their continental subjects. John's successes in Wales, Scotland, and Ireland contrast sharply with his failures in France. The frontiers of the English kingdom were unsettled in the early thirteenth century, and England's relations with the Welsh and the Scots were ill-defined. Also John saw a need for some permanent pattern of government for the other British Isle, his lordship of Ireland which he had visited in 1185, and to define its relationship with the English kingdom. By John's time, a royal policy of legal definition of feudal relationships was widespread. Just as John's Capetian overlord on the

19. Painter (1949) p. 228.

Continent was trying to tighten control over his vassals, so the English king sought to specify his rights over his Welsh, Scottish, and Irish vassals. Their vague ties of personal dependence on the English king, which had not implied conditional tenure of their lands, were being transformed into specific obligations of feudal services as conditions for landholding, often spelled out in charters.

John's loss of Normandy impelled him towards consolidating his control over the British Isles. Barons who had lost Norman lands also sought recompense for themselves and for their knights on the Celtic fringe, since little land was available elsewhere. Their efforts to carve out liberties sometimes conflicted with the king's own policies in Wales and Ireland, feeding his suspicion of potentially over-mighty subjects. Marcher lords' relations with the various peoples and principalities occupying the fringes of Britain and relations of both natives and Anglo-Norman settlers with the English king caused tensions, requiring John's attention. During the years 1209–12 especially, the king showed great strength in asserting authority over the Celtic fringe, leading military expeditions to Wales, Scotland, and Ireland. John's efforts produced little permanent change in the pattern of relations between the centre and the Gaelic edges, however, since much of this achievement of his middle years was to be undone after 1212.

John's possession of the earldom of Gloucester during his brother's reign had brought him the Welsh marcher lordship of Glamorgan, giving him an awareness of Welsh conditions; and after 1204, he frequently visited the border counties, adding to his knowledge. Wales was still a very different society from England during John's time, its economy under-developed in comparison to England's, ruled by almost a dozen princes who were frequently in conflict with each other, yet recognizing the English king's loose overlordship. The Norman conquest had resulted in creation of marcher lordships to defend the Welsh frontier, and Anglo-Norman marcher barons saw an opportunity to expand militarily into Welsh territory without much royal supervision. Their incomplete conquests resulted in uneven Anglo-Norman settlement along the eastern edges and southern coast, dispersed among large stretches where Gaelic natives remained almost untouched by outside influences.

Kings of England had as much to fear from the Anglo-Norman barons of the Welsh marches with their castles, armed retainers, and freedom from royal supervision as they did from the native Welsh princes, and their alarm grew once marcher lords began to expand into Ireland by 1169. Some marcher lords were also Norman landholders, who were seeking after 1204 to make up for their losses in the duchy by expanding their holdings in Wales and Ireland, carving out fees for household knights, and increasing agricultural income through replacing traditional farming and livestock-raising with more profitable grain production on a manorial basis. Expansion of lands, revenues, and knights by marcher lords such as William de Braose, Earl Ranulf of Chester, or William Marshal, who as earl of Pembroke held the scattered Clare family estates, would be worrying to King John.

Because the marcher lords' lands lay on a military frontier, they needed the service of fighting men, bound to them by homage; and a feudal mentality, hostile towards the Angevins' centralized administration, survived on the Welsh marches and in Ireland. The feudal lordships of those territories were great liberties, free of much of the close control by royal agents that had characterized England since Henry II's last years. Because of hostile frontier conditions, the monarch allowed the marcher lords rights to wage private war and arrange peace terms that other royal vassals had lost. One marcher baron exclaimed in 1199 that 'neither the king nor the justiciar nor the sheriff ought to interfere in his liberty'.[20] Their policies of 'intrusion or *colonisation*' in both Ireland and the Welsh marches conflicted with John's 'policies of *assimilation*'.[21]

20. Davies, R.R. (1979) 'Kings, lords and liberties in the March of Wales, 1066–1272', *Transactions of the Royal Historical Society*, 5th Ser., 29, p. 56, citing *Rotulae Curiae Regis*, vol. 1, p. 426.
21. Crouch, D. (1988) 'Strategies of Lordship in Angevin England and the Career of William Marshal'. In Harper-Bill, C., Harvey, R. (eds) *The Ideals and Practice of Medieval Knighthood*, vol. 2, Boydell & Brewer, Woodbridge, p. 6, his italics.

John's response to the Welsh marcher barons was a policy of encouraging rivalries between them and also counter-balancing them with the native Welsh and Irish princes. In South Wales, John at first built up William de Braose in an effort to offset William Marshal's power, and Braose won control of a number of Welsh castles and land in Ireland as well. By 1207, Braose's domination of almost all southeastern Wales was increasingly worrisome to John, however. The king turned against his former friend and stripped him of his Welsh possessions, forcing him into flight to Ireland, and pursuing him there in 1210.

Elsewhere in Wales, three native principalities counted most. Deheubarth in the south had fallen into fratricidal feuds since the death of its great lord, Rhys, in 1197. Leadership then passed northwards to Powys under Gwenwynwyn, although he had been defeated in the last year of Richard I's reign. He later would seek to take advantage of the confusion occasioned by John's pursuit of William de Braose. By 1208 John suspected the lord of Powys of seeking to dominate native Wales, and he had Gwenwynwyn brought under his royal court's jurisdiction, confiscating his estates and only restoring them under humiliating terms. The third Welsh princedom was Gwynedd in the northwest corner of Wales, ruled by Llywelyn ap Iorwerth or Llywelyn the Great. He became the most powerful lord in North Wales, possessing potential for uniting the Welsh into a single principality under his overlordship and fashioning a relationship with the English crown similar to Scotland's vague vassalage. Llywelyn and John made a treaty in 1201, and he enjoyed the king's favour as a check on Gwenwynwyn. He had no hesitation in doing homage and fealty to the English king; and in 1204 John betrothed Joan, his illegitimate daughter, to him.

Enjoying the English king's favour, Llywelyn was able to expand his rule widely in native Wales. Eventually, however, John decided that his son-in-law was growing too powerful; for Llywelyn in 1209–10 apparently was seeking to extend his power into South Wales. At the same time, John was seeking to strengthen his lordship over the Welsh, spelling out the Welsh princes' obligations to him in charters of submission. In 1209 after John had intimidated the Scottish king with a threatened invasion, most Welsh princes went to his court at Woodstock to do homage to him. In the summer of 1211, two campaigns were launched from England against Llywelyn in northern Wales. The first, like so many English expeditions into Wales, failed when the Welsh adopted their usual tactic of retreat into rugged terrain. John personally led the second 1211 invasion two months later, which penetrated deep into Gwynnedd, deeper than any earlier royal expedition. He imposed humiliating terms on the Welsh prince, mitigated only because of his daughter's pleas, forcing Llywelyn to surrender the North Welsh region known as the Four Cantrefs, considerable cattle, and hostages. To cement control over the southern marches of Wales, the king installed three of his alien mercenary captains: first Gerard d'Athée and then Engelard de Cigogne as sheriffs of Hereford and Gloucestershire, and Fawkes de Breauté as bailiff of Glamorgan.

Lesser Welsh princes were alarmed at castle-building by these men, and in 1212 they allowed Llywelyn ap Iorwerth to rally them into rebellion. When John's plans for an expedition to Poitou that year miscarried, he decided to march his feudal host instead against North Wales. He planned to bring it under his direct control, collecting men and supplies for a large-scale expedition that included thousands of workers to construct castles as he advanced. Such elaborate preparations foreshadow Edward I's campaigns at the end of the century. Before setting forth for Wales, John demonstrated his brutality by hanging twenty-eight hostages, sons of Welsh leaders. Rumours of a conspiracy among the English baronage diverted the king's attention, however; and difficulties with his barons forced cancellation of the campaign in August 1212. The Welsh prince was able to take advantage of baronial hostility and civil war in John's last years to recoup his losses and recover his position in Wales. Llywelyn allied with other Welsh princes and with the English rebels, and they secured a number of concessions concerning Wales in Magna Carta, returning lands, liberties, and hostages to Welsh lords.

The pattern of Welsh relations with the English monarchs

is repeated with some variations in other Celtic lands, less so in Scotland than in Ireland. Unlike Wales and Ireland, Scotland was a kingdom under a single monarch; the Scottish Church successfully defended itself from subjection to English archbishops; the native aristocracy assimilated Anglo-Norman settlers without allowing them to dominate; and the Scots kings imported Norman institutions in an effort to strengthen their kingdom. The Scottish royal family and other Scots nobles held lands south of the border as vassals of the English monarch. Either the king or his brother held the earldom of Huntingdon in the east Midlands as a fief of the English crown. At least in the Lowlands, the civilization of Scotland with its growing towns and trade was much like that of England.

Political and military conflict with England had two sources: Scottish attempts to extend their frontier southwards, and the English monarchs' claims to overlordship over the Scottish rulers. Periodically the Scots pushed into northern English shires, laying claim to them. The Scottish king had taken advantage of King Stephen's feebleness to seize control of Northumberland, Cumberland, and Westmorland. The kings of the Scots had long recognized a vague vassalage to the kings of England; their homage signified an inferior position, but did not commit them to any concrete obligations. The Angevin monarchs would seek clearer definition of their overlordship.

In 1157 Henry II compelled the young king of the Scots, Malcolm IV, to surrender northern counties occupied during the Anarchy. Then after King William the Lion had joined the 1173–74 rebellion in hope of recovering Northumbria, he had the bad luck to be captured. Henry saw that the nature of his vassalage was clearly spelled out in a treaty; the captive king was coerced into declaring himself 'the liegeman of the [English] king against all men, for Scotland, and for all his other lands'.[22] He, his brother, the Scottish prelates and magnates all did homage to the English monarch; in addition, he handed hostages

---

22. Stones, E.L.G. (ed. and trans.) (1965) *Anglo-Scottish Relations 1174–1328: Some Selected Documents*, Oxford UP, p. 3, doc. 1.

and five castles into Henry's custody. Despite chroniclers' complaints of Scotland lying under 'the heavy yoke of domination and of servitude',[23] Henry wanted little more from the Scottish kings than a peaceful northern frontier. He and his successor were too absorbed with defence of their continental possessions to give too much attention to Scotland. Richard Lionheart in his search for cash for the Third Crusade cancelled the 1174 treaty, releasing the Scottish king from his earlier agreements in exchange for 10,000 marks, although he hesitated to honour William's claims to northern English counties.

William the Lion sought to profit from the uncertain succession to the English throne in 1199, and he expected to pressure John for return of Northumbria as the price for his support. John characteristically promised satisfaction and then stretched out the discussions without any intention of resolving Scottish claims. Meanwhile, he worked to extend effective royal control in the far North of England. Barons of Northumbria had long sought to play one king off against the other to preserve their independence. Feudal honors dominated by their lords' castles had kept their significance there longer than in the rest of the kingdom, since the process of shiring the North was only being completed in the late twelfth century. John's own honor of Lancaster became a county with the usual machinery of government now that he was king. John, unlike his predecessors, made visits to the North a regular part of his circuits about his kingdom. He sought to secure the Scots border by excluding old families in favour of new appointments as sheriffs and constables of such trusted agents as Robert de Vipont in 1204–05.

Although William the Lion came to Lincoln in November 1200 to do homage to the English king, their relations remained strained. In August 1209 John apparently got wind of William's participation in a conspiracy concocted by Philip Augustus and some English barons. He marched to the banks of the Tweed with a large army, and the

23. Chronicle of Melrose, Anderson, A.O. (ed.) (1922) *Early Sources of Scottish History A.D. 500 to 1286*, Oliver and Boyd, vol. 2, p. 323.

aged Scottish ruler dared not oppose him. The Scottish ruler submitted completely, offering John liege homage, promising a 15,000-mark fine for his goodwill, and sending his two daughters to the English court for marriage to John's sons. Although the 1209 treaty does not mention the three northern counties that William claimed, it appears that they were promised to his son Alexander. Another treaty in 1212 agreed to the marriage of the English king's daughter to Alexander, who would succeed William in 1214. John continued to tantalize the Scottish king and his heir with the possibility of restoring Northumbria. Neither the marriage nor return of the northern counties took place, however; and Alexander II would seek revenge by joining the rebels and Prince Louis of France in 1215–16. He invaded England twice; but his invasions accomplished nothing, and he abandoned his claims to northern English counties.

John had been lord of Ireland since his father gave him that title as a lad and sent him off on an Irish campaign at the age of eighteen. The island lacked the defensible terrain that protected the Welsh, and it failed to achieve the political unity of the Scots under a single king. Like Wales, it was ruled by a number of petty kings, whose warfare soaked early Irish society with blood. It was also subject to colonization by Anglo-Norman nobles, chiefly lords of the southern Welsh marches who had begun moving into eastern Ireland by 1169. Henry II seems to have long contemplated a conquest of Ireland, but his fears of the growth of the Welsh marcher lords' power there led him to exert his authority over the island with an expedition in 1171. The Irish kings submitted readily, offering their allegiance to him as lord. He came as their protector, establishing order in the land, imposing his authority over the Anglo-Norman adventurers, and ensuring that they would not enjoy the liberties that the marcher lords had in Wales.

Henry's selection of John as lord of Ireland in 1177 shows his interest in maintaining Angevin control over both the settlers and the natives there. Central control remained ineffective, however, with nonentities as justiciars at Dublin during Richard I's reign. The Anglo-Norman adventurer-settlers felt that they should be the English ruler's deputies in Ireland, and they viewed professional royal officers as hindrances to their expansion and exploitation of their estates. Their expansion continued, carrying the threat that the combined English and Irish resources of over-mighty subjects such as Walter and Hugh de Lacy, William de Braose, or William Marshal would prevent imposition of any effective royal authority on the island. Richard Lionheart had granted John's lordship of Leinster to William Marshal in 1189 over his objections, and the Marshal pursued on his Irish honor 'a policy of colonisation at its most harsh'.[24]

Once John became king, he attempted to assert his authority in Ireland, introducing English legal processes for natives and newcomers alike. He appointed a new justiciar, Meiler fitz Henry, who worked until 1207 – largely unsuccessfully – to limit the Anglo-Norman barons' growing power. Apparently, the aim was to create 'an arc of royal bases and king's men' to act as a buffer between the rival principalities,[25] but this attempt failed. Nonetheless, King John succeeded in extracting revenues from Ireland for defence of his continental possessions, levying the thirteenth of 1207 there as well as in England.

In 1200, John began a brief experiment of governing Ireland through 'a feudal structure of great baronies'.[26] He needed the military support in Normandy of William Marshal and the Lacy brothers, lords of Meath and later of Ulster; and he granted William de Broase the lordship of Limerick, in exchange for 5000 marks. He made an agreement with the Gaelic king of Connacht, bringing him into a feudal relationship for part of his kingdom, although he continued to hold other territory as a traditional client-king.

After a few years, John rejected this policy in favour of direct royal rule. The quest of barons who had lost their Norman holdings after 1204 for new resources for

24. Crouch (1988) p. 21.
25. Warren, W.L. (1981) 'King John and Ireland'. In Lydon, J. (ed.) *England and Ireland in the Later Middle Ages, Essays in honour of Jocelyn Otway-Ruthven*, Irish Academic Press, Dublin, p. 28.
26. Warren (1981) p. 33.

themselves and their retainers in Ireland led to quarrels with the king, and eventually to his expedition of 1210. Following John de Courcy's forfeiture of his lordship of Ulster in 1205, Hugh de Lacy took the deposed earl's title and estates, dangerously strengthening the power of the Lacy brothers. When William Marshal angered King John, he retired to his lordship of Leinster to sit out his fall from favour, 1208–13. Such quarrels, plus John's pursuit of William de Braose, convinced him that he must bring his over-ambitious Anglo-Norman barons in Ireland to heel. In the spring of 1210 the king summoned his feudal host and Flemish mercenaries, and a fleet of 700 ships sailed on his first expedition to his Irish lordship since 1185. In a two-month campaign, he managed to crush most of his Anglo-Norman opponents. He expropriated William de Braose's lands and those of the Lacy brothers, Walter and Hugh, for sheltering Braose; he did not disseize William Marshal of his Irish estates, but demanded hostages from him.

John's campaign was a success, completely cowing the Anglo-Norman baronage, making him truly 'Lord of Ireland'. He won the quick submission of most native Irish kings, who accompanied him on his march about the country, anxious to show their loyalty. The expedition's success placed him in a position to introduce an ordered pattern of royal government with personnel and practices closely modelled on English administration. Simon of Pattishall, one of England's most experienced judges, came to Ireland with John in 1210, bringing a register of writs to help establish English law and custom. Although only one Irish pipe roll (1211–12) survives from John's reign, there was an exchequer located at Dublin Castle, which was rebuilt in stone to serve as a centre of royal government. Other royal castles were constructed at such key points as Athlone on the Shannon.

John aimed at an administration strong enough to stand between the two rival groups of Anglo-Norman settlers and native Gaelic nobility. A modern authority on medieval Ireland finds it a great irony that in Ireland of all John's possessions, he should have demonstrated 'qualities of foresight and constructive leadership'. The author continues, 'John, so often described as the worst of the kings of England, was, paradoxically, the best for Ireland.'[27] Whether or not one accepts this judgment, John made a strong impact, perhaps stronger than any other medieval English monarch.

John appointed churchmen as Irish justiciars to replace the barons who had used the office for expanding their own estates. One of John's confidants and most trusted friends, John de Gray, bishop of Norwich, held the justiciarship from 1208 to 1213, putting him in a post beyond the papal interdict placed on England, where he could serve the king safely. Then he was replaced by Henry of London, 1213–15, another career royal clerk in the king's confidence, who became archbishop of Dublin and papal legate also; he functioned as both the leading secular authority and spiritual authority in Angevin-dominated Ireland. The archbishop lacked the sympathy needed to implement John's policy of assimilating the native Irish kings into the baronage as equals beside the Anglo-Norman nobility. Abetted by his deputy Geoffrey Marsh and by William Marshal, he pursued a policy of favouring the settlers over the native population. Archbishop Henry would be a ruthless advocate of promotion for Anglo-Norman clerics in the Irish Church over native Gaelic clergy, giving the Irish a frightening foretaste of the discrimination that lay ahead. By 1213, however, John was preoccupied with his quarrel with the papacy and a threatened French invasion; and he accepted the new policy of Anglo-Norman preference as the price of co-operation with the settlers. He would need the loyalty of his Norman barons in Ireland and the Welsh marcher lords in the approaching confrontation with his English barons.

Yet Ireland remained at peace, prospering, and largely contented with King John's lordship, while rebellion broke out in England in 1215. Royalist support from barons with extensive Irish lands, sometimes former adversaries such as Walter de Lacy, gave John an edge during the civil war. Had his attempt at a *modus vivendi* between Anglo-Norman

27. Martin, F.X. (1987) 'John, Lord of Ireland, 1185–1216'. Chapter 5 in Cosgrove, A. (ed.) *A New History of Ireland*, vol. 2, *Medieval Ireland 1169–1534*, Oxford UP, p. 132.

newcomers and native Irish nobles remained in force throughout the thirteenth century, a new Ireland might have emerged with an assimilated ruling class, a healthy ethnic and cultural mixture. For a time, it seemed that Wales might have a similar future as well. John disclosed the possibilities open to an English monarch with the will to concentrate his energies on Britain.

Chapter 6

CRISES OF JOHN'S REIGN: THE STRUGGLE WITH THE PAPACY

. . .

KING JOHN AND THE CHURCH IN ENGLAND AND NORMANDY BEFORE 1205

King John was heir to a tradition of strong royal control over the Church in his domains, which had survived Henry II's quarrel with Thomas Becket. John had the bad luck to be a contemporary of Pope Innocent III, however, one of the most ambitious and aggressive of the lawyer-popes who occupied the papal throne in the high Middle Ages. Christopher Cheney, the foremost modern authority on Innocent's relations with England, wrote of Innocent: 'This pope, by his ceaseless concern with the affairs of all Christendom and by his insistence on his rights and duties as God's vicegerent, summed up all the efforts of his predecessors.'[1] The result was a bitter conflict in the middle years of John's reign, 1207–1213, a papal challenge to royal authority over the English Church.

This contest coloured contemporary accounts of the king, written chiefly by monastic chroniclers. John's excommunication and exploitation of church property led them to judge him harshly and to dwell upon his immorality and irreligion. Their application of standards of private morality and piety in judging John's performance as ruler continued to influence historians for

1. Cheney, C.R., Semple, W.H. (eds and trans.) (1953) *Selected Letters of Pope Innocent III concerning England (1198–1216)*, Thomas Nelson (Medieval Texts), Walton-on-Thames, p. x.

centuries. His personal immorality weighed heavily in both thirteenth-century chroniclers' and Victorian scholars' evaluations. Some even denied that John was a believing Christian. The monk who authored a biography of St Hugh, bishop of Lincoln, took care to portray King John as superstitious and lacking Christian piety, certain to be damned. His work, written in 1213, notes that John failed to communicate at masses on the great feastdays, and that according to his friends, 'He had never done so since attaining to the years of discretion.'[2] Matthew Paris recorded irreligious remarks that John allegedly made, questioning basic Christian teachings. The mid-thirteenth-century chronicler adds an implausible account of an embassy supposedly sent by John to the sultan of Morocco and Spain to express his willingness to submit to him and convert to Islam.

Other sources present quite a different picture of John's religious practices. Although no model of piety, he was conventionally pious, devoted to St Wulfstan of Worcester, and capable of friendships with distinguished churchmen. The death of St Hugh of Lincoln in 1200 deeply moved John, who had visited him in his final illness. According to Hugh's biographer, miracles following the bishop's death inspired the king to reconcile with Cistercian abbots with whom he was quarrelling and to found a Cistercian abbey, Beaulieu, his only monastic foundation. John chose as his confessor a Cistercian abbot and devotional writer, John of Forde (d. 1214).

Official records depict John observing the Church's feasts and fasts and participating in its penitential practices. The king made arrangements for feeding hundreds of paupers, perhaps 3500 a year, usually for his and his friends' freedom to eat meat and to hunt on fastdays or during Lent. John's frequent gifts to small and obscure religious houses, often convents, suggested to Lady Stenton his 'uncalculating generosity'.[3] Even when

---

2. Douie, D.L., Farmer, H. (eds and trans.) (1961–2) *The Life of St Hugh of Lincoln* (2 vols), Thomas Nelson (Medieval Texts), Walton-on-Thames, vol. 2, p. 143.

3. Stenton, D.M. (general ed.) (1933–64) *Great Roll of the Pipe, 1–17 John*, Pipe Roll Society, new ser. 18, pp. xxxvi–vii [Pipe Roll 6 John].

he was preoccupied with problems, for example in the midst of his unsuccessful 1203 defence of Normandy, he found time for ecclesiastical benefactions. Almsgiving was a normal part of the royal household's expenses.

In addition, regular allowances from royal revenues at about £1450 annually went to the Church, mainly to monastic houses. Some of these payments were doubtless obligations inherited from his predecessors, so institutionalized that they reflect little of the king's personal feelings. John's continuation of them without protest in a time of financial crisis, however, says something for his acceptance of the Church's teachings on charity. A study of John's charitable practices concludes, 'Even a king with a reputation for impiety accepted the Christian obligations of . . . giving substantial sums in tithe, small voluntary gifts, penitential alms, regular Household alms, and fixed alms upon his revenues.'[4] Like his father, his brother, and most medieval nobles, John followed the forms of Christian practice without necessarily comprehending the substance of true Christianity. Chroniclers' reports of his blasphemy can be discounted.

Like his predecessors, King John was conscious of his prerogatives over the Church within his domains. Old concepts of interdependence for *regnum* and *sacerdotium* that the lawyer-popes of the twelfth century considered outdated lingered long in the Angevin domains. Henry II once boasted after Thomas Becket's flight that he had recovered 'the privileges of his grandfather Henry I, who was king, apostolic legate, patriarch, emperor, and all that he wished in his land'.[5] The boundary between royal authority and the Church's autonomy was still unclear even after the Becket conflict.

The English clergy's attitude toward Rome was ambivalent with few expressing markedly pro-papal views, and even fewer openly resisting royal control of the Church. The reality of numerous royal servants in clerical orders

4. Young, C.R. (1960) 'King John and England: an illustration of the medieval practice of charity', *Church History*, 29, pp. 267–8.
5. Millor, W.J., Brooke, C.N.L. (eds) (1979) *The Letters of John of Salisbury* (2 vols), vol. 2, *The Later Letters (1163–1180)*, Clarendon Press, Oxford, p. 508, no. 275.

conflicted with ecclesiastical councils' decrees against the clergy's entanglement in secular government. Many clerics in King John's employ clung to an exalted view of service to an anointed and crowned monarch that reformers at Rome, seeking the Church's freedom from lay control, considered old-fashioned. Royal clerks could see the competition between royal and ecclesiastical courts, yet they sought to protect the *corona et dignitas domini regis* from the church courts' incursions.

Because prelates ranked as barons, with great financial and military resources and with a place among the king's counsellors, England's rulers sought to maintain control over episcopal elections. They felt a bishopric to be a suitable reward for officials who had proven faithful in executing royal commands, and they had considerable success in securing election of royal *familiares*. Twenty of the forty-three bishops elected between Becket's death and 1213 came from the kings' service, and the episcopate of Normandy also was closely linked to the king/duke. The Angevin monarchs' record in dominating episcopal appointments in greater Anjou and Aquitaine is less impressive.

Usually the king could win election for his nominee while following the form of canonical election by the cathedral chapter. Monastic chapters at some English cathedrals occasionally needed prodding before agreeing to his choice, however, especially the monks of Christ Church, Canterbury, who had caused problems for John's predecessors, preferring monastic candidates over secular clerks. Periodic attempts to create a rival college of secular clerks to replace them as archiepiscopal electors made them all the more prickly about their prerogative. Also they had to combat claims by the bishops of the province of Canterbury for a role in elections.

Richard Lionheart was as determined as any of his predecessors to maintain royal control over episcopal elections. At a great council shortly before his departure on crusade, he named four bishops, all of them royal *curiales*. Richard stated his view on episcopal elections in 1195, when he heard that the monks at Durham Cathedral had held an unauthorized election. He claimed that it was 'no small offence to our royal majesty'; and he sought to guard against 'any diminution of the right and dignity which our ancestors had in the choice of bishops of England and which is due to us'.[6] Richard's record for Normandy is similar to his English one: appointment of four bishops, all closely associated with him. Bishops chosen from the *curia regis* are often dismissed as mere time-servers, more attuned to the king's interests than to spiritual matters, yet they often handled ecclesiastical affairs ably and zealously guarded their churches' property and privileges.

Generally, relations between the royal government and Church were smooth during King John's early years, doubtless due to Archbishop Hubert Walter's skills. Nonetheless, the king showed early on that he shared his predecessors' determination to impose his will in episcopal elections. Of eight episcopal elections in the years before the interdict of 1207, royal *curiales* filled five sees, and members of noble families two.[7] Only at Winchester in 1205 did John have any problem in securing election of one of his *curiales*. Part of the monastic chapter elected the royal candidate, Peter des Roches; but a faction among the monks favoured another candidate. John insisted that Peter had been elected properly and moved with brutal speed against the dissenting monks. When the dispute reached Rome, the pope rejected both elections and held a third under his supervision, which conveniently chose the royal candidate. Of the two nobles elected to bishoprics, Giles de Braose won Hereford as a royal reward to his father; but William of Blois, brother of the earl of Leicester, the canons' choice for Lincoln, was opposed by the king. The eighth see, Carlisle, went to the exiled archbishop of Ragusa as John's grant 'until [the king] shall provide him with a richer benefice'.[8] How or

---

6. Ralph Diceto. Stubbs, W. (ed.) (1876) *Radulphi de Diceto, Opera Historica* (2 vols), Rolls Series, vol. 2, pp. 128–9; translation, Cheney, C.R. (1979) *Innocent III and England*, Hiersemann, Stuttgart, p. 125.

7. *Curiales* are Jocelin of Wells to Bath and Wells; Simon, archdeacon of Wells, to Chichester; John de Gray to Norwich; Peter des Roches to Winchester; Mauger, Richard I's physician, to Worcester.

8. *Rot. Chart.* Hardy, T.D. (ed.) (1837) *Rotuli Chartarum, 1199–1216*, Record Commission, p. 96b.

why the Dalmatian prelate wound his way to the Scottish borders is a mystery.

Struggles to impose the royal will on episcopal elections took a more dramatic turn in John's continental lands than in England. King John sent a letter to the dean and chapter of Lisieux in autumn 1200, stating strongly his right to appoint to vacant cathedral churches. He pointed out that appointment to Lisieux 'depends by old custom and for manifold reasons on our will and assent as its prince'. Perhaps naively, he appealed to the pope against the electors, lest they act 'in prejudice of our right and in damage to our dignity'.[9] Eventually the son of John's constable of Normandy secured the appointment. Early in 1202, the king sent his seneschals of Anjou and Normandy to Angers, 'since we are too busy to take part ourselves', to assist the dean and chapter in electing the royal candidate, brother of the seneschal of Anjou.[10]

Foreshadowing the disputed succession to the archbishopric of Canterbury is the dispute over the bishopric of Sées, Normandy, 1201–03. It reveals John's determination to defend his rights in episcopal elections and Innocent III's disregard for such supposed royal rights. John's eventual acceptance of defeat in the Sées election may have convinced the pope that he could pressure the king into accepting Stephen Langton at Canterbury. The chapter of Sées, after the bishop's death in September 1201, agreed to elect one of themselves without notifying either King John or the archbishop of Rouen. John sent messengers instructing the chapter to elect as bishop his nominee, the dean of Lisieux, but the canons refused, even after meeting with the king. John then proposed that the chapter nominate three canons and three outsiders from whom he could choose. Their response was to name five candidates, all members of the chapter. Early in 1202, the prior and representatives of the chapter set out for Rome, accompanied by their candidate, Silvester, archdeacon of Sées, to appeal to the pope. John,

9. *Rot. Chart.* Hardy (1837) p. 99.
10. *Rot. Lit. Pat.* Hardy, T.D. (ed.) (1835) *Rotuli Litterarum Patentium 1201–1216*, Record Commission, p. 14; John's candidate was William de Beaumont.

meanwhile, proposed a third candidate and secured his election by a faction of canons remaining in Normandy. Throughout late 1202, he was seeking to prevent confirmation of the chapter's nominee, which he maintained to be 'contrary to written law and equally contrary to our dignity' if given without his consent.[11]

Innocent III's threat to place Normandy under an interdict in spring 1203 damaged John's already dangerously weak position in the duchy, and by October he had submitted to the pope's demand and accepted Silvester at Sées. In his letter to his seneschal of Normandy admitting Silvester to the bishopric, the king wrote that electing and consecrating a bishop without his assent 'is contrary to our dignity and the liberty of our land', that he was only allowing Silvester's installation out of reverence for the pope, and that he planned to explain to the pontiff that his rights in the process, 'according to right and our dignity and old and approved custom', must be recognized.[12] The contrast between John's crude assertion of his rights and Philip Augustus's promise of free elections helped win the Norman episcopate to the Capetian's side.

John's most serious ecclesiastical conflict in his early years was not over episcopal elections, but over England's carucage of 1200, from which the Cistercian order claimed exemption, offering instead a lump sum of 1000 marks. The king refused and threatened severe reprisals. In October 1200 when John returned to England, he contemplated seizing all the white monks' sheep grazing in royal forests. They staunchly resisted the king, however, and Archbishop Hubert Walter interceded on their behalf. In late November, the Cistercian abbots met King John at Lincoln, where he gave up his demands, sought their pardon for damages, and promised to found a new Cistercian house. Contemporaries attributed his change of heart to the death of Hugh of Avalon, saintly bishop of Lincoln. The Cistercians would again suffer for their resistance to John's financial exactions in 1210.

---

11. *Rot. Lit. Pat.* Hardy (1835) p. 16b, 13 Aug. 1202; pp. 22–22b, 29 Dec. 1202.
12. *Rot. de Lib. ac de Mis.* Hardy, T.D. (ed.) (1844) *Rotuli de Liberate ac de Misis et Praestitis*, Record Commission, p. 72, 9 Oct. 1203.

During King John's early years, diplomatic factors favoured good relations with Pope Innocent III. The pope wished to secure election of the English king's nephew, Otto of Brunswick, as Holy Roman Emperor instead of the Hohenstaufen candidate. Since Philip Augustus of France was supporting Philip of Hohenstaufen, diplomatic considerations drew John and Innocent together. John never lost sight of his and his nephew's shared interests in preventing a Capetian-Hohenstaufen alliance, but Italian political factors caused the pope eventually to reconsider his support for Otto.

Before John's loss of Normandy, the pope misjudged him, charitably overlooking character faults that he would again ignore after settlement of their long quarrel in 1213. John undertook devotional acts to win the pope's good opinion as his situation in Normandy deteriorated, confessing all his sins since manhood, promising to support a hundred knights in the Holy Land for a year, and to build a Cistercian abbey. Innocent composed a little homily for John in March 1202, commending his resolve, and encouraging works of piety in order that 'your kingdom will prosper and your royal honour even in this life will be enhanced'.[13] John's ploy proved profitable, for the pope wrote to the archbishop of Rouen in May 1202 condemning Norman rebels against their king/duke and pressing him to impose ecclesiastical censures on them. About a year later, however, the pope was losing patience with the English king; he wrote a letter of 'fatherly warning' for his faults,[14] including his conduct during the episcopal election at Sées, and recalling him from evil. Nonetheless, as John's position in Normandy deteriorated, he turned to Innocent III as a peacemaker, seeking a truce with Philip Augustus; and the pope appointed envoys to Philip in May 1203, urging peace between the warring monarchs. The Capetian king, who was overrunning Normandy, wanted no papal attempt at mediation halting his advance. He reminded Innocent that John was a contumacious vassal who had rejected the judgment of his lord's court.

13. Cheney, Semple (1953) p. 39.
14. Cheney, Semple (1953) pp. 48–53, 20 Feb. 1203.

. . .

THE DISPUTED CANTERBURY ELECTION, INTERDICT, AND EXCOMMUNICATION, 1205–13

The central event in spiritual-temporal relations during John's reign was the long and bitter Canterbury succession crisis that followed Archbishop Hubert Walter's death in July 1205. This appears to be a replay of earlier conflicts between royal defenders of old custom and canon lawyers' defence of the Church's independence, limiting the king to a largely formal role in episcopal elections. King John assumed that, like his Anglo-Saxon and Norman predecessors, he could engineer the election of his choice as archbishop; and his point of view did not lack supporters. While England had numerous *magistri* learned in canon law, few were willing to endorse Innocent III's extreme claims to papal power. The king even found a clerk to counter papal theories with old doctrines of the king as God's scourge, punishing the people's sins.

By 1208 John himself was girding for the debate with the pope by sending for his collection of theological works housed at Reading abbey. In a letter to Innocent, he stated, 'All my predecessors conferred archbishoprics, bishoprics and abbeys in their chamber;'[15] and in another, he urged the pope to protect 'our dignities which we and our predecessors had in providing for the church of Canterbury and for other episcopal sees, as is evident from the letters of the English bishops and other trustworthy men'.[16] John appealed to the Anglo-Saxon past, arguing that Edward the Confessor's appointment of St Wulfstan to Worcester provided a precedent for election of his own bishops in the royal chapel. This was a particularly apt precedent, since Innocent had recently canonized Wulfstan. Later in the crisis, John had a letter drafted in his barons' name, declaring their support and arguing from history, 'It is notorious that in ancient times before the coming of the Normans, the kings of England,

---

15. Translation, Powicke, F.M. (1928) *Stephen Langton*, Oxford UP, p. 86; Luard, H.R. (ed.) (1864–9) *Annales Monastici* (5 vols), Rolls Series, vol. 1, p. 211 (Burton).
16. *Rot. Lit. Pat.* Hardy (1835) p. 65b.

even those now canonised, granted cathedral churches to archbishops and bishops entirely at their pleasure. Since the conquest elections have been subject to the king's assent and hitherto have been carried out strictly in this form.'[17]

As Sidney Painter noted, 'The fiercely intransigent attitude of the king . . . can only be understood in the light of his relations with Hubert Walter.'[18] The archbishop had enormous expertise in royal government, having served Richard I as justiciar and John as chancellor. He had insisted on being consulted about important matters of state, and he often got his way, perhaps restraining some of John's more extreme impulses. The king must have felt somewhat overshadowed by the experienced Hubert Walter, and he looked forward to choosing as his own archbishop of Canterbury someone who had his complete confidence and who would be willing to carry out his wishes. His furious reaction to the Christ Church monks' duplicity in seeking to deny him what he felt was his legitimate right to select his own man for Canterbury is hardly surprising.

Details of the Canterbury election are complicated, involving three separate elections and a number of irregularities, all of which ensured appeals to Rome. Soon after Hubert Walter's death, King John came to Canterbury, and the Christ Church monks claimed their right of election and their wish to choose one of their number. Spokesmen for the bishops of the province of Canterbury also claimed a share in the election. The king convinced both parties to postpone any election until December 1205, and meanwhile both monks and bishops appealed to Rome for recognition of their rights. Then a faction among the monks, seeking to safeguard their right, met secretly and without royal licence to elect their sub-prior, Reginald. He then set off to Rome, promising to make public his election only if necessary to prevent papal

17. Latin text, Richardson, H.G., Sayles, G.O. (1952) *The Irish Parliament in the Middle Ages*, Pennsylvania UP, Philadelphia, pp. 286–7; translation, Richardson, H.G., Sayles, G.O. (1963) *The Governance of Mediaeval England*, Edinburgh UP, pp. 341–2.
18. Painter, S. (1949) *The Reign of King John*, Johns Hopkins UP, Baltimore, p. 163.

approval of an episcopal or royal role in the election. Once Reginald landed on the Continent, however, he publicized his election without revealing its conditional nature. This first Canterbury election was irregular in three ways: the monks had no royal licence to elect; they had elected while an appeal to Rome was pending; and they had made the election conditional.

The bishops' agent at Rome opposed the election on grounds that it had taken place after an appeal was already underway. News reached King John, and in early December he went to Canterbury, questioned the monks and received their assurances that no election had taken place. They renounced their appeal to the pope and held another election in the king's presence, electing this time the king's choice, Bishop John de Gray of Norwich, a longtime royal *familiaris*. Innocent III early in 1206 refused to recognize John de Gray's election, however, finding it invalid because it had taken place while the earlier one was under appeal at Rome.

In March, the pope summoned additional Christ Church monks to Rome to hold a third election, should Reginald's be quashed. In the autumn of 1206 Innocent rejected the bishops' claim to participate in the archiepiscopal election. At the same time, he annulled the monks' first election of Reginald the sub-prior, having discovered that it was conditional, not absolute. Since both elections were ruled invalid, he called on the Christ Church representatives at Rome to hold a new election. With the monks still split between their sub-prior and the bishop of Norwich, Innocent III proposed a third candidate, the newly-named cardinal Stephen Langton, an Englishman who had made his career on the Continent at the schools of Paris and at the papal *curia*, and assumed by the pope to be an ardent supporter of papal plenitude of power. One modern authority suspects heavy papal pressure on the electors; Christopher Cheney wrote, 'To a party of harassed English monks, far from home, a proposal made by the Holy Father in the precincts of the Vatican Palace might seem as compelling as the recommendation of their king delivered at Nottingham Castle or the Tower of London.'[19]

19. Cheney (1979) p. 151; p. 153, 'For his influence on their choice cannot be doubted.'

In December 1206, the pope demanded John's assent to the election of Stephen Langton. When royal assent was not forthcoming, Innocent announced in May 1207 that he would consecrate Langton at Rome without waiting for John's approval. He pointed out that a prince's agreement was not needed in elections held at the Holy See because the pope has 'plenary authority [*plenitudo potestatis*] over the church of Canterbury'.[20] Cheney speculated that electing a bishop at the papal court without royal assent was a 'custom' of Innocent's own making, aimed at preventing the monks from having time for second thoughts. The pope was not so naive as to think that the selection of an archbishop of Canterbury was a purely ecclesiastical matter and that royal assent was simply a formality. Clearly, Innocent wanted to prevent the installation of a royal *curialis* as archbishop, for he could have convinced the electors to choose King John's candidate. His decision to impose his choice on the English king was 'deliberately provocative and politically maladroit',[21] bound to bring on a confrontation between the two powers. Although it was evident that royal assent would be withheld, Innocent III consecrated Langton on 17 June 1207.

John was furious at being foiled in electing his own candidate to the archbishopric; rarely had an English monarch ever failed to influence the election to Canterbury. He protested on two grounds. First, he maintained that Stephen Langton was personally unacceptable to him, a man who had lived for years in his chief enemy's capital. Langton's associations at Paris were enough to arouse John's hostility; he belonged to a circle of Parisian masters with pro-French views, who contrasted the Capetians' just rule with Angevin tyranny, and who manifested deep devotion to the martyred Thomas Becket. Second, John argued that his traditional right of patronage had been denied, that his predecessors had appointed bishops and abbots. Innocent III rejected both objections. He dismissed John's complaints that Langton was a man unknown to him who had lived among the French as

---

20. Cheney, Semple (1953). pp. 86–8.
21. Richardson, Sayles (1963) p. 341.

'paltry reasons';[22] he insisted that John must have known Langton at least by reputation, and he vouched for his loyalty and devotion to the English king and kingdom. Innocent viewed the second complaint as irrelevant, since royal assent to elections was simply a courtesy. Because Stephen Langton had been canonically elected and consecrated, royal objections had no legal force.

The St Albans chroniclers writing in the thirteenth century applied their own prejudices to the Canterbury succession crisis, making Stephen Langton into a hero to fit their anti-royalist, anti-papal, and pro-baronial bias. They spread 'a haze of sentimental affection' about him that still influences historians.[23] Langton shared with fellow Paris theologians, the school of Peter the Chanter, a pragmatic turn of mind; and their attempts to apply theology to practical moral problems have impressed modern scholars. Yet the evidence of Langton's surviving sermons, biblical commentaries, and *quaestiones* portrays him as a man of little originality, a thoroughly conventional academic, a casuist in his thought. Indeed, he showed little practical sense in accepting the archbishopric of Canterbury under such awkward circumstances. Since he could never expect to be on good terms with King John, he was either very arrogant or very obtuse to think that he could function effectively as primate in the face of royal enmity. As archbishop, Langton would experience difficulties and disappointments at the hands of the king, his fellow bishops, the pope and papal legates.

When John learned of Innocent's consecration of Stephen Langton, he vented his anger on the monks of Christ Church, expelling them and forcing them into exile. He denied Langton entry into the kingdom and took the Canterbury estates into his hand. Also he moved against the pope, seizing Italian clerics' benefices in England and barring papal judges-delegate from English church courts. Nonetheless, Innocent set in motion negotiations by August 1207. He named three English bishops as commissioners to persuade the king to accept Langton as archbishop; if he refused, they were to proclaim an

22. Cheney, Semple (1953) 86–9.
23. Richardson, Sayles (1963) p. 352.

interdict. Imposition of an interdict supposedly would make a prince's Christian subjects, denied access to the sacraments, put pressure on him to submit to the papal will.

The pope skilfully chose as commissioners William de Sainte-Mère-Eglise of London, Eustace of Ely, and Mauger of Worcester, men who had begun their careers in the royal service, but who owed their appointments to John's predecessor. Despite their backgrounds as *curiales*, they proved staunch supporters of papal policy. They tried throughout the winter of 1207–08 to persuade John to accept Langton, visiting him 'often, sometimes tearfully, and on bended knee'.[24] According to Roger of Wendover the king 'became nearly mad with rage, and broke forth in words of blasphemy . . . swearing by God's teeth'. He threatened that if the pope proclaimed an interdict, he would send all the English clergy off to the pope and confiscate their property; and all Roman or papal clerks in England would be sent back 'with their eyes plucked out, and their noses slit'.[25] In fact, John skilfully dragged out discussions to delay the interdict's taking effect. In January 1208, he informed the commissioners that he was willing to obey the pope 'saving to us and our heirs in all things our right, dignity and liberties'.[26] Then in March, the king had a meeting with Stephen Langton's brother, Simon. In open letters to the shires, he reported Simon's harsh statement that nothing could be done to safeguard the royal dignity unless the king placed himself totally in his mercy. Not long after Simon Langton's departure, on 23 March 1208, the commissioners pronounced the interdict.

King John viewed the interdict as the equivalent of a papal declaration of war on him, and he quickly retaliated. The St Albans chroniclers' account of John's violent retaliation is greatly exaggerated, like much that they wrote about him, although other sources are contra-

24. Luard (1864–9) vol. 2, p. 210.
25. Roger of Wendover. Hewlett, H.G. (ed.) (1886–9) *Chronica Rogeri de Wendover . . . Flores Historiarum* (3 vols), Rolls Series, vol. 2, p. 46; translation Giles, J.A. (1846) *Roger of Wendover*, Henry G. Bohn (Bohn's Antiquarian Library) vol. 2, p. 245–6.
26. *Rot. Lit. Pat.* Hardy (1835) p. 78b.

dictory. It seems that Romans resident in England were arrested and that the clergy may have had reason for fear at the outset, since John seems to have condoned some violence in his first fury; but the king wanted to convince the English clergy that his quarrel was with the pope, not with them. He quickly issued letters of protection for the religious, threatening to 'have hanged on the nearest oak' any violators of his proclamation.[27] John did punish his clergy in a particularly appropriate way, showing a sense of humour and spurious moral indignation at the same time. He ordered the arrest of all priests' and clerks' mistresses, whom they had persisted in keeping despite the Church's repeated legislation mandating celibacy. Because the clerics were allowed to purchase their lovers' release, the king also gained revenue.

Royal reprisals mainly took the form of confiscation of clerical property. John prepared public opinion by sending agents to the shires to spread his own version of his quarrel with the pope. Next he commanded that royal custodians take into their hand 'all the lands and goods of abbots, priors, and all religious, and the clergy of [those dioceses] who do not wish to celebrate divine services'.[28] John's confiscation of ecclesiastical wealth improved his financial position at a time when he was seeking to replenish his treasury. Yet his subjects could quickly grasp the reasoning behind such an act, since they were familiar with the feudal concept of confiscation for default of service.

It is possible that John first gave the English clergy the simple alternative of either redeeming their property or forfeiting it by fleeing into exile. Within a few weeks of the orders for confiscation, the king's friends among the clergy recovered their property freely, while others redeemed their lands with gifts. Other clerics' property was handled in three ways. First, a royal custodian in each diocese had charge of property not given to anyone else; he was to collect revenues, provide for the clergy's maintenance, and keep the rest for the king. Second,

---

27. *Rot. Lit. Claus.* Hardy, T.D. (ed.) (1833–4) *Rotuli Litteranum Clausarum* (2 vols), Record Commission, vol. 1, p. 111.
28. *Rot. Lit. Pat.* Hardy (1835) p. 80b.

some landholders took charge of religious property on their own lands, and royal officials took custody of favoured religious bodies; for example, the justiciar was custodian of the Templars' property. Finally, many abbeys were simply turned over to their own abbots' custody in return for a fine; thus they found themselves in effect royal 'farmers' of their own land. Royal policy chiefly aimed at punishing clerics who fled the country, and the exiles' property remained in the king's hand until 1213. Supervising hundreds of ecclesiastical estates and thousands of parish churches' incomes would have proven beyond the capability of the royal administration. There can be no doubt, however, that profits from church properties during the years of the interdict helped to relieve John's financial distress.

It was to King John's advantage that religious life in the kingdom continue as normally as possible during the interdict. He made a show of his own devotion, and the clergy encouraged private religious practices among the laity, continuing to preach and hear confessions. Aside from the interdict's restrictions on public religious services and burial in consecrated ground, much of the Church's business seems to have continued nearly as in normal times. Clergy continued to bring actions in the royal courts and to engage in other legal business, and the ecclesiastical courts continued to function, except for a prohibition on appeals to Rome. None of this means that the interdict was being openly disobeyed, however, simply that clergy and laity learned to accommodate to it.

Elections were held during the interdict to fill five vacant bishoprics.[29] Indeed, the pope ordered them, threatening otherwise to fill vacancies with his own candidates. In three elections, the royal candidate, a *curialis*, won; at Chichester, the elect was not a *curialis*, although he had John's approval; while at Durham, the chapter rejected several of the king's candidates, only to have John de Gray, the former royal nominee for Canterbury, imposed on them once king and pope came to terms in 1213. In three of the four elections

29. Chichester, Coventry and Lichfield, Durham, Exeter, and Lincoln.

concluded, Langton as archbishop quashed them on grounds of unlawful royal interference. One of these elections, Coventry and Lichfield in 1209, shows John's vigorous efforts to win election for his candidate, the royal chancellor Walter de Gray, who was eventually elected. One of John's knights even locked the electors in a room, warning them, 'By God's tongue, you shall not leave until you have made a bishop as the king wants; so go and act quickly.'[30]

The annalist of a Welsh abbey remarked that all the laity, most of the secular clergy, and many monks supported the king's side in the Canterbury succession dispute. Perhaps he was ill-informed about conditions beyond the Welsh marches, perhaps not. Few of the king's subjects, lay or clerical, had much sympathy for the Church's problems. They felt little excitement about the issue of free episcopal elections, although the baronage seems to have supported John's demands during the 1209 negotiations that respect for the royal dignity be guaranteed. They had reason to fear for their own rights to patronage over churches on their estates. Stephen Langton sent an ill-considered letter in 1207 to the barons that failed in its purpose. He reminded them that their first loyalty was not to their temporal lord but to 'their superior lord, the eternal king who is king of kings and lord of lords',[31] and that they were absolved from their fealty to John, a rebel persisting in schism. Since they too were lords of men, wary of such appeals to higher authority, it seems a tactless argument for seeking their support.

Even though proclamation of the interdict meant warfare between king and pope, their hostility did not preclude negotiations. It was to John's advantage to stretch out discussions as long as possible to prevent Innocent from imposing more severe sanctions. In April 1208, John sent the abbot of Beaulieu as his envoy to Rome. The king agreed to receive Langton as archbishop and to restore the Canterbury monks if the pope would

30. Cheney (1979) pp. 130–1.
31. Major, K. (ed.) (1950) *Acta Stephani Langton Cantuariensis Archiepiscopi*, Canterbury-York Society, vol. 1 (1950) p. 5, no. 2.

issue formal letters recognizing royal rights, that is, assuring that Langton's election would not become a precedent. Innocent deposited such a bull at the abbey of Clairmarais, conveniently near Channel crossings. John could not bring himself to invest Stephen personally with his regalia, however; he agreed that the pope or his commissioners could perform that ceremony. Both pope and king appeared fairly confident that an accommodation could be reached. Then in July, the three English bishops serving as papal commissioners crossed to England with Simon Langton, his brother's proctor, and they waited eight weeks for a meeting with John that never took place. Since the central issue for John was protecting his prerogative, the sticking point was deposit of the papal bull outside England. He wanted guarantees that Langton's election would not constitute a precedent for filling future episcopal vacancies.

By early the next year, 1209, Innocent III had to conclude that King John had no intention of abiding by the agreement that the abbot of Beaulieu had negotiated the previous spring. He concluded that he must threaten excommunication in order to apply more pressure. John still held out the possibility of an accommodation to stave off his excommunication, authorizing another visit by Simon Langton to England around Easter. Discussions with Simon Langton, if they were held, failed to settle the dispute; however, by mid-summer more meetings were underway. Apparently, John's closest advisers, including the justiciar, Geoffrey fitz Peter; the bishop of Winchester, Peter des Roches; Jocelin of Wells, bishop of Bath; and his brother, Hugh, elect of Lincoln, were urging a settlement before the king's excommunication could be proclaimed. They did not wish to face the dilemma of either serving an excommunicate or enduring the Church's censure.

A conference began at Dover in late July 1209 between the king's most trusted counsellors and the three papal commissioners. These royal agents stood for conciliation and a quick end to the conflict with the Church. The negotiators reached an agreement by 10 August, offering terms that came close to satisfying the pope's and Langton's conditions. The king would accept Stephen Langton as archbishop and take his fealty, and restitution was promised for church property seized during the interdict. Distrust on both sides continued, however. The three bishops doubted the king's intention to make full restitution, and he was concerned because they could not produce the papal bull guaranteeing that his acceptance of Langton would not constitute a precedent for future episcopal elections. He hesitated and, seeking to stall, proposed to meet personally with the three bishops acting as papal agents. Fearing for their safety, they refused the meeting, although they did postpone proclaiming his excommunication.

Then King John proposed that Stephen Langton himself come to England for discussions. In early October, Langton sailed to Dover; but John decided against seeing him, sending Geoffrey fitz Peter and Peter des Roches instead. They demanded guarantees of respect for the royal dignity, but the archbishop could not go beyond the previous Dover terms, and the only result of Langton's visit was more bitterness between the king and the archbishop-elect. The papal commissioners formally published John's excommunication on 8 November 1209.

The king's excommunication failed to make much impact on England. Because the Church's overuse of the ban as a political weapon was making it less frightening to the faithful, John experienced little concern. Two of his allies, Otto of Brunswick and Count Raymond VI of Toulouse, were also excommunicates. Doubtless, Innocent III hoped that the king's excommunication would arouse acts by the already restless English baronage that might persuade him to surrender; but at a great council the barons ratified King John's stand that a papal guarantee for royal rights must be a part of any settlement. At the least, the pope expected excommunication to drive John's servants away, making it difficult for him to govern. More bishops went into exile, and some royal clerks, fearful of being placed under the ban, felt obliged to leave his service. But two bishops continued to serve the king, and two Cistercian abbots, Knights Templars and Hospitallers, and numerous secular clerks remained at court. If anything, the interdict and excommunication strengthened King John's political position by separating two powerful groups in his realm – Church and baronage

– capable of mounting political opposition to his increasingly arbitrary acts, if they should make common cause. The Canterbury chronicler wrote, 'It was as if he alone were mighty upon earth, and he neither feared God nor regarded man.'[32]

Innocent III never anticipated that John could hold out for so long. He had miscalculated, perhaps misled by the king's willingness throughout the interdict to negotiate. Possibly he failed to realize how much the king's enjoyment of the flow of the Church's wealth into his treasury dampened his enthusiasm for peace. By 1213 seven vacant bishoprics and seventeen abbacies were providing valued injections of money.

Not even the king's excommunication ended efforts to negotiate a settlement. In the early months of 1210 a number of royal envoys visited the papal court. Royal letters invited the archbishop-elect again for discussions with King John at Dover in May, but Langton distrusted John's safe-conduct and refused to cross the Channel. Langton's failure to meet the king at Dover so angered John that he commanded that the trees on all the archbishopric's manors be chopped down. Papal nuncios arrived in England in summer 1211 with new peace proposals. The king would be required to take an oath 'unreservedly to obey [papal] commands in respect of the matters for which he now stands excommunicated';[33] he must receive the archbishop-elect and his fellow exiles, accept the archbishop's fealty and invest him with his temporal possessions; and he must restore all losses the Church had suffered during the interdict. The papal agents' visit achieved no purpose, for John refused such a complete surrender, and discussions stopped for a time.

. . .

PEACE WITH THE POPE AND AFTER

Negotiations went on intermittently throughout the interdict, and they resumed in autumn 1212, with an embassy sent by John to Rome. The king's circumstances had

32. Gervase of Canterbury. Stubbs, W. (ed.) (1879–80) *Gervase of Canterbury, Historical Works* (2 vols), Rolls Series, vol. 2, p. 100; translation, Norgate, K. (1902) *John Lackland*, Macmillan, p. 137.
33. Cheney, Semple (1953), p. 126.

worsened with wide discontent that summer, even a conspiracy among some of his barons. Abroad a diplomatic revolution was strengthening his enemy Philip Augustus's position, posing the possibility of a Capetian, Hohenstaufen, and papal alliance. Rumours were circulating that the pope planned to release John's subjects from their fealty to him. John may well have felt that he had too many enemies, and as Sidney Painter phrased it, 'The cheapest of these to buy off and the most effective ally when bought was obviously Pope Innocent.'[34] The king agreed to accept papal terms that he had rejected a year earlier, and his envoys arrived at Rome early in 1213.

By 27 February, Innocent III drafted a letter to King John setting forth new terms for settlement; they repeated those rejected in 1211, but contained some new provisions. John must now receive back into his kingdom not only the exiled clerics, but also exiled laymen, including two barons who had fled following their failed conspiracy in the summer of 1212. He must make a down-payment of £8000 on the Church's compensation for damages. John did win the right to require Langton and his colleagues to swear that they would do nothing against the king's person or crown.

John's position was weakening throughout the spring of 1213, for Philip Augustus was preparing to invade England, and the English king feared papal support for him. Indeed, contemporary or near-contemporary English chroniclers claim that Innocent declared John deposed and authorized Philip's planned invasion as a means of carrying out the deposition. Because French chronicles are silent, and no letters or other documentary evidence for a papal declaration of deposition survives, recent scholarly opinion is against it. Christopher Cheney concluded that 'the French project had no official or public support from the pope. It was sufficiently alarming to King John without having the character of a crusade against him.'[35] Apparently Innocent did prepare secret letters in February 1213 as ammunition against John, a

34. Painter (1949), p. 189.
35. Cheney (1979) p. 339.

means of pressuring him in case he repudiated the peace settlement, and probably they authorized deposition as an ultimate sanction. These letters may be the source of chroniclers' tales that the pope deposed John.

On 13 May, the papal nuncio Pandulf landed at Dover, and two days later John accepted the pope's proposal for peace, agreeing to go beyond the papal terms. He surrendered his crowns of England and Ireland, putting himself and his two realms under apostolic suzerainty, receiving them back as fiefs to be held by him and his heirs of the popes. To make concrete his submission, he would pay an annual tribute of 1000 marks for the two territories. He stated that he took such a step:

> ... being in great need of the divine mercy, and having nothing but ourselves and our kingdoms that we can worthily offer as due amends to God and the Church, we desire to humble ourselves for Him who humbled Himself for us even unto death; and inspired by the grace of the Holy Spirit – not induced by force or compelled by fear, but of our own free and spontaneous will, and *by the common counsel of our barons* – we offer and freely yield to God, and His holy apostles Peter and Paul, and to the Holy Roman Church our mother, and to the lord pope Innocent and his catholic successors, the whole kingdom of England and the whole kingdom of Ireland . . .[36]

The spectacle of an English monarch doing homage to Innocent III before his legate in England appeared humiliating to the anti-papal and anti-John chroniclers at St Albans Abbey in the mid-thirteenth century. It seemed even more disgraceful to Protestants in the sixteenth century and nationalists in the nineteenth century. Some scholars still follow Matthew Paris in maintaining that Stephen Langton disapproved of John's paying tribute to the pope, and that 'only a remnant' of the barons approved of the king's surrender.[37] In its own day, however, John's action aroused little opposition; papal overlordship had not damaged the prestige of the kings

36. *Rot. Chart.* Hardy (1837), p. 195: translation Warren, W.L. (1961) *King John*, California UP, Berkeley, Ca./Eyre Methuen, p. 208; my own italics.
37. Powicke (1928), p. 101.

of Sicily or Hungary. The Barnwell annalist probably sums up informed contemporary opinion:

> The king provided wisely for himself and his people by this deed, although to many it seemed ignominious and a monstrous yoke of servitude. For matters were in such extremity . . . that there was no shorter way – perhaps no other way – of evading the impending danger. For from the moment he put himself under apostolic protection and made his kingdom part of St Peter's Patrimony, there was no prince in the Roman world who would dare attack him or invade his lands to the damage of the Apostolic see, since everyone stood in greater awe of Pope Innocent than of his predecessors for many years past.'[38]

The bulk of modern scholarship weighs in with the Barnwell writer; recent scholarship acclaims John's surrender as 'a brilliant manoeuvre', 'a diplomatic stroke of genius', or 'prudent and wise'.[39] Although the Barnwell author states that initiative for papal vassalage originated with John, the possibility must be considered that it was the pope's suggestion. Both had something to gain from it. Securing papal suzerainty over England clearly enhanced Innocent III's prestige, and a 1000-mark annual addition to papal funds was not insignificant. Also he hoped that his position as overlord would give him some control over England's foreign policy. Innocent was now opposing John's nephew, Emperor Otto IV, in Italy, seeking to replace him with young Frederick of Hohenstaufen; and he wished to prevent the English king from lending aid to his imperial kinsman.

John gained more from his submission. His calculation that it would flatter Innocent greatly, earn his gratitude, and bind him to support of his political interests proved correct; overnight John converted an implacable enemy into a devoted friend and protector at a time when he was in need of powerful friends. After John's submission, Innocent set aside any doubts about his trustworthiness,

---

38. Barnwell Chronicle. Stubbs, W. (ed.) (1872–3) *Memoriale Walteri de Coventria* (2 vols), Rolls Series, vol. 2, p. 210; translation, Cheney (1979), p. 333.
39. Painter (1949) p. 194; Cheney (1979) p. 335; Poole, A.L. (1955) *From Domesday Book to Magna Carta*, 2nd edn, Oxford UP, p. 458.

and he regarded his new vassal with the same unrealistic indulgence that he had shown before the Canterbury crisis. For the last three years of John's reign, the king could be confident of support from his new protector against both the English baronage and the French king. His vassalage meant that the barons would have an overlord, the pope, who insisted that they respect and obey their king, their immediate lord. As early as October 1213, the pope was writing to warn them 'not . . . to move a step against the king, until you have consulted the Roman pontiff'.[40] On the eve of civil war in August 1215, Innocent rebuked the barons for their support of John during the interdict, pointing out that 'with a wicked inconsistency' they had supported the king in his rebellion against the Church only to rebel against him once he made peace with the Church.[41] Perhaps John's most immediate advantage was preventing a papal blessing for the French king's threatened 1213 invasion of England, securing instead papal calls on Philip to make peace.

John's submission to Innocent meant that he would confront Stephen Langton on his arrival in England as the pope's ally, and the archbishop could not threaten the king with ecclesiastical censures unless the pope approved. A papal letter to John in November 1213 states the situation plainly, 'Do not wrangle with the archbishops and bishops of your kingdom, particularly over spiritual matters and ecclesiastical law, when you can have recourse to us, and through us can honourably achieve much that you could not honourably achieve by yourself.'[42] Langton arrived in England on 9 July 1213 to take up his post of primate, and he headed west for a meeting with King John at Winchester. John proved capable of feigning contrition before his absolution and exchanging the kiss of peace with the primate. Langton then led him into Winchester Cathedral to hear mass, although the interdict still barred public celebrations of the eucharist.

The king flattered Innocent III by asking that a papal legate be sent to England, and in May 1213 the pope

40. Cheney, Semple (1953) p. 163.
41. Cheney, Semple (1953) p. 213.
42. Cheney, Semple (1953) pp. 169–70.

sent Cardinal Pandulf, followed in the autumn by Nicholas of Tusculum. Friction soon developed between Cardinal Nicholas and the archbishop. Papal letters that had come into Langton's possession, apparently authorizing extreme measures in case John should repudiate his agreement, contributed to their quarrel. Innocent, evidently trusting John more than his archbishop, directed that Nicholas of Tusculum retrieve those letters and destroy them. Langton hesitated to surrender the documents, for he wanted to use them as weapons for forcing the king to pay promptly and fully for damages to the Church during the interdict.

The interdict remained in effect following King John's reconciliation with the pope and Langton's arrival in England, its relaxation awaiting final agreement on royal payment of reparations to the English Church. John, preparing for his great continental campaign of 1214, wished to avoid paying any more than necessary. Langton and the bishops returning from exile mistrusted the king, and the archbishop refused to lift the interdict until full reparation was made. His refusal put him in an awkward position, continuing to deny to the English people the comfort of the sacrament that their king, no longer excommunicate, was not denied.

Innocent III was eager to bring the conflict to a close, and he was beginning to view Langton as an obstacle. This enabled John to stall on paying without fear of reprisal. He enjoyed the papal legate's support against the archbishop and also the diplomatic skills of ambassadors at the papal court. To supplement his diplomacy, John distributed funds among the pope's courtiers to purchase friends. Also in autumn 1213, John promised to make payments for projects close to the pope's heart once the ban was lifted: 10,000 marks for a proposed crusade, and annual contributions to papal building programmes at Rome. Painter commented, 'One hesitates to use the term bribery . . . But it certainly looks as if money well spent smoothed the way for the pope's change of heart.'[43]

Negotiations over payment for damages to ecclesiastical property prevented lifting of the interdict for over a year.

43. Painter (1949) pp. 201–2.

On the exiled bishops' return, King John had promised to pay 15,000 marks by Christmas 1213 and the balance by Easter 1214, but they could not agree on a final figure. In January 1214, the pope imposed a settlement whereby John would raise 100,000 marks for paying off all claims. The king, who soon sailed for Poitou, could not spare a penny from his continental expedition; nonetheless, he levied a tallage to raise money for the Church's claims. He sent an embassy to Rome to negotiate better terms, and in late spring 1214, Innocent III agreed to relaxation of the interdict on payment of 40,000 marks, with the balance to be determined by a papal inquiry and paid in semi-annual instalments of 6000 marks. Finally on 2 July, the papal legate declared the interdict lifted. John paid 6000 marks in October 1214, but it is unlikely that he made any additional payments. His treasury was nearly empty following the defeat of his coalition against Philip Augustus, and he was facing baronial discontent that would erupt in civil war by the next spring. John seems to have bargained away any further compensation to the English Church in exchange for a promise of free elections to bishoprics and abbacies.

The issue of filling episcopal vacancies was another topic for friction between Stephen Langton and the king, and also between Langton and the papal legate. Since John had an archbishop whom he disliked and distrusted, he sought to fill bishoprics with his own men. Innocent III obliged with instructions to his legate to secure election of candidates 'who should be men not only distinguished by their life and learning, but also loyal to the king, profitable to the kingdom, and capable of giving counsel and help – the king's assent having been requested'.[44] Further letters stressed the need to consider 'proper requests from princes' and to choose candidates 'faithful to the king and useful to the kingdom'.[45] With the pope and Nicholas of Tusculum proving so co-operative, the only stumbling block that John encountered in getting his way

44. Cheney, Semple (1953) p. 166.
45. Cheney, C.R., Cheney, M.G. (eds) (1967) *Letters of Pope Innocent III concerning England and Wales*, Clarendon Press, Oxford, p. 265, no. 939.

in episcopal elections was the archbishop of Canterbury. Langton feared that the principle of free election that had been the purpose for his long struggle with John was being sacrificed to papal expediency. The archbishop proposed a formula for elections to which the king responded in January 1214, on the eve of his departure for the Continent. John concluded, 'Rest assured that there is no disagreement between us.' In fact, Langton cannot have agreed with such clauses as 'saving our right' and 'saving our dignity'.[46] Other churchmen resented renewed royal demands that episcopal and abbatial elections take place in the presence of the king's representatives, and royal agents' crude attempts to impose the king's will led Langton to complain to the papal court.

John's weakening political position following his return from France in autumn 1214 made him willing to placate his bishops with a charter for free elections, later confirmed in the first chapter of Magna Carta. The Charter did not have its intended effect, for royal influence on episcopal elections did not end. The formality of royal consent to an election remained, enabling the king lawfully to withhold his consent from a bishop-elect; and his right of appeal to the papacy about an unacceptable candidate gave popes added cause for intervention in English episcopal elections. Perhaps the 'strangest sequel' to the long Canterbury succession quarrel is that John got his way in all six episcopal elections held after the 1213 peace.[47] Royal clerks won election to three sees; papal nominees acceptable to John took two; and the archbishop's nominee was installed at Rochester with royal assent in an attempt to purchase Stephen Langton's goodwill.[48] Innocent opposed John only once, refusing to translate Peter des Roches from Winchester to the archbishopric of York. The pope supported John's opposition to the York chapter's election of Simon Langton,

---

46. *Rot. Lit. Claus.* Hardy (1833–4) vol. 1, p. 160.
47. Barlow, F. (1988) *The Feudal Kingdom of England 1042–1216*, 4th edn, Longman, p. 414.
48. *Curiales* were William of Cornhill at Coventry, Walter de Gray at Worcester, who was soon translated to York; papal selections were Richard Poore at Chichester and Pandulf at Norwich.

however; and he had no objection to translating another *curialis*, Walter de Gray, from Worcester to York.

Innocent III succeeded in imposing his own choice for archbishop of Canterbury on King John, but he neither succeeded in ending the king's role in English episcopal elections nor in compensating the English Church for its financial losses suffered during the interdict. Henry III could still get his way in episcopal elections, gaining financially all the while from vacancies, as his 1238–44 struggle to impose his candidate on the Winchester canons shows. In English kings' eyes, their bishops still had dual status as barons; and they could exercise *coercio propter baroniam*, seizure of their temporal possessions. Innocent had not been battling for freedom of the English Church from royal oppression so much as for principles of papal supremacy. Like other lawyer-popes of the high Middle Ages, he was largely content with 'a formal victory reinforced with resounding generalizations'.[49] Royal acknowledgement of papal suzerainty over England and Ireland was victory enough for him. Meanwhile John had enjoyed the Church's wealth for years, had thwarted a potential Franco-papal alliance against him, and had won a valuable friend and ally for the coming struggle against his barons and archbishop. It is not difficult to decide which one – monarch or pontiff – won more.

49. Southern, R.W. (1970a) *Western Society and the Church in the Middle Ages*, Penguin Books, Harmondsworth, p. 132.

Chapter 7

CRISES OF JOHN'S REIGN: INCREASING BARONIAL DISCONTENT

. . .

THE CHANGING POSITION OF THE BARONAGE IN ANGEVIN ENGLAND

One of the most common accusations made by historians against King John is his inability to manage his magnates. Any successful medieval monarch had to keep his barons contented if he was to govern successfully, and English kings in the later Middle Ages often created a 'court party' of favoured nobles. Yet John recruited only a handful of great men for his household, and mutual mistrust characterized his relations with his barons. John's mistreatment of William de Braose, a favourite early in his reign, is infamous; but he also quarrelled with other barons, some of whom would be his stalwarts in the crisis of 1215–16, among them William Marshal, earl of Pembroke, Walter de Lacy, another marcher lord with large Irish holdings, and Ranulf III, earl of Chester. His shunning of the earl of Pembroke for several years is notorious because the Marshal's verse biography attributes it to the king's small-minded jealousy of his superior in chivalric conduct.

If John could not get along with leading loyalist barons, his troubles with others should be no surprise. While his suspicious character contributed to troubles with his great men and individual grievances roused some barons to rebellion, the Angevin revolution in government generated a broad baronial reaction. By the second decade of the thirteenth century, Angevin habits of arbitrary government were building a sense of community among

175

the baronage. Accumulated grievances against monarchs' actions *sine judicio* or *per voluntatem* and their failure to govern *per consilium baronum* made a rebellion predictable. Resentment of arbitrary and exploitative tendencies in Angevin government, exacerbated by John's frenzied quest for funds and his prickly personality, brought on civil war by spring 1215.

A truism of textbooks is that king and baronage were natural enemies, and they often depict the barons as reactionaries retarding progress toward construction of a strong nation-state. Nowadays, scholars are more likely to see some community of interest between king and baronage in exploiting the kingdom and its resources, protecting their property from foreign threats, and seeing that the people rendered their payments and services. The English baronage from its origins as companions and kinsmen of William the Conqueror had shared with the king an interest in keeping a subject population under control. Nonetheless, baronial rebellions had punctuated the reigns of earlier English monarchs, although the rebels had rarely co-operated, fighting because of personal wrongs, not on account of political issues. Not even in the great rebellion of 1173–74 had they presented a united front against Henry II, and neither would they against John in 1215–16.

Since earls and barons controlled a major portion of medieval England's resources, including knights and castles, they had the potential for resisting a monarch threatening their privileges, seeking to gather too much power into his own hands. Medieval kings faced a contradiction: they sought to suppress disorder and to enhance their authority; yet to do this, they had to rely on their nobility's resources, including armed forces, that might be used in rebelling against them. A result was that quarrels between king and magnates often ended in an accommodation without any severe punishment for the rebel. While feudal law allowed for formal renunciation of a vassal's homage and taking arms against a lord who had treated him cruelly or unjustly, it did not sanction compacts or conspiracies by bands of vassals. By the early thirteenth century, however, the baronage was beginning to think of itself as a corporate body with collective rights and responsibilities. John would face by early 1215 a *conjuratio* or sworn band of barons, bound together not simply by private complaints but by broad opposition to his rule based on principle.

On John's accession, some 165 men could be ranked as barons, including those holding halves or thirds of baronies previously partitioned. Defining the baronage of England in this period is not easy, however; the Latin word *baro* did not denote a clearly defined rank. Unfortunately, no precise scheme of classification works effectively to fit the barons into ranks or categories. At the top in social standing were the earls, of whom there were sixteen or seventeen on John's accession in 1199.[1] Barons varied widely in wealth and power, with some holding only one knight's fee in-chief of the king and others holding over a hundred fees plus lands held of other lords. Aside from lists of knights' fees made for assessing scutages, little evidence exists to make any meaningful calculation of barons' and earls' wealth. Yet numbers of fees held of the king do not present an accurate measure of resources, for they could vary in extent and income; also some barons held many fees of lords other than the king.

Scutage lists, inaccurate as they are, afford some figures for comparison. They show that barons without comital titles could equal earls in landholdings and wealth, for example, Robert fitz Walter of Little Dunmow, Essex, with

1. Confusion about numbers arises because Baldwin of Béthune (d. 1212) and his successor William de Forz (d. 1241) lords of Skipton and Cockermouth, bore a Norman title 'count of Aumale', formerly rendered as 'earl of Albemarle'. Other earls are William d'Aubigny of Sussex (d. 1221); Robert de Beaumont of Leicester (d. 1204); Roger Bigod of Norfolk (d. 1221); Henry de Bohun of Hereford (d. 1220); Ranulf of Chester (d. 1232); Richard de Clare of Hertford (d. 1217); William de Ferrers of Derby (d. 1247); Geoffrey fitz Peter of Essex (d. 1213), succeeded by his son Geoffrey de Mandeville; David of Huntingdon (d. 1215); William Longsword of Salisbury (d. 1226); William Marshal of Pembroke (d. 1219); Waleran de Newburgh of Warwick (d. 1204), succeeded by a minor son, Henry de Newburgh; Hamelin Plantagenet of Surrey (d. 1202), succeeded by his son William de Warenne; William de Redvers of Devon (d. 1217); Aubrey de Vere of Oxford (d. 1214), succeeded by his brother Robert; Saher de Quency (d. 1219), created earl of Winchester, 1206.

over a hundred fees, and Gilbert de Gant's Lincolnshire honor or William de Mowbray's holdings in Yorkshire amounting to about ninety fees each. About ten barons owed scutage on over ninety fees in 1199, while some seventy held fewer than fifteen. A good-sized baronial holding seems to have consisted of about thirty fees total. Although baronial incomes can only be estimated, they seem in King John's time to have ranged from over £800 annually to less than £100 with an average income of £202. By whatever measure applied, it is clear that the baronage controlled most of the kingdom's landed wealth. Wealthiest of all by John's middle years was Earl Ranulf of Chester, who controlled his county free from royal officers' interference; he also held a great Lincolnshire legacy, the honor of Bolingbroke; and he regained his former wife's honor of Richmond, Yorkshire.

Textbook accounts of the English baronage usually give an impression of a static, closed class, proud of its ancestry and mindful of its privileges. A strong sense of aristocratic self-consciousness would not flower fully until the fourteenth century, when an hereditary right to a summons to Parliament became the mark of nobility. Yet the patrilineal pattern for descent of lands that appeared by the time of the Conquest was strengthening their solidarity, and adoption of patronymics derived from ancestral lands in Normandy points to pride in their predecessors. For many baronial families, protecting the lineage began to take precedence over service to their lord the king. Grants of feudal tenures to younger sons or as marriage-portions to daughters were obscuring the clear military basis for landholdings.

The barons remained a fluid group, however, with many noble families disappearing after three or four generations because of failure to produce sons. From Henry I's time on, new men had entered the aristocracy through royal service. When the king's favour won them grants of extinct titles or marriages to heiresses, their success does not seem to have aroused great resentment. William Marshal, earl of Pembroke, and Geoffrey fitz Peter, earl of Essex, who secured earldoms through service to the Angevins seem to have won easy acceptance by their fellow magnates.

By the twelfth and thirteenth centuries, noble families throughout Europe were absorbing the chivalric outlook of their retainers, and their military role took precedence over public responsibilities, which had survived in attenuated form from Roman times down into the Carolingian age. Barons and knights, despite disparities in wealth, were coming to identify themselves as a single class based on their military function. Preachers and vernacular poets were teaching that all *milites*, fighting men who lived by the chivalric code, belonged to a single superior caste. This emphasis on martial tradition took hold among the English baronage, as the Barnwell chronicler's account of the rebellion against King John illustrates. He explained that sons and nephews of magnates became rebels because 'they wanted to make their name through warlike deeds'.[2]

The Anglo-Norman baronage originated as a military caste imposed on a defeated population, but also holding governmental responsibilities: exercising jurisdictional and fiscal rights over the assemblage of knightly and manorial tenants that made up their honor. The honor or aggregation of a baron's holdings had its own court, which played a significant part in peace-keeping and dispute settlement. Military service by barons and their knights contributed to the kingdom's defence, and barons constructed castles to control the countryside. Many, especially on the Welsh borders and in the North, continued in the late twelfth century to build castles, maintain large armed forces, and hold liberties beyond the reach of sheriffs and royal justices. The Norman kings had chosen their intimate counsellors from barons and earls, summoning them to councils on the great feasts of the ecclesiastical calendar. This concept of the magnates as the monarch's 'natural advisers' was embedded deeply in medieval tradition, but the twelfth-century revolution in government was altering the position of the barons and their relations with the king. With Henry II, a trend toward centralization was taking authority away from traditional local officials or feudal lords and placing it under the royal government.

---

2. Barnwell Chronicle. Stubbs, W. (ed.) (1872–3) *Memoriale Walteri de Coventria* (2 vols), Rolls Series, vol. 2, p. 220.

Angevin castle policy brings into clear focus the tilt in the balance of power away from the baronage. Castles, 'the bones of the kingdom' in a chronicler's words,[3] expressed physically and symbolically domination over the countryside and its inhabitants. Henry II and his sons embarked upon a large-scale programme of castle construction and renovation, which made it the largest regular item of royal expenses in the period 1154–1216. These expenditures reached a peak under King John, notably his spending on northern castles, which was due as much to increasing internal tensions as to a Scottish threat. John and his predecessors also confiscated barons' castles, sometimes in their eagerness riding rough-shod over customary law and tradition, for example, denying hereditary claims to castles when heirs succeeded to their baronies. The result of this Plantagenet policy is a shift in the proportion of royal fortresses to baronial ones from one royal castle in five in 1154 to one in only two by 1214. Their programme of reducing the proportion of baronial castles clearly fits into a general policy of royal centralization.

Angevin innovations in government were undermining the traditional feudal pattern of baronial justice for the men owing them homage. Honor courts were declining in influence throughout the twelfth century, but Henry II's legal reforms hastened their decline, allowing baronial tenants easy transfers of their suits into the *curia regis*. Sheriffs and itinerant justices connected the king directly with knightly landholders, undermining the barons' old role as intermediaries between their men and the royal government. Increasingly, knights of the counties had direct contacts with the central government, suing in the royal courts, serving on commissions and juries, holding new local offices.

Cementing a new direct link between the monarch and the countryside without local lords as intermediaries were networks of *curiales* or *familiares regis*, circulating

---

3. William of Newburgh. Howlett, R. (ed.) (1885–90) *Historia Return Anglicarum of William of Newburgh*. In *Chronicles, Stephen, Henry II and Richard I* (4 vols), Rolls Series, vol. 1, p. 331.

constantly between the royal court and the counties. Royal government had been growing more complex since Henry I's time, with literate and numerate servants needed to staff offices such as the exchequer. Changes in military science by the late twelfth century also meant that traditional cavalrymen were less needed than soldiers with new skills as crossbowmen or siege engineers. Creation of a corps of specialist soldiers and administrators threatened the great men's places as the king's chief deputies. No longer needing to rely upon them to keep his kingdom functioning effectively, he called upon their counsel only occasionally and named them only to honorific offices.

A minority of barons did succeed in becoming *curiales*, however, and 'new men' in the king's service frequently moved into the baronial class. Yet baronial discontent during John's reign was more than mere jealousy of 'outs' towards 'ins'. A result of Angevin innovations in government was a cleavage within the baronial ranks similar to the seventeenth-century split of the gentry into 'court' and 'country' factions. Some barons, such as Peter de Brus or Simon de Kyme, tried without success to adapt to changing conditions, but they failed to win the advantages that came with royal favour and had to seek other means of improving their families' economic prospects. Northern barons in particular had little taste for the court and administrative responsibilities; and they remained in the countryside, preoccupied with their estates and family matters. Yet they knew that local office brought wealth and power, and they resented royal favourites taking such posts as sheriff. Their inability to compete with new men with new skills sometimes embittered them toward the king and his *familiares*, whom they viewed as something akin to the 'parasitic bureaucracy' of the early Stuarts.[4] Typical is John fitz Robert, baron of Whalton, Northumberland, and an East Anglian landholder as well. Although his father had been

---

4. Trevor Roper, H.R. (1965) 'The general crisis of the seventeenth century'. In Aston, T. (ed.) *Crisis in Europe 1560–1660*, Routledge & Kegan Paul. Reprint (1967) Anchor Books, New York, NY, pp. 83, 100.

one of John's *familiares*, he shunned the court and royal office except for a short spell as sheriff of Norfolk and Suffolk, and he avoided offering fines to purchase favours. His estates linked him with both northern and East Anglian rebel leaders, and he followed them into rebellion.

The Angevins' precocious administration bound tightly the shires and the central government, while the monarchs' energetic travel about England meant that they could learn about conditions in the kingdom firsthand by consulting barons and knights individually in the counties. A result of such royal means of information gathering was that the Angevins saw little need for formal meetings of a great council of magnates. King John's discussions with *familiares regis* or *curiales* who were in daily attendance on the king decided many matters. His reliance upon a corps of household officials and new men instead of spokesmen for the corporate body of the baronage, aroused fears of secret government. The complaint that the king neglected their counsel in favour of 'evil advisers' marks the appearance of an issue that would resurface in all the rebellions of the later Middle Ages.

Of course, the royal court remained the centre of social life, and some magnates still became *familiares regis*, joining John's court on its travels about the country. Warfare brought others into the king's presence in the course of fulfilling their military obligation. Among the fifty-five or so most frequent witnesses to King John's charters were eleven earls. Of these, three were new men who had acquired their earldoms by marriage: Geoffrey fitz Peter, who was also justiciar, William Marshal, and Saher de Quency, earl of Winchester. A fourth – William Longsword, earl of Salisbury – was John's bastard half-brother. Seven had credentials as magnates of old family: Aubrey de Vere, David of Huntingdon, Ranulf of Chester, Robert of Leicester, William d'Aubigny of Arundel, William de Ferrers, and William de Warenne. Of eleven bishops among the frequent attestors, all were former royal clerks, several of whom continued to hold posts in John's administration; they include Archbishop Geoffrey of York, another illegitimate half-brother of the king. Most of the remaining fifty-five witnesses to royal charters were *familiares*, not of baronial background; some such as Hugh de Neville, the chief forester, William Briwerre or Robert de Vipont, were multi-purpose royal servants and self-made barons.

The 'country' barons were suspicious of the *curiales*, and their suspicions grew during John's reign. They felt vaguely, without verbalizing coherently, 'a crisis in the martial values of an aristocratic society confronted by a bureaucratic monarchy'.[5] Those north of the Trent especially felt their traditional autonomy threatened by encroaching central authority. Professionals staffing new offices often held an exalted view of the royal power that owed more to old traditions of sacral kingship or Roman law than to feudal custom, making them punctilious in applying John's harsh policies. Also their approach to their work might be termed bureaucratic or even proto-bourgeois, with their knowledge of letters and numbers making them more calculating and rational, more concerned with material gain than with chivalric virtues.

Medieval monarchs wanted to select as administrators or soldiers men with needed skills, and not be limited in their choices to a group whom accident of birth alone made eligible for office. Kings also sought obscure knights and clerks to staff their government because their complete dependence on royal favour made them more pliable than great nobles with castles and troops of their own. The Angevin kings paid little attention to conservatives' complaints about their choices for royal offices. By the time of Henry II, an administration staffed by lesser ranking agents had proceeded so far that some scholars refer to 'household government' or government by royal *familiares*. None of John's great officers of state or senior household officials came from the old nobility; neither did his inner corps of multi-purpose royal servants whose influence equalled that of formal office-holders.

The ambition of new men alarmed conservative critics at the Angevin court, who complained that they were

5. Baldwin, J.W. (1986a) 'The Capetian Court at work under Philip Augustus'. In Haymes, E. (ed.) *The Medieval Court in Europe*, Wilhelm Fink Verlag, Munich.

threatening a stable social order. Such critics saw John's *curiales* or *familiares* as a narrow clique enjoying royal favour at barons' expense. They sought to discredit new men in the king's service by pointing to their base birth despite the fact that they came largely from the knightly class. This new corps of specialist royal servants, enjoying easy access to the king's person, competed with barons for office, threatening their political power, wealth, and social dominance. The Angevin *familiares'* tendency to crowd the barons out of the king's presence was becoming more apparent under John, and competition for access to royal patronage fuelled resentments.

Chroniclers also complained about John's promotion of aliens, Poitevin mercenary captains, to posts. A chronicler wrote of Fawkes de Breauté, 'King John had raised him with others from being a poor attendant into a knight, and then made him the equal of an earl.'[6] Actually, such complaints date from the mid-thirteenth century, written under the influence of anti-foreign feelings aroused by Henry III's promotion of his Poitevin and Savoyard relatives. Although John faced the problem of finding posts for friends who had followed him from the Continent after 1203, writers exaggerated the impact of aliens. Nonetheless, military men were taking prominent places in John's government during his em-battled last years, among them Anglo-Normans such as Hubert de Burgh, Robert de Vipont, or Brien de Insula, who were not precisely aliens. Most resented were several mercenary soldiers from Poitou and Touraine who took posts in England after 1207; a chapter of Magna Carta named them and called for their removal from office. The most powerful alien was probably Peter des Roches, bishop of Winchester, whose appointment as justiciar in 1214 aroused baronial resentment, but hardly more than had Richard I's Norman favourite, William Longchamp.

Third- or fourth-generation barons, little interested in holding office at court or Westminster, nonetheless felt entitled to a special place in the kingdom because of great landholdings, military power, and also distinguished

6. Barnwell Chronicle. Stubbs (1872–3) vol. 2, p. 253.

ancestry. By the mid-twelfth century some Anglo-Norman families were asserting special prestige because their ancestors had fought with William at Hastings, sensing that their superior status and military service required that they be summoned to counsel the king. Depictions of King Arthur and his knights of the Round-table in romances perhaps represent nobles' anti-administrative fantasy of a monarchy in which the king was merely *primus inter pares* with no professional civil servants about. Poets' praise of largess in epics and romances made the aristocracy feel entitled to share in royal generosity simply on the basis of rank. When barons did win appointment to the new administrative posts, they felt that undertaking new duties beyond traditional military obligations entitled them to additional reward, just as new men were earning from their service to the king.

For monarchs, on the other hand, ancient lineage alone did not justify privileges. John and his predecessors felt that their barons owed loyalty and services, especially military and monetary ones, as a condition for holding the great estates and other privileges that their families had amassed, not in order to gain more. Angevin kings had to distribute patronage very carefully, rewarding their growing staffs of royal officials adequately, but not lavishly enough to arouse the barons' jealousy. Also they needed to purchase the loyalty of their barons, who still had power to threaten rebellion if they grew too dissatisfied; yet they had to take care not to create over-mighty magnates capable of threatening royal authority. At the same time, they needed to husband a royal demesne shrunken from previous royal grants. Little was left for rewarding magnates; or perhaps a better way of expressing it is that little was left for bribing the magnates to remain peaceful.

Since little land was available for grants, the Angevins had to depend on wardship and marriage, escheated honors, or local offices as instruments of patronage. Obtaining custody of an heiress and then marrying her was a common path for royal servants seeking to rise in wealth and social status, but barons also sought heiresses to marry to their non-inheriting younger sons. In such a situation, competition arose between *curiales* and country barons. Henry II and his sons adopted more stringent policies to bring more and more custodies and marriages into their hands. Royal tinkering with rules of succession alarmed the barons, who also needed resources for their sons and for rewarding their retainers. The novel custom of prerogative wardship denied to barons rights to custody of the lands of any tenant who was also a tenant-in-chief of the king, losing them substantial income from wardships and marriages. Henry II and John also sometimes restricted the principle of *parage*, or partition of inheritances equally among daughters. In John's own marriage to Isabelle of Gloucester, an older feudal custom was revived that left married daughters only whatever portion their father had granted them at the time of their marriage, denying them an equal partition of the patrimony.

The magnates still kept retinues of armed men, who were less likely to be their own tenants because they no longer had free land for enfeoffing landless soldiers. They maintained such bands of retainers without tenurial ties by means of annual money payments that foreshadow the indentures of retinue of the later Middle Ages. Many barons, no longer holding surplus land with which to enfeof their retainers, competed with *curiales* for disputed inheritances, lucrative custodies, or escheats. Some barons, Walter de Lacy or William Marshal, for example, looked for new lands in Ireland or Wales to carve out fees for rewarding their retainers, creating more friction with King John over policies in those principalities. Perhaps the 'ideological conflict' between these warrior nobles and royal agents appears most vividly in Gerald of Wales' work, *Expugnatio Hibernica*. The Anglo-Norman settlers in Ireland felt that they could recreate a truly feudal world for themselves, and their 'anti-bureaucratic sentiment' caused them to see the king's officials as hindering their work of carving out estates for themselves and their retainers.[7]

7. Flanagan, M.T. (1989) *Irish Society, Anglo-Norman Settlers, Angevin Kingship: Interactions in Ireland in the Late Twelfth Century*, Oxford UP, pp. 304, 299.

Competition for patronage was bound to be strong, and some claimants would be inevitably disappointed. Royal *familiares* enjoying access to the king's presence had an advantage over barons in the counties in acquiring custodies and marriages of heirs or marriages to widows with dower lands that must have aroused resentment. New men such as William Briwerre could accumulate baronial-sized holdings. This problem of disappointed patronage seekers was greater for John than for his predecessors. As absentee rulers, they could distance themselves from unpopular or impolitic distributions of favours, rescinding them if necessary. John, continually present in England, insisted on personal involvement in patronage matters and had to bear personally the blame of the disappointed. A number of the barons rebelling in 1215, then, saw competition with John's *curiales* frustrating their ambitions, denying them lands or making exorbitant financial demands.

Probably the major factor in John's troubles with his barons was his insistence on increasing their contribution to royal revenues and their resistance to any change in their feudal obligations. Of course, his father and brother had sought to increase revenues with oppressive financial policies; but by 1208 and 1209, John's abuses seem to have surpassed those of his predecessors, and his policies were more and more those of 'a suspicious ruler, keeping his subjects in hand through fear'.[8] His tightening or loosening of pressure for repayment of crown debts proved a powerful incentive for a noble's good behaviour. Barons enjoying royal favour felt little or no pressure to repay their debts, and they might find them pardoned entirely. John aroused greater hostility than his predecessors because he insisted on involving himself directly in the details of raising money by means that his subjects saw as extortionate.

Any medieval king ran the risk of confronting an over-mighty magnate who refused to obey royal commands, but traditional feudal processes offered few instruments for

8. Stenton, D.M. (1958) 'King John and The Courts of Justice', *Proceedings of the British Academy*, 44, p. 101. Also reprinted (1964) *English Justice, 1066–1215* (Raleigh Lecture).

dealing with such defiance short of force. By the Angevin period in England, however, the royal government was devising new means of bringing down the powerful, entangling them in a web of administrative procedures. Besides using crown debts as an excuse to subject his barons to the exchequer's confiscation of their lands, or even their imprisonment, King John knew how to use lawsuits to threaten loss of inheritances. While Henry II's legal reforms had deprived the barons of their right to discipline their tenants by dispossessing them, he and his sons were keeping the baronage insecure in their tenures. Disputed successions to baronies brought demands for large fines from contending claimants, if not more direct intervention by John.

Perhaps arbitrary and authoritarian methods adopted by the Angevin kings were the only workable ones available to control the baronage and to prevent chaos. The confusion of Stephen's reign was still a reminder to many in early thirteenth-century England of the price paid for a compliant king. Until late in John's reign, it seemed that the barons were sufficiently cowed by his methods. The Angevin programme had not completely broken baronial power, however; and the risk of pushing the barons into armed revolt was always present. John risked provoking a rebellion by reducing the barons' opportunities for royal patronage at the same time that he was making greater financial demands on them. Rebellion resulted in 1215.

. . .

RIVAL VIEWS OF KINGSHIP AMONG KING, *CURIALES*, AND BARONAGE

Barons' perception of Angevin oppression forced them to consider new ideas on government that could place limits on King John's power. Their problem was that medieval political thought was often a jumble of contradictory ideas about kingship; doctrines that the monarch was answerable only to God co-existed with doctrines of the supremacy of law. The lawbook *Glanvill*, for example, presents conflicting pictures of kingship typical of much medieval political thought. On the one hand, its author states the Roman law maxim, 'What pleases the prince has the force of law'; and on the other, he asserts that England's laws are made 'on the advice of the magnates'.[9]

Many scholars today assume the dominance of 'an "ancient" feudal mentality' among the aristocracy of Angevin England,[10] and they find that Henry II's legislation grew out of his feudal overlordship. It is just as likely, however, that it followed from older traditions of sacral monarchy stretching back from Anglo-Saxon kings to Charlemagne and beyond to Constantine. The English coronation oath emphasized royal responsibility for justice. Often overlooked is the heritage from Norman dukes and Angevin counts, which supplied 'a Gallo-Roman and Frankish substratum' of concepts of the state and public authority.[11] This tradition sanctioned royal intervention in lesser courts, public or feudal, to amend defaults of justice or unjust judgments. Thus it is likely that Henry II's assizes originated not as outgrowths of feudal custom but as quasi-criminal processes.

King John's statements show that his notion of the royal power is consistent with a stream in twelfth-century political thought that placed the king, 'a certain image on earth of divine majesty', above enacted law.[12] Henry II and Richard Lionheart had already introduced a new vocabulary of power into royal documents, continued by John's chancery. Henry added the term *Dei gratia* to his title on charters, and Richard adopted the 'plural of majesty'. John went further in a 1202 letter to the English clergy in which he claimed almost imperial status for England, *regnum Anglicanum quasi imperio adequetur*.[13]

9. Hall, G.D.G. (1965) (ed. and trans.) *Tractatus de Legibus et Consuetudinibus Regni Anglie qui Glanvilla vocatur*, Thomas Nelson (Medieval Texts), Walton-on-Thames, Prologue.
10. Milsom, S.F.C. (1976) *The Legal Framework of English Feudalism*, Cambridge UP, pp. 46, 52, 60.
11. Boussard, J. (1956) *Le gouvernement d'Henri II Plantegenêt*, Librarie d'Argences, Paris, p. 588.
12. Nederman, C.J. (ed. and trans.) (1990) *John of Salisbury Policraticus*, Cambridge UP, p. 28, lib. iv, cap. 1 (Cambridge Texts in the History of Political Thought).
13. *Rymer's Foedera*. Clarke, A., Caley, J., Bayley, F., Holbrooke, F., Clarke, F.W. (eds) (1816–30, 1869) *Foedera, Conventiones, Litterae, etc.* or *Rymer Foedera, 1066–1383* (4 vols in 7), Record Commission, vol. 1, p. 87.

Medieval political thinkers, fearful of chaos, tolerated a large sphere for operation of the king's will. Well known was a 'tutelary' view of kingship reaching back to St Augustine, which viewed the ruler-subject relationship as like that of guardian to a minor; as the *Dialogus de Scaccario* expresses it, God has entrusted the king with 'the general care of his subjects'.[14] Among the books that King John sought out in 1208, seeking ammunition for arguments against Pope Innocent III, was Augustine's *De Civitate Dei*. Because the monarch is responsible to God for his subjects, but not to them, the Angevins' subjects accepted the *benevolentia, malevolentia regis*, the *gratia, ira regis* as political facts of life. The *Dialogus de Scaccario* admitted that although monarchs sometimes acquired wealth through arbitrary acts, 'Their subjects have no right to question or condemn their actions.'[15]

In contrast, another stream of medieval political thought stressed the king's subjection to the law. An interpolation of the *Leges Edwardi Confessoris* from early thirteenth-century London contrasted will and law, 'Law is always made by right [*jus*]; but will and violence and force are not right.'[16] Contemporary chroniclers depicted John as a tyrant because he ruled by will, not as a true prince in accord with the law. Typical is the Waverley annalist's statement, 'He disinherited some without judgment of their peers, and he condemned others to a dire death; he violated their wives and daughters – his only law was his despotic will.'[17] Although this doctrine of the law's supremacy recognized that a king could do wrong, it provided no means of righting wrongs suffered by his subjects, no machinery for enforcing a tyrant's obedience to the law. The only remedy was to await God's judgment.

14. Johnson, C. (ed. and trans.) (1950) *Dialogus de Scaccario*, Oxford UP (Oxford Medieval Texts), p. 101; also *Glanvill*. Hall (1965) p. 28, lib. 2, cap 7.
15. Johnson (1950), p. 1.
16. Liebermann, F. (ed.) (1898–1916) *Die Gesetze der Angelsachsen* (3 vols), M. Niemeyer, Halle vol. 1, p. 635; translation Holt, J.C. (1992) *Magna Carta*, 2nd edn, Cambridge UP, p. 93.
17. Luard, H.R. (ed.) (1864–9) *Annales Monastici* (5 vols), Rolls Series, vol. 2, p. 282.

Official records of the Angevin kings reflect this ambivalence about law and will. John himself occasionally submitted questions of royal right to property to his justices for settlement by juries, but he did not make very wide use of the common law courts, except for asserting his rights to advowsons of churches. Doubtless, he wished to stay on the solid ground of legality in such pleas to avoid the Church courts' claims to jurisdiction. Yet the Angevin kings made disseizin *per voluntatem regis* into a common disciplinary measure that they did not view as requiring a previous judgment. The plea rolls refer matter-of-factly to disseizins *per preceptum regis*, and tenants defending their right pleaded that they had possession by royal precept. In 1191, those governing in Richard Lionheart's absence conceded that royal officials ought not to take free tenants' land, that it should only be seized 'by judgment of the king's court according to lawful customs and assizes of the kingdom *or* by the king's command'.[18] Apparently, they accepted either as equally lawful.

A king who was both above the law and below it posed an insoluble problem for his subjects seeking legal remedies for his wilful acts. King John in 1213 ordered an inquiry into whether one of his subjects had been disseized 'by our will or by judgment of our court';[19] if he was found to have been disseized by the king's will, then he was to be placed in possession. At the beginning of John's reign, he promised several important continental vassals that he would not disseize them 'unless by judgment of our court';[20] other subjects offered fines

18. Roger of Howden. Stubbs, W. (ed.) (1868–71) *Chronica Rogeri de Hovedene* (4 vols), Rolls Series, vol. 3, p. 136.
19. *Rot. Lit. Claus.* Hardy, T.D. (ed.) (1833–4) *Rotuli Litterarum Clausarum* (2 vols), Record Commission, vol. 1, p. 136b.
20. E.g. charters for the count of La March; the count of Eu; the viscount of Thouars, *Rymer's Foedera*. Clarke, Caley, Bayley, Holbrooke, Clarke (1816–30, 1869) vol. 1, 79; the counts of Armagnac, 1202, *Rot. Lit. Pat.* Hardy, T.D. (ed) (1835) *Rotuli Litterarum Patentium 1201–1216*, Record Commission, p. 11; the king of Connacht, Ireland in 1215, *Rot. Chart.* Hardy, T.D. (ed.) (1837) *Rotuli Chartarum, 1199–1216*, Record Commission, p. 219.

for a similar promise. In lawsuits, litigants sometimes petitioned the king to 'do his will'; seeing the king's will as a means for setting aside the rigidity of customary law or redressing grievances for which the common law gave no remedy.

Scholars have depicted the English baronage of 1215 as brutish reactionaries simply seeking to regain their dominant place in a feudal structure, lacking any sense of public responsibility and incapable of espousing the broad political principles expressed in Magna Carta. Like many sweeping generalizations, this depiction of the rebel barons as feudal reactionaries contains a kernel of truth. Basic beliefs that the king should rule *per judicium* and *per consilium* came to them from feudal tradition. Yet scholars have turned to clerics for sources of the political principles set forth in Magna Carta, chiefly to Archbishop Stephen Langton, but also to an antiquarian circle of churchmen centred at St Paul's Cathedral, who had contacts with discontented barons as early as 1212. Clerical allies could reinforce the barons' views, aid them in spelling out their ideas more clearly, and broaden their reform programme's appeal beyond the feudal aristocracy.

The barons were capable of grasping their clerical colleagues' ideas about government, applying the experience that Angevin innovations had given them. Barons' practical experience presiding over honor courts and attending shire courts had taught them that any petitioner had a right to justice, 'to a reasonable application of legal process to his own particular case'.[21] For example a fine offered in the course of a 1206 lawsuit shows a plaintiff's optimism that the king could be persuaded to allow law to prevail over royal will. He complained that the tenant had his land *per preceptum regis*, and he offered the large sum of 300 marks and two palfreys to have the suit proceed 'according to the custom and assize of the kingdom'.[22]

21. Holt (1992), p. 92.
22. *Rot. de Obl. et fin.* Hardy, T.D. (ed.) (1835a) *Rotuli de Oblatis et Finibus*, Record Commission, p. 352.

The barons were beginning to see themselves as defenders of the custom of the realm, but in their view good custom predated the Angevins who had departed from the good old law of Edward the Confessor and Henry I. Their appeal to Anglo-Saxon and Norman precedent was a subtle means of charging the Angevin kings with unlawful innovations. For example, some maintained that custom obliged them to fight overseas only in defence of the old Anglo-Norman realm, not in defence of the Angevin patrimony or Aquitaine.

By the second decade of the thirteenth century, two notions were taking root among the baronage that challenged endorsement of the king's will: demands for government *per judicium* and *per consilium*. The barons' feudal tradition, reinforced by churchmen's writings, was teaching them that no one should be dispossessed of goods or lands except by judgment. Langton's teachings at Paris had stressed that rulers must proceed only after lawful judgment, and once at Canterbury, he pushed for acceptance of the idea. The early thirteenth-century London collection of old English laws included among its texts the *Leges Henrici Primi*, stating that nothing ought to be demanded or taken from anyone 'unless by right [*de jure*] and reason, by law of the land and justice and by a court's judgment'.[23] Feudal tradition taught the barons that a freeman, *liber homo*, had privileges denied the unfree, most important, protection from arbitrary punishments by his lord. A lord ought to proceed against his free tenant only *per judicium*, by regular legal process in which his other tenants participated. As Sir James Holt recognized, 'The idea of a right to judgement was so ingrained in the medieval mind that judgement was almost equated with justice.'[24] This insistence on proceeding *per judicium* appears in chapter 39 of the Great Charter as the germ of the 'due process' concept.

---

23. *Leges Henrici Primi*. 8.1.b.; Liebermann (1898–1916) vol. 1, p. 554.
24. Holt, J.C. (1955) 'The barons and The Great Charter', *English Historical Review*, 70, p. 15. Reprinted in Holt (1985) *Magna Carta and Medieval Government*, Hambledon Press.

A second concept influencing baronial thought about government was the great men's right to advise king, and that their advice represented the *commune consilium regni*. Henry I had promised in his coronation charter that he would not change the law without his barons' counsel, and the term 'common counsel of the realm' appears in chapters 12, 14, and 47 of Magna Carta. This phrase 'counsel' (Latin *consilium*), not 'council' (Latin *concilium*), has caused much confusion over the centuries. It referred to an activity, giving counsel, not to an assembly or council; and giving counsel, *consilium*, was not the same as giving consent, *consensus* or *assensus*. The assumption that the assembled baronage constituted the king's natural advisers followed from the feudal tradition of the lord's obligation to seek his men's counsel, and poetry recited at noble courts depicted Arthur or Charlemagne soliciting their barons' advice.

No assembly of royal tenants-in-chief met in Angevin England unless summoned by the king; it was an event, not an institution. One scholar has written, 'The great council which has played such a role in English historiography is largely a myth, a myth which has served to support the view that large assemblies were expansions of the *curia regis* or the king's small council – or rather counsel.'[25] The barons were beginning to seek an assembly that could speak for them collectively, once familiarity with such corporations as communes and chartered boroughs allowed them to see themselves as a corporate body. It was not difficult for the barons to conceive of the kingdom of England as a *communa*, not a subversive sworn association, but a collectivity or community of all the king's subjects possessing certain liberties. A significant step towards such thinking came while Richard I was away on crusade, when crises forced the *communitas Angliae* – magnates and royal officials working together – to make new arrangements for government. Not surprisingly, John's barons claimed that a baronial assembly not only could protect their own interests, but could represent the 'community of

---

25. Langmuir, G. (1972) 'Per Commune Consilium Regni in Magna Carta', *Studia Gratiana*, 15, p. 472.

the realm'. Possibly this concept of a *communa totius terrae* possessing corporate liberties with themselves as its spokesmen is the barons' most original contribution.

Feudal custom hardly distinguished between judgment and counsel; lords settled disputes with their vassals more often by negotiation than by formal legal process, and matters of justice often slipped into administrative or political spheres. The London collection of early English laws shows clearly this confusion, stating that the king ought to render justice 'by counsel of the magnates of the realm'. The barons linked these two ideas into a demand for *judicium parium*, that is, arrogating for themselves a role in the process of judging cases involving their own class. The new baronial ideal for England's government was in many ways an old one: an honor court for the whole kingdom at which great tenants-in-chief would counsel the king and collectively make judgments.

John's barons may have had current theory on their side; however, the king had traditional doctrines on his side. Royal officials sought to protect the *corona et dignitas domini regi*, a phrase that indicates their grasping for a concept approaching the later royal prerogative. Some royal clerks voiced proto-absolutist notions of royal authority derived from old traditions of sacral kingship. John found a *pseudotheologus*, Master Alexander the Mason, who preached that the king is 'the rod of the wrath of the Lord, ruling his people like a rod of iron and dashing them in pieces like a potter's vessel'.[26] A more influential adviser than Master Alexander was Peter des Roches, who also held views that placed the king above his barons.

John himself encouraged such views with his reinstatement of ceremonial crown-wearings and chanting of the *Christus vincit* at Christmas, Easter, and Pentecost. Evidently the king intended a particularly impressive celebration of Christmas in 1207. In early December, he received a complete set of regal costumes, designed

---

26. Roger of Howden, Stubbs (ed) (1868–71) vol. 2, p. 53; translation Powicke, F.M. (1927) 'Alexander of St Albans: a literary muddle'. In Davis, H.W.C. (ed.) (1927) *Essays in History Presented to Reginald Lane Poole*, Oxford UP, p. 257.

according to the imperial tradition of emphasizing the monarch's semi-priestly character. The regalia included Empress Matilda's great crown from Germany, a sceptre, a golden rod surmounted by a dove, silk cloth to be borne before the crowned king, and garments of purple silk worked with gold.

A number of the Angevins' clerks were *magistri* whose schooling had acquainted them with civil and canon law, which revealed to them Roman principles of public authority. They recognized royal responsibility for the *utilitas reipublicae*, the public or common good, and subjects' reciprocal obligation to contribute resources for it. The king's responsibility for the general welfare entitled him to override the law in case of emergency or *necessitas* and to impose extraordinary levies on his subjects. Certain phrases in the *Dialogus de Scaccario* and *Glanvill* reveal familiarity with this concept; and chancery documents show John himself using such terminology, describing one of his servants as 'useful to the realm'.[27] The Romanist vocabulary of public power reinforced old theocratic teachings of the king's supreme protection, advancing political thought beyond the purely personal relationships of feudal monarchy. By John's reign, the proto-Machiavellian concept of *necessitas* could justify extreme measures in the face of the threat from Philip Augustus and the pope. A 1205 summons to a great council used the phrase, 'common utility of our realm'. The notion appears in the writ authorizing levy of the thirteenth in 1207, 'for the defence of our realm and recovery of our rights'.[28] In brief, a concept of public obligation assisted in providing a legal basis for general taxation.

A term applied to the public power or common utility was the term *corona* or crown, for example, 'pleas of the crown', which gave the English monarch authority to suppress crime, to keep the king's peace, linking his

---

27. *Rot. Lit. Pat.* Hardy (1835) p. 139, describing Richard Marsh.
28. Stubbs, W. (ed.) (1913) *Select Charters and Other Illustrations of English Constitutional History*, 9th edn, Clarendon Press, Oxford, pp. 277, 278.

dignity with peace-keeping responsibility. Both Roman and canon law contributed to the concept, but the Angevins' practical activity in creating a complex of royal rights was crucial. Henry II applied the term *corona* to the royal castles, manors, and fiscal and jurisdictional rights that he sought to recover after 1154. Angevin officials began to distinguish between the king and his crown, for example, separating lands held *de corona* from lands taken temporarily in the king's hand. Later this would lead to a separation of the person of the king from the institution of kingship. In John's day, however, *corona* still meant the sum of inalienable rights and properties inseparable from their persons that enabled them to rule effectively, what would later be called the royal prerogative.

John appealed to custom in attempting to protect this prerogative, especially to fend off encroachments of the canon law. As seen in Chapter 6, John was confident in the Canterbury succession conflict that custom favoured his position, and he appealed to the Anglo-Saxon past for support. In 1207, it was barons in Ireland who threatened royal privileges. When they sought to apply the assize of novel disseizin against disseizins *per preceptum regis*, John accused them of trying to create new law *sine assensu principis terre illius*. He complained that their action was 'unjust indeed and unaccustomed', and 'unheard of in the time of our ancestors and our own'.[29] Again when the northern barons objected to military service overseas in 1213–14, John replied that custom sanctioned their obligation to serve.

John acknowledged the force of custom, and he usually succeeded in placing his exactions within the letter of the law, but the problem was, whose law? Frequently it was not the ancient custom, laws of Edward the Confessor or Henry I, desired by the barons. It was instead the *lex scaccarii*. The king could refer to law of the exchequer and custom of the realm, as if they had equal legitimacy, as he did in a letter explaining his seizure of William de Braose's lands. If he wanted one of his enemies outlawed, he could bring the ancient process of outlawry against him

29. *Rot. Lit. Pat.* Hardy (1835) p. 72.

in county court, as he did against William de Braose and later against Robert fitz Walter and Eustace de Vesci, following their plot against him.

John sprinkled his documents with the phrase *secundum legem et consuetudinem regni* or *secundum consuetudinem Anglie*. The fact that he found it necessary to issue such instructions suggests that at times he ordered his officials to act contrary to custom, or his justices to deviate from common law procedures. Indeed, his subjects sometimes offered fines that their lawsuits might proceed 'justly and according to the custom of England', for example, William de Mowbray's 2000-mark fine early in John's reign. Several times John's instructions to his justices constrasted custom of the realm with royal commands; writs ordered pleas to proceed 'justly and without delay unless it should be forbidden by special precept of the lord king'.[30] Sometimes the king insisted that his commands take precedence over custom, but other times he commanded that custom prevail over his orders. Whatever the significance of such phrases in royal documents, they hardly signify any deep respect for law and custom. Probably they simply represent his attempt to 'place royal actions within the letter of the law'.[31]

Also John claimed that he was careful to seek counsel, and his documents refer often to decisions taken *consilio baronum et fidelium nostrorum* or *communi consensu baronum nostrorum*. While such phrases can mean that he had consulted with some of the baronage, they do not necessarily mean discussions with a formally summoned assembly of the great men of the realm. The Angevin monarchs made no distinction between a court composed of professional royal servants and a tribunal including barons and bishops; both were equally *curie regis* in their view. During the Canterbury succession crisis, John wrote that he had taken counsel with three barons and a royal

---

30. E.g. Stenton, D.M. (ed.) (1948–67) *Pleas before the King or his Justices 1198–1212* (4 vols). Selden Society, 67–8, 83–4, vol. 2, p. 227, no. 759; Flower, C.T. (ed.) (1923–) *Curia Regis Rolls* (17 vols in course), HMSO, vol. 3, p. 215.
31. Holt (1955). p. 8.

clerk, 'then residing at our exchequer and other barons of our exchequer'.[32] All were new men who had risen through service to the king; it is unlikely that the English baronage viewed them as qualified to be their spokesmen. Occasionally John had no barons in his company, and he turned to his 'bachelors' or household knights for counsel.

In fact, the line between rules requiring baronial consent and those enacted solely on the king's initiative was vague. Perhaps a 1207 assize regulating the price of lampreys indicates John's notion of the monarch's predominant role in framing new law; he announced that it was enacted *per preceptum nostrum et per consilium Baronum nostrorum*.[33] John took care to strengthen his position in ecclesiastical controversies by taking baronial counsel. When surrendering his kingdom to the pope in 1213, he declared that he was acting 'by the common counsel [*consilio*] of our barons';[34] the witness-list, however, indicates that few barons other than royal *familiares* advised him. The barons seemed most concerned about approval of taxation and about trials to which they were parties. John recognized that the thirteenth of 1207 was an extraordinary levy, unlike scutages or tallages, that demanded discussion with his great men and their consent; and he secured its authorization *per commune consilium et assensum concilii nostri*.[35] According to the Waverley annalist, this Oxford council consisted of 'a great multitude of prelates of the Church and magnates of the realm'.[36]

On the few occasions when John consulted his great men about court cases, it was not to apply the principle of *judicium parium*. King John initiated no proceedings before councils of great men that could be called 'state trials', such as Henry II's prosecution of Thomas Becket. Crimes of *laesio majestatis* rarely appear on the plea rolls of John's reign; one of the few is an appeal lodged in 1214

32. *Rot. Lit. Claus.* Hardy (1833–4) vol. 1, p. 132b.
33. *Rot. Lit. Pat.* Hardy (1835), p. 68b.
34. *Rot. Chart.* Hardy (1837) p. 195.
35. Stubbs (1913), p. 278.
36. Luard (1864–9) vol. 2, p. 258.

for spreading a rumour of the king's death, probably part of the plot in the summer of 1212. Although the action came before the justices at Westminster, apparently it was never concluded, despite the judges' warning to the sheriff who had failed to secure the accusers' appearance 'to take all heed lest the king have cause to bestir himself . . . in the matter'.[37]

The plea rolls of John's reign yield only three cases coming before the royal justices which the king sought to have heard before a council of his barons, all three dating from early in his reign, before the end of 1204. Two disputes lay between great men whom he wanted to avoid offending: Earl Ranulf of Chester versus William de Béthune, an important vassal of the count of Flanders; and William Marshal versus the wife of William de Redvers, earl of Devon, while the third raised the question of royal rights within the liberty of the bishop of Durham. A chronicle account of a fourth case, a dispute over the honor of Mowbray in January 1201 in which both claimants offered very large fines, hints at a conclusion reached by baronial counsel. Roger of Howden wrote that the contenders settled their case *consilio regni et voluntate regis*.[38]

Barons who did not frequent the court complained that John governed arbitrarily, proceeding without judgment. They wanted the *lex terrae*, the common law procedures available to their tenants against them, applied in their quarrels with the king, not law that sprang from the royal will. They also complained that John sought counsel from his intimate counsellors, officials, courtiers, and those few magnates accompanying the king, not from a baronial body. In their view, his government fell short of the new standard that was being defined.

King John acknowledged an obligation to take counsel, but with counsellors of his own choosing; he also recognized custom and law, but found them to support

37. Flower (1923–) vol. 7, p. 95; translation, Flower, C.T. (1943) *Introduction to the Curia Regis Rolls*, Selden Society, 62, p. 81.
38. Roger of Howden. Stubbs, W. (ed.) (1868–71) *Chronica Rogeri de Hovedene* (4 vols), Rolls Series, vol. 4, p. 118; Holt (1992) interprets the phrase *consilio regni* as a great council.

longstanding royal rights and privileges. W.L. Warren labelled John's dual concern for law and custom and for free exercise of the royal will a case of 'royal schizophrenia',[39] but it is quite sane when seen in the context of his dual legacy of political thought. John's statements about the *corona*, the *dignitas regis*, and his adoption of elaborate court ceremonial indicate a lofty concept of kingship. Like his father and brother, he felt that feudal custom allowed arbitrary seizure of property as an administrative measure; but feudal tradition was not the only source of his authoritarian approach to government. Romanist-influenced clerics introduced concepts of *utilitas reipublicae* or *necessitas* to justify arbitrary royal measures.

. . .

KING JOHN AND GOVERNMENT *PER JUDICIUM*

Many barons' complaints against King John centred on their failure to secure justice and demands that in his dealings with them he proceed *per judicium*. Chapter 39 of Magna Carta, the 'due process' clause, seems to stand as an indictment of his standard of justice, as does Chapter 40, in which John promised that he would not sell, deny, or delay justice to anyone. Other chapters reveal the barons' fears that John was threatening their lawful rights with his seizures of lands *per voluntatem* and exorbitant reliefs for inheritances. Such complaints were not new; critics had levelled them at Henry II and Richard I as well.

Yet more and more landholders were bringing suits – the possessory assizes or proprietary actions – before John's justices, many involving people of little power and plots of only a few acres. Small freeholders discovered that they could win suits against powerful landlords, including their own lords. The courts' reputation and volume of business were increasing rapidly in the first decade of the thirteenth century; indeed, final concords arranged before royal justices were becoming standard instruments for small freeholders' transfers of land. Here is one of

---

39. Warren, W.L. (1961) *King John*, California UP, Berkeley, Ca./Eyre Methuen, p. 178.

the paradoxes of John's reign, for at the same time that barons' cries against defaults of justice grew louder, the Bench at Westminster and the itinerant justices achieved a degree of autonomy and maintained a respected standard of justice.

This paradox is explained by two levels of justice operating under John. The bulk of the common law courts' business involved knights and lesser freeholders settling disputes not directly involving the king, often conflicts with their lords. The *curia regis* also served as the king's own honor court, however, resolving disagreements between him and his barons that were as much political as legal. Perhaps this explains how John's contemporaries and later historians can have such diverse views of his accomplishments in the sphere of justice. A recent encyclopedia entry condemns John's 'manipulation of royal justice to destroy those he disliked'.[40] On the other hand Doris M. Stenton, deeply immersed in judicial and financial records of the reign, felt that 'in the matter of judicial administration King John deserves credit rather than blame'. In her view, 'His interest in legal development, his untiring activity in hearing pleas, and his readiness to admit litigants not only to his court but to his presence must be remembered in his favour.'[41] Because of the two distinct spheres of judicial activity – pleas involving the king and his magnates and common pleas, those between individual freeholders – both statements can be true.

A key question is John's personal responsibility for his courts at a time when they were gaining a professional staff and operating apart from direct royal control. During the Angevin kings' absences overseas, English government had functioned largely under the justiciar's

40. Lyon, B. 'John King of England'. In Strayer, J.R. (general ed.) (1982–9) *Dictionary of the Middle Ages*, Scribners, New York, NY, vol. 7, p. 130.
41. Stenton, D.M. (1964) *English Justice between the Norman Conquest and the Great Charter*, American Philosophical Society, Philadelphia, pp. 113–14; *Great Roll of the Pipe, 1–17 John*, Pipe Roll Society, Stenton, D.M. (general ed.) (1933–64), new ser. 18, p. xxxiii, introduction [Pipe Roll 6 John].

supervision, without direct intervention from the king; and it grew steadily subject to the routine of professionals, settling into fixed procedures that guaranteed a high standard. John's justices were mainly appointees of the justiciar, many having been appointed by Hubert Walter when he was Richard I's justiciar. Eventually, his successor, Geoffrey fitz Peter, brought several of his men to the bench. As chief judicial officer in the kingdom, the earl of Essex presided over the four annual terms of the Bench at Westminster; he also organized the general eyres, groups of royal judges on circuits carrying justice to the counties, one underway when Richard I died, another following in 1201–03, and a third in 1208–09. A steady stream of instructions flowed from Geoffrey to the judges at Westminster, to the itinerant justices, and to the sheriffs, treating such routine matters as the scheduling of suits or appointments of jurors and attorneys. While most suits at Westminster or on eyres held no interest for the king and proceeded without his intervention, occasionally the justices had to consult him about royal grants and charters or cases involving his servants.

During Geoffrey fitz Peter's tenure of the justiciarship, his office underwent deep change. Once King John was driven from Normandy, he resided almost continuously in England, leaving the kingdom for only a few months in 1206, 1210, and 1214. Inevitably, the office of justiciar weakened; John, distrustful by nature, was scarcely the sort of ruler who would want to share authority with a chief minister. John's almost permanent residence in England gave him greater opportunity to involve himself personally in the work of justice. Perhaps the clearest sign of the change is the shaping of the court *coram rege*, predecessor of the Court of King's Bench, first into an alternative and then, 1209–14, a replacement for the Bench at Westminster, later called the Court of Common Pleas. John's *curia regis coram rege* was not composed of great men whom the barons could recognize as their peers; it consisted of a few professional justices and household officials following the king. The two courts – Bench and *coram rege* – represent two distinct trends in tension during the Angevin period. The process of specialization and professionalization at work since

Henry I's time accounts for the Bench's origin, but John's court *coram rege* indicates royal resistance to that tendency and a desire to preserve 'familiar' government more responsive to the king's will.

No noticeable differences in procedure distinguished the two courts, both following the pattern of writs, plaints, and juries that had evolved in the twelfth century. John and his judges made no attempt to make the court *coram rege* into a 'prerogative court' with special procedures to make it more malleable to the king's will. Neither can any significant difference in the nature of cases be discerned. The judges were especially careful to consult the king in cases that touched his interest in some way, involving his barons or bishops, his *familiares*, or raising questions of royal lands and rights; and *loquendum cum rege* is a notation found frequently on John's plea rolls. Of course, suits often hinged upon a royal grant or charter for which the king could be called to give warranty. The chief factor determining whether or not a plea should be heard *coram rege*, however, was John's wish to have it heard there. While most suits held no interest for the king and proceeded without his intervention, some legal historians have attributed this dual system of royal courts to John's concern for his subjects' convenience; litigants' fines to bring pleas before the king enabled them to obtain justice when he came near, avoiding the expense of travel to Westminster. Sometimes unusual circumstances account for the fines – a difficult point of law or a politically sensitive suit – but often no ready explanation appears for fines to have pleas not touching the king heard *coram rege*. John sometimes simply wished a plea heard before him because one of the parties offered a fine, however, and he likely encouraged such fines as a fund-raising measure. In 1204 John accepted £100 from Alexander of Caldbeck to hear a plea *coram rege*.

In 1207–09, more and more cases were being removed from the Bench for hearing *coram rege*, and by spring 1209, the court at Westminster had closed. This seems in keeping with John's suspicious temperament, further evidence for his desire to deal personally with as much of government as he could, and not unexpected, if political conditions at the time are recalled. During the years

1208–13 occurred the interdict, John's excommunication, barons' treachery, and threats of foreign invasion. A more specific political circumstance, a possible rift between the king and his chief justiciar, may explain the closing of the Bench. Some sources hint at hostility, although evidence is mixed and dates from only two or three years before Geoffrey fitz Peter's death in October 1213. Geoffrey's years in office and learning in the law may have given him a respect for custom and orderly process that clashed with John's increasingly arbitrary behaviour. Yet two of John's justices *coram rege*, Simon of Pattishall and James of Potterne, were experienced judges from Westminster with longstanding ties to the justiciar. Early in 1214, less than a year after Geoffrey's death, the king departed for Poitou, and his justices returned to Westminster, where a revived Bench operated until summer 1215. Whatever the reason for John's suspension of the Bench, his subjects had grown accustomed to easy access to courts either at Westminster or on itinerant justices' eyres; and Chapter 17 of the Great Charter called for common pleas to be heard 'in some fixed place'.

The plea rolls and royal writs reveal King John's active role in his courts' work. Of course, many writs to the judges were purchased by litigants for a fee, copied out from a formulary by chancery clerks, and issued without the king's direct knowledge. Yet the phrase *per preceptum regis* was not always merely a matter of form. Even during 1202–03, when John was continuously in Normandy, commands came to the justiciar *de ultra mare*, obviously originating with royal household clerks. Sometimes a word of explanation was added, making clear that the command came directly from the king. Several cases were adjourned on account of the king's desire to hear them on his return to England.

Many times King John took part in judgments, as he advised his justices on uncertain points of law, modified procedures, or showed his benevolence. The king's *voluntas* could modify the letter of the law; his *gratia* could relax its full harshness and provide remedies not supplied by ordinary procedures. In 1205, a royal judge sought to place himself on the grand assize, although he was the plaintiff and only tenants could ask for that procedure.

To secure this dispensation, he offered 100 marks and a knight for the king's service. The records reveal John occasionally 'moved by mercy', for example, pardoning those who had committed involuntary homicide, causing deaths by misadventure. In the troubled last days of his reign, a woman seeking recovery of land approached the king and 'so cried upon the lord king that he gave her possession'.[42]

Surprisingly, King John rarely used his courts for taking action directly against individuals who had fallen from his favour. The explanation is simple. Because the jurisdiction of the common law courts was largely limited to the possessory and proprietary actions, John found it easier to prosecute his victims at the Exchequer, whose law was often little more than enforcement of the royal will. Or he might proceed extralegally, venting his *ira* or *malevolentia* through arbitrary administrative measures. For those who opposed the king with violence, the old criminal process of outlawry in county court still proved a powerful weapon, precipitating the flight by the plotters of 1212 from the kingdom.

Nonetheless, John made his courts instruments of royal policy to be used to frustrate his enemies and to favour his friends. Suits between individual subjects, common pleas, can reveal operation of the royal will, directly or indirectly. The royal courts opened or closed to suitors at the king's pleasure. The *Dialogus de Scaccario* states of Henry II, 'To some he does full justice for nothing, in consideration of their past services or out of mere goodness of heart; but to others (and it is only human nature) he will not give way for love or money.'[43] This was true of John as well; an example is an entry from the 1207 plea roll commanding dismissal of a suit because the king 'does not wish that plea to be held'.[44] The pipe roll explains why; one of the parties to the suit had offered three horses to have it dismissed. This case is

42. Stenton, D.M. (ed.) (1934) *Rolls of the Justices in Eyre for Lincolnshire (1218–1219) and Worcestershire (1221)*, Selden Society, 53, pp. 145–6.
43. Johnson (1950), p. 120.
44. *Curia Regis Rolls*. Flower (1923–) vol. 5, p. 72.

far from unique. That same year, John accepted £1000 and 15 palfreys from Gerard de Furnival 'for having our good will and in order that a suit between him and his wife against Nigel Luvetot should stand over'.[45]

Just as the king could deny access to his courts, so he could slow or speed the course of suits, or transfer them from one panel of justices to another. One of the most frequent royal commands received by the judges was to adjourn actions involving persons absent in the king's service. Usually these were writs issued by royal clerks without the king's personal intervention. In 1203 in the midst of the failing campaign in Normandy, however, John issued commands not only postponing cases of knights fighting for the king across the sea but also suits of those whose *denarii*, moneys, were in the king's service across the sea. Clearly, John's preoccupation with financing his struggle for Normandy took priority over his obligation to render swift justice to all his subjects.

Sometimes King John gave general instructions, setting judicial policies; such commands are important in evaluating his supervision of the courts. He continued his father's efforts to restrict lords' disciplinary powers over their tenants, introducing a new common law procedure for tenants' recovery of distrained chattels, withername. By John's middle years, he was encouraging the sale of writs which would bring more pleas into his courts; for example, increasing numbers of creditors were seeking to collect debts through the royal courts, paying the king a quarter to a third of the debt. Another innovation was the writ for a jury of attaint. If a litigant believed that a jury had rendered a wrongful decision, based on its prejudices, he could purchase a writ *de odio et atia* to empanel a jury of twenty-four to convict the earlier jury of false judgment due to hate and malice. The first reference to such a jury dates from 1202 in a writ from the king in Normandy, indicating John's part in its formulation. This new procedure proved popular, for payments for juries of attaint occur regularly in the pipe rolls for the rest of

45. *Rot. Lit. Claus.* Hardy (1833–4) vol. 1, p. 78; Stenton (1933–64), new ser. 22, p. 74 [Pipe Roll 9 John].

John's reign; and Chapter 38 of Magna Carta called for it to be made freely available.

Pipe rolls of John's reign record frequent fines *ut bene tractetur* for smoothing the course of justice in one way or another. Because the common law courts' procedures in proprietary actions provided for innumerable delays, with cases dragging on for periods measured not in weeks or months, but years, it is hardly surprising that many offerings were made for writs 'to hasten the course of justice'. William de Braose offered the king 300 cows, 30 bulls, and 10 horses for expediting a 1205 plea challenging his right to the barony of Totnes, Devon. Purchasers of such writs for speedy justice normally did not approach the king directly; nonetheless, approval of the policy rested with him, and it again shows his search for revenues extending to his courts of justice.

Oblations of ordinary free tenants for writs for simple favours such as postponements, transfers of pleas, or permission to settle by final concord may be considered simply court fees. They were no more than half a mark or a mark, although the price could vary according to the king's whim; an earl might pay £100 for an assize. In other instances, persons of little consequence found it prudent to offer fines for special juries or some other departure from standard procedure without, however, expecting to purchase any influence on their case's outcome. Certainly the king had no hand in soliciting or collecting them; nonetheless, the volume of these fines leads to the conclusion that accusations of John's sale of justice have a sound basis in people's experience. Litigants with well-filled purses purchased real advantages over their opponents, sometimes managing to get suits brought against them postponed indefinitely. Offerings for departures from ordinary procedures became common after 1207 and reached a peak about 1210–12. John's frantic search for funds in those years was driving him to a policy of increasing revenues from the common law courts.

Since John rarely intervened in suits of no special concern to him except to receive a fine for some minor adjustment in the courts' routine, most litigants still found good quality justice at the *curia regis*, though more costly.

Evidently, most litigants accepted these payments as part of the normal costs of lawsuits, and they never seriously threatened the common law courts' reputation. The editor of many *curia regis* rolls concluded that 'the object of these oblations was not the perversion of royal justice, but at most the diversion of its course'.[46] Yet this policy of seeking to increase revenues from the common law courts raises serious questions of their impartiality and accessibility.

Besides paying for writs and special procedures, litigants at the *curia regis* ran the risk of falling into 'the king's mercy', owing an amercement (in today's terms, a fine). Itinerant justices' visits to the shires resulted in many amercements, not only for parties to pleas but also for jurors and entire communities. In Lincolnshire, the general eyre of 1202 produced £633 in amercements, compared with some £250 in the first eyre of 1166. The 1210 'autumnal justices' probably went out under the king's orders rather than the justiciar's, apparently with instructions to make as many amercements as possible; and they found new offences, such as 'false speaking', which they amerced at 200 marks. According to *Glanvill*, amercements were to be set 'by the oath of lawful men of the neighbourhood'.[47] However assessed, the average amercement of half a mark (a third of a pound) was a heavy blow to common people with annual incomes of less than five pounds. The barons' view, expressed in Chapter 21 of Magna Carta, was that they were to be amerced by their peers. In practice, the barons of the exchequer had amerced them, and apparently the magnates found their assessments too high. The pipe roll for 1206 records a number of amercements made *per Regem*. While most range from 20 to 40 marks, one levied against the count of Boulogne was for 1000 marks.

King John's subjects faced a dilemma, for he was the source of all justice in the kingdom and also a great and greedy landlord, who often acted out of anger or ill-will. His tenants-in-chief could find themselves embroiled in

46. Flower (1943) pp. 495–6.
47. Hall (1965) p. 114, lib. 9, cap. 11.

conflict with him, yet they could not expect an impartial hearing in the *curia regis* before justices eager to promote his interests. Almost the characteristic complaint against King John was default of justice. Tenants whose land he had taken arbitrarily obviously could not purchase a royal writ of novel disseizin summoning a jury to state that the king had disseized them 'unjustly and without judgment'.

Nonetheless, King John's justices did occasionally deal with instances of disseizin by the will of King John or one of his predecessors. It was possible through a third party action, suing the current tenant of the land, to correct unjust or unlawful disseizin by Henry II or Richard I. It is an irony that the plaintiffs in some suits were men disseized by the Lionheart in reprisal for their support of John's rebellion. Yet such actions were rare, brought only by prominent persons; and they received special attention, with the justices consulting the king before pronouncing judgment. Also the plaintiff offered a hefty oblation for such a hearing. Examples are the 1208 offer by Roald fitz Alan, constable of Richmond, of £100 and two palfreys for an inquest into Henry II's alleged disseizin of his grandfather and Alan of Galloway and his mother's offer in 1211 of 600 marks and six palfreys for an inquest into Henry II's disseizin of her father.

Only one plea brought before John's justices alleged disseizin by the king himself. In that 1204 case, the plaintiff was the wife of William de Redvers, earl of Devon, who was countess of Meulan in her own right, and her opponent was William Marshal, earl of Pembroke. Both claimed the manor of Sturminster, Devonshire, which was in the king's hand. She claimed that she had held it previously, but had been disseized *per preceptum regis*. John was cautious and sought counsel. His *familiares* suggested postponement until 'the lord archbishop [of Canterbury] and other great and wise men of the land' should be present,[48] a rare example of John's intimates declaring themselves unqualified and seeking counsel from the magnates.

---

48. *Curia Regis Rolls.* Flower (1923–) vol. 3, p. 124.

Plea rolls from John's reign, then, almost never show victims of his arbitrary acts having recourse to his courts, although occasionally victims of disseizins by his father or brother brought suits. A safer way of winning redress was extra-judicial, simply approaching the king with a fine *pro benevolentia regis*, for regaining his goodwill. The fine rolls record numbers of offerings for remission of the king's anger and return of lands, ranging from 10 marks to 4000 marks offered by Walter de Lacy in 1215 for his Irish lands.

Baronial families who held their estates directly of the king did not have access to the writs and assizes that their own tenants had against them. While their tenants were enjoying greater security of proprietary right, they felt that King John was trampling underfoot their lawful rights of inheritance, making them less and less secure in their tenures. He, like his father and brother, held the old view that an heir to a barony had no hereditary right under the law to succeed to his ancestor's property, only a customary right to be accepted as tenant. Although the common law justices were working out rules of seniority for heirs and heiresses, the king insisted on playing a part in successions to great lordships.

Because John wanted some share in deciding succession to baronies and earldoms, political advantage weighed as heavily as legal reasoning in determining the heir, although genuine uncertainty could invite royal intervention. Sometimes conflicting royal grants as long ago as the confusion of Stephen's reign raised questions. Cases where no direct descendants – only collateral heirs – survived could raise tangled questions about priority of hereditary right, and in the early thirteenth century their rights were still considered negotiable rather than fixed by law. John might choose to follow customary rules of succession or not, depending on what heir – or heiress – chances of heredity tossed up, and depending on whether or not he wished to keep a barony intact.

Such a dispute was the *casus regis*, named for King John's succession to the English crown as Henry II's fourth son despite the claim of his nephew, Arthur of Brittany, son of his deceased elder brother. Such uncertainty gave the king considerable freedom of action, and he demanded exorbitant fines such as Nicholas de Stuteville's 10,000-mark fine to be preferred over his nephew as heir to his brother's barony, Robert de Vere's later fine of 1000 marks for his brother's earldom of Oxford, or Roger Bigod's 700-mark fine that he not be disseized 'unless by judgment of the King's court' in a dispute with his half-brother for the honor of Framlingham. In a dispute over succession to the honor of Topcliffe, Yorkshire, John wished to favour the nephew, William de Percy, who was a ward of his 'evil counsellor' William Briwerre. Yet he dared not deny entirely the claim of the boy's uncle, Richard de Percy, which resembled all too closely his own claim to the English crown. The king decided upon a partition of the honor, even though partitions between male heirs were rare.

It is not surprising to find these barons among the rebels in 1215–16. While sons usually succeeded to their father's baronies without incident, they too sometimes had to offer fines or purchase the political influence of *curiales* to gain what they considered rightfully theirs. The pipe rolls record numerous fines offered to John for inheritances, and reliefs often shot far above the customary £100 figure, even for undoubted heirs.

Partition of honors among female heirs in default of male heirs provided the king with lands for patronage to family, friends, or officials without making any one of them too powerful. When lordships descended to daughters, the Angevins usually followed the custom of equal partition among co-heirs, but not always. In 1213, a co-heir to the baron of Cavendish, Suffolk, who had died leaving only sisters as heirs sought division of the barony 'according to the custom of England into two equal parts'.[49] Such a partition may have been customary, yet her husband still thought it prudent to proffer 500 marks to John. Perhaps more significant is what is omitted from the record; it makes no mention of a widowed third sister whose rights were being ignored.

The financial inducement of a large fine, the desire for an estate with which to reward a faithful *familiaris*,

49. *Rot. de Obl. et Fin.* Hardy (1835a) p. 507.

or fear of concentrating too much power in a baron's hands might influence the royal will more strongly than strict hereditary right. Rarely were these decisions made in the common law courts; they were the result of political haggling with intimate counsellors or of financial bargaining at the exchequer. Competition between rival claimants could result in bidding that drove costs of their suits higher and higher. Once a suit was settled, the king still had considerable scope for disputing the settlement should the victorious party cross him, since the uncertainty of laws governing inheritance of baronies offered opportunity for reviving unsuccessful claims.

Barons with some shadow over their title never knew when King John might revive a long dormant claim to their baronies. The uncertainty of Geoffrey fitz Peter's claim to the great Mandeville honor, for example, gave the king a weapon to hold over him, a means of keeping him loyal and obedient. John did not have to bring such suits himself, for he could simply encourage claimants to estates eager to challenge rivals who had lost royal favour. He permitted Geoffrey de Say, a nephew of William de Mandeville and cousin of Geoffrey fitz Peter's first wife, to re-open his case claiming the earldom of Essex in 1212, shortly before the justiciar's death, probably as a means of harassing him. That same year the earl of Salisbury, the king's half-brother, brought suit against Henry de Bohun, earl of Hereford, challenging his possession of the barony of Trowbridge; again the king's connivance can be suspected.

Often royal intervention in such disputed successions to baronies came not on the king's initiative, but was inspired by his counsellors. They most likely saw the opportunity first and then persuaded the king to favour their cause, or claimants sought out some *curialis*, enlisting his support in guiding them through the complexities of pleading in the *curia regis*, advancing them funds, or acting as pledges for their fines. The role of *curiales* as custodians of minors drew them into such disputes. With their easy access to the king, they secured custodies of heiresses, either took them for wives or married them off to their sons, and then launched lawsuits to add as much of the inheritance as possible to their families' holdings.

William Briwerre obtained wardship of the widowed Rose of Dover, who had a claim to half the Lucy inheritance. He bankrolled her lawsuits and exerted his influence at court, and on her success in recovering her legacy, she promptly granted him eleven knights' fees. Sidney Painter commented, 'Thus Rose recovered her inheritance at the expense of giving most of it to William Brewer as a fief.'[50]

It cannot be denied that litigants with connections to *curiales* had very real advantages over their opponents, sometimes succeeding in getting their suits dismissed entirely. One of Stephen Langton's Paris sermons witnesses to suitors' need to turn to royal *familiares* to smooth the way. He advised those seeking reconciliation with the monarch to 'approach one of the king's familiars, and seek out his aid and counsel; and . . . listen to him in all things so that he shall obtain the king's favor.'[51] Neither can it be denied, however, that for every instance of royal pressure or courtiers' undue influence many other actions went forward without incident except for fees for writs, fines to expedite proceedings, and gifts to judges. Today such payments would be viewed as bribery, but medieval litigants found them normal and acceptable. The common law courts were considered by contemporaries to be less venal than the papal *curia* at Rome, where costs could run to thousands of marks.

John's reign saw two levels of justice. One, headed by a corps of judges whose outlook approached that of professionals, settled suits between private individuals; they followed a routine reaching back to Henry II's justices. John saw little reason to interfere with their work, except to seek greater revenues. The other level involved suits of the barons and other significant tenants-in-chief of the king, which touched the king's interest directly. Such cases often involved his rights and privileges as feudal lord, and he was hesitant to allow his own tenants the advantages that the common law was extending to

50. Painter, S. (1949) *The Reign of King John*, Johns Hopkins UP, Baltimore, p. 76.
51. Roberts, P.B. (1968) *Studies in the Sermons of Stephen Langton*, Pontifical Institute of Mediaeval Studies, Toronto. p. 129.

tenants of other lords. Barons found their suits settled neither before a body comparable to an honor court of royal tenants-in-chief nor before the common law courts, but by John's informal counsel with his *familiares* or by bidding at the exchequer.

King John saw justice as an instrument of his own policies, for favouring his friends and pursuing his enemies and for raising revenues. Not surprisingly, many of the king's victims felt that he was tampering with justice in order to persecute them, trampling on their legitimate rights of inheritance. This accounts for the paradox of a high level of satisfaction with royal justice by the mass of suitors, whose cases were of no concern to John, and great dissatisfaction by his baronage. A number of those in the ranks of the rebels in 1215 had suffered from what they perceived to be injustices in the royal courts through the king's intervention. They include such baronial leaders as Eustace de Vesci, William de Mowbray, and Roger de Montbegon.

. . .

FORMATION OF A BARONIAL OPPOSITION PARTY

The 1214 failure of John's master plan for reconquest on the Continent meant that on his return from Poitou barons would be more willing to risk rebellion than they had been under the first two Angevins. Opposition to fighting overseas and to frequent scutages, which John took at ever higher rates and sometimes unconnected to military campaigns, had encouraged the baronial interest in the concept of government *per consilium*. Although many barons and knights had grievances, only a minority of them would take part actively in a movement for rebellion against King John in the winter of 1214–15. An embittered nucleus had reasons beyond political or financial ones that drove them to take up arms; they appear to have had personal grievances against John. At least two claimed that their wives or daughters had been objects of John's lust, and others had relatives who had been victims of his cruelty.

Chroniclers' condemnation of John's lustfulness is hardly shocking, for it was a complaint that monastic writers commonly levelled; but even a minstrel serving with John's Flemish mercenaries noted that the king 'de bieles femes estoit trop couvoiteus'.[52] The accusation against John was not simply that he was a seducer of women, but that his victims were noble ladies, a charge that modern scholars tend to accept. Like most nobles of his day, John kept mistresses, and the mothers of two of his five bastards may have been noblewomen. Some stories of John's sexual adventures, however, appear to have been invented after the fact to explain barons' taking up arms against the king. Among several different explanations that Robert fitz Walter gave for his 1212 flight to France was that King John had stolen his daughter, wife of young Geoffrey de Mandeville, to have her 'a force a amie'.[53] Also John supposedly tried to seduce Eustace de Vesci's wife, but her honour was saved when a common woman replaced her in the royal bed. According to the French royal chronicler, John had his way with the wife of his half-brother, William Longsword, while the earl was in France waiting to be ransomed after his capture at Bouvines. More readily substantiated are charges of John's cruelty; certainly the friends and family of the Braoses knew well that he could be merciless on occasion.

A more plausible explanation for rebellion is the expense of warfare to defend the Angevins' continental lands. Increasingly, English barons and knights had more interest in improving and enlarging their own estates than in performing the military services by which they supposedly held them. Under John, or even earlier, barons rarely came to battle followed by their full complement of knights; usually no more than twenty knights accompanied the greatest of barons. Even so, resistance against performance of personal military service overseas was rising. The barons showed so little enthu-siasm for John's projected expedition to Poitou in 1205 that he had to abandon it, but levied a scutage anyway. Barons resented this, feeling that custom decreed that scutages be collected only in connection with an actual

52. Michel, F. (ed.) (1848) *Histoire des ducs de Normandie et des rois d'Angleterre*, Société de l'histoire de France, Paris, p. 105.
53. Michel (1848) p. 119.

campaign; Roger Bigod and Robert fitz Walter, both later prominent rebels, first broke with the king after the 1205 scutage.

Baronial reluctance to participate contributed to John's postponement of Poitevin campaigns in 1212 and 1213. First, a number refused to follow him on grounds of his excommunicate status. After his absolution, they appealed to what they considered custom, admitting longstanding obligations to serve in Normandy and Brittany but objecting to service in greater Anjou or Aquitaine. When the king summoned his feudal levy to gather at Portsmouth in late July 1213, a number of northern barons refused to cross to Poitou, forcing him to postpone his expedition and costing him a military advantage. Since the king was certain that custom sanctioned their obligation to serve him across the sea, he saw their refusal as tantamount to rebellion, and he proposed to take military action against them. John prepared to march northwards with a mercenary force to punish his recalcitrant barons until Stephen Langton, newly arrived in England, insisted that the king proceed against them only 'in accordance with the best judgment of his court' and threatened to excommunicate John's soldiers.[54] When John's expedition to Poitou finally embarked in 1214, however, most barons' chivalric and feudal ethos of military service outweighed their dissatisfaction, and they dutifully set sail. Undertaking the campaign were a number who would later become rebels; only a few northern barons refused to serve or to send their knights.

Wounded as John was in October 1214 on his return to England, he insisted on payment of scutage at three marks per fee from barons who had not participated in his expedition. His exchequer had achieved little success in collecting the money since the first attempts in May. The barons again argued that they neither owed service in Poitou nor scutage in lieu of service, and they appealed to the pope, but got no support. Innocent III considered scutage to be a customary service to which the king had a right; only once it was paid would he agree to arbitrate between king and barons. Demands for a hefty scutage

---

54. Roger of Wendover. Hewlett (1886–9) vol. 2, p. 81–3.

from those who had not crossed the sea in 1214 aroused wide protest, especially in the North and East Anglia, regions that later became rebel centres.

Other financial concerns, evident earlier than 1214, were also feeding baronial discontent. As seen in Chapter 4, Angevin policies meant that the feudal relationship between king and barons was changing more and more into a financial one. Like other feudal lords, John was enforcing his tenants' performance of feudal services and payment of the feudal incidents by extra-judicial seizure of chattels, distraint; and like his father, he also made seizure of lands into an administrative measure. The barons found in their feudal tradition, however, arguments that declared any distraint of land *sine judicio* unlawful; and churchmen's teachings strengthened their demands that the king only proceed against them after judgment.

Most of the northern barons who joined the rebellion owed large fines or reliefs and were deeply in debt to the king or to the Jews; indeed, Lincoln and York were centres for Jewish money-lending in England. A Lincolnshire baron, Gilbert de Gant, owed over £800 to the Jews; but it was not only northerners who fell into debt to the Jews. Henry d'Oilly, an Oxfordshire baron who joined the rebels, owed over £1000 in 1208, which he was paying off in annual instalments of 200 marks. Many debtor barons were bound together by serving as pledges for one another's debts. Sir James Holt states of the baronial opposition, 'It was a rebellion of the king's debtors.'[55] While this is an overstatement, the burden of debt gave added weight to other baronial grievances. Many barons blamed John for forcing them into debt because he had demanded high payments for feudal incidents, which they regarded as fixed by custom. *Glanvill*, however, noted the king's claim to 'primer seisin',[56] the right to take a barony into his hand and grant it to the heir only once homage was done and arrangements made for paying relief.

Others risked falling into the exchequer's clutches because of speculative ventures. Barons such as Peter de

---

55. Holt, J.C. (1961) *The Northerners. A Study in the Reign of King John*, Oxford UP, p. 34.
56. Hall (1965), p. 110, lib. 9, cap. 6.

Brus competed with *curiales* in offering extravagant fines to purchase custodies, rights to marriages, and other means of enlarging their estates that they thought would prove profitable. When Peter inherited his honor during Richard I's reign, his relief was £500, and then he promised John £1000 for return of the Brus family seat, the manor of Danby, Yorkshire. In 1205–06 he purchased custody of the heir to a Northumberland barony by assuming £1300 in debts of a prominent royal *familiaris*, the boy's former custodian. He managed to make some payments, and by 1208 the exchequer had consolidated his various debts into a figure of £1235, five palfreys and two greyhounds. It is little wonder that he become alienated from John's system of government and vented his frustration in rebellion in 1215. Some who were deeply in debt continued blithely to make offers for such privileges, plunging themselves even deeper into debt. Saher de Quency competed with the dowager countess of Leicester in bidding for lands, eventually offering 5000 marks even though already indebted to the Jews

Not even John's friends got an office, an heiress, or similar favour for nothing, and bidders mistakenly assumed that their high station or standing in the king's eyes would protect them from having to pay the full amount, that the king would eventually forgive the debt or at least a part of it. King John was not always so forgiving. Men such as Simon of Kyme tried to play the game of fining for profitable favours, only to fall into the clutches of the exchequer. Such men saw themselves as outsiders, their ambitions thwarted because they were denied the royal patronage that was enriching the king's friends and should at least have relieved their burden of debt.

Barons, prominent royal officials, and others fell into debt to the king also because of political miscalculations. Amercements were a means of disciplining political offenders, or they could purchase the king's forgiveness with a fine. The pipe rolls record fines for *benevolentia regis* offered by many people, including royal servants who in performing their duties had displeased their master. Some, such as Robert de Ros, sheriff of Cumberland, joined the rebels. He proved careless about custody of prisoners and offered a 1200-mark fine in 1200, then in 1207 incurred a 300-mark amercement for escape of prisoners from his gaol. A West Country sheriff who joined Robert de Ros among the rebels was William de Montague of Dorset and Somerset, who offered £800 in 1207 for the king's goodwill. Fines of 1000 marks by less than prominent officials were not uncommon, for example, William of Cornborough's fine in 1209 for failings as a forester in Yorkshire. Thomas de St Valery, an Oxfordshire baron, offered 1000 marks in 1209 for the king's goodwill, most likely merely because he was the fallen William de Braose's brother-in-law.

The Angevin kings, and especially John, became masters at enmeshing those who lost their favour in administrative difficulties that could result in financial ruin. John made the most of his ability to entangle his subjects in debt and then use their indebtedness to impose political discipline. A baron or bishop who offended him would find royal agents suddenly much less accommodating. Over half the barons at any one time were in debt to the king, and those who lost royal favour would find themselves subjected to the full force of the *lex scaccarii*. That meant distraint of lands, even imprisonment, arbitrary acts from the victim's point of view, although well within the law in the king's eyes. William of Cornborough died in prison, apparently because he could not pay a fine offered for John's goodwill. His fate probably accounts for the presence of his kinsman, Walter of Cornborough, among the rebels.

The most shocking instance of King John's harrying a royal debtor was his harsh treatment of William de Braose, 1208–11. John, however, sought to put his pursuit of Braose within the bounds of the law in a letter 'to all who may read it'. He maintained that William's outlawry was 'according to the law and custom of England' because of his default on debts and his violent resistance against distraint of his lands on failure to pay a 40,000-mark fine. The king held that all his actions concerning debt collection had been 'according to the custom of our kingdom and by our law of the exchequer'.[57] William

---

57. *Rymer's Foedera*. Clarke, Caley, Bayley, Holbrooke, Clarke (1816–30, 1869) vol. 1, pp. 107–8.

de Braose died in exile at Paris in 1211; his wife and eldest son fell into John's hands to suffer imprisonment and death by starvation; and his grandsons remained in prison until 1218. The hounding of Braose and his family to exile and death was a lesson that the king would exact the hefty payments his exchequer demanded from the greatest crown debtors, even barons who had previously basked in royal favour. It taught John's leading subjects that his notion of lawful procedure bore little resemblance to their own perception of proceeding *per judicium*.

By autumn 1214, a party of barons opposing King John was beginning to take shape. Identifying the rebels is important, but difficult. Royal letters naming individuals in arms against the king who had their lands seized provide some names, while chroniclers' lists are incomplete and partially incorrect. Confusion is compounded by listing among the rebel barons some men not technically of baronial rank; for example, Simon of Kyme had only knightly rank, although he held some thirty fees. Temporary switching of sides during the rebellion adds to the difficulty in defining the baronial party; some went over to the rebels only briefly in order to safeguard lands in rebel-held regions. By spring of 1215, shortly before Magna Carta it seems that no more than forty-five significant landholders were rebels, only thirty-nine of whom had definite baronial rank; by 1216, when John died, the number of rebel barons had risen to ninety-seven. The number of rebels for 1215 includes less than half of the most important barons, thirteen of twenty-seven; however, by 1216 the number of major barons had fallen to only eight. It seems likely, then, that the majority of the English baronage never defected to the rebels, although perhaps more passively sympathized with the baronial cause than with the royalists.

Of course, knights as well as barons were significant in making up a fighting force to oppose the king. Earlier baronial rebellions had centred on personal grievances of a few magnates, whose knights followed them into battle because of ties of fealty. By the early thirteenth century, however, many knightly landholders no longer felt so tightly bound to their lords, in part because so many held lands of several lords. The rebel barons had to rely upon landless retainers for a fighting force. King John recognized the divergence in interests of barons and knights, and he sought to take advantage of it to win knightly support. In August 1212 and again in November 1213, he summoned representatives of knights from the shires to meetings; at the first, sheriffs were to summon six from each shire 'to do what we shall tell them', and at the second four from each shire were summoned 'to speak with us concerning the affairs of our realm'.[58] These meetings may have been 'the first well recorded occasion of a national assembly of knights of the shire';[59] but they have never earned John any credit as one of the fathers of the English Parliament.

Chivalric literature sought to create a common outlook for barons and knights, depicting them as members of a single fighting élite. In fact, many knights were abandoning their military life for that of rural aristocrats, ancestors of the class later known as the 'gentry'. Many knightly landholders doubtless shared the outlook of their lords, to whom they often were bound by ties of kinship as well as lordship; knights were often cousins of barons, descendants of younger sons of baronial families. Some took up arms against John, following their lord, or one of their lords; others, however, joined the rebel cause even though their lords remained loyal to the king.

It is more difficult to identify rebel knights than barons. Writs reinstating former rebels record the names of some 1380 out of some 6500 knights in the entire kingdom. About a quarter of the knights held at least one fee in-chief of the king, and they experienced for themselves harsh treatment by the king's agents. The knightly class had grievances of its own against John that, unlike specific baronial complaints, could not be remedied through private arrangements between the king and individual barons. These knightly grievances would force the negotiators framing Magna Carta to think in

58. *Rot. Lit. Claus.* Hardy (1833–4) vol. 1, p. 132; Stubbs (1913) p. 282.
59. Holt, J.C. (1981) 'The prehistory of Parliament'. In Davies, R.G., Denton, J.H. (eds) *The English Parliament in the Middle Ages: A Tribute to J.S. Roskell*, Manchester UP, p. 5.

terms of general remedies, and they would have some impact on the character of the Charter as a set of general political principles, aimed at a large group.

Opposition was concentrated in three regions: The North of England, the West, and East Anglia. A group of eighteen northern barons held lands as far south as Lincolnshire, including Eustace de Vesci, who had fled England in 1212 to return with exiled clerics the next year, two other great barons, John de Lacy and William de Mowbray, and intermittently, William de Forz, count of Aumale. A less well-defined group of ten or so scattered in western shires included Earl Henry de Bohun of Hereford and the earl marshal's eldest son, even though William Marshal senior remained a staunch royalist. Centred in Essex and East Anglia was a group of twelve great barons that included Robert fitz Walter; Geoffrey de Mandeville, earl of Essex; Earl Richard de Clare of Hertford with his son, Gilbert; Roger Bigod; earl of Norfolk; and Robert de Vere, whose chief castle stood in Essex, although his title was earl of Oxford. Two barons fail to fall into these regional categories: Saher de Quency, earl of Winchester, whose lands lay mainly in Northampton and Cambridgeshire; and William de Beauchamp, whose lands were concentrated in Bedfordshire.

While much of the rebel leadership came from the eastern region, with twelve East Anglians as members of the committee of twenty-five charged with enforcing Magna Carta, the most extreme in hostility toward John were northern barons. They appeared to contemporaries to form the core of baronial opposition; indeed, contemporary writers continued to call the rebels 'Northerners' even after it was clear that the movement extended beyond that region. Perhaps one reason is that northern barons' resistance manifested itself so early; they formed the core of opposition to overseas service and payment of scutage in 1213–14. Ties of kinship and friendship may have bound this group of barons together; several leading rebels were connected by marriages. More significant, however, was their shared hatred of King John on account of personal wrongs done to them. A number felt that the king had wrongfully withheld from them lands, castles, or other privileges that rightfully belonged to them, or if he had granted them, that they had been required to pay too high a price. John's insistent demands for repayment of their debts helped push them into rebellion by 1215. In their view, the law of the exchequer did not constitute government *per judicium* but simply ratified arbitrary royal will.

Chapter 8

CULMINATION OF CRISES: MAGNA CARTA AND CIVIL WAR

. . .

CONFRONTATIONS CULMINATING IN REBELLION

John's reign culminated in a baronial uprising, 1215–16, that imposed Magna Carta on him, an attempt to place limits on his authority. By 1208 and 1209, signs of the king's abuses were more and more evident. Soon rumblings of baronial discontent sounded, and a number of incidents signalled simmering friction between king and barons. While quarrels with individual barons were not uncommon, summer of 1212 saw a conspiracy that marks a kindling of the crisis in royal-baronial relations that would burst into civil war. Settlement of the Canterbury succession crisis the next year gave baronial critics of the king clerical allies in formulating a reform programme based on return to good old custom. Not until John's return in defeat from Poitou in autumn 1214, however, did a large-scale rising take shape. This baronial rebellion would differ from earlier ones in representing itself as a broad-based movement, expanding its aim from mere amendment of private grievances to political reform. As such, it points towards the rebel programme in the middle years of John's son and to similar reform efforts in the late Middle Ages.

King John had reason to feel insecure about frontier territories, where great liberties held potential as centres of opposition. The marcher barons of South Wales who also had substantial Irish lands made John uneasy, and the almost autonomous barons in the North of England

225

also caused him a sense of insecurity. Northern barons resented the king's efforts at bringing their honors under closer royal control; moreover, several had suffered injustices or financial exactions at his hands. A letter of Philip Augustus in 1209 to the lord of Pontefract, John de Lacy, hints that nobles of the North were conspiring with the French monarch. Evidently, John had some inkling of a conspiracy that summer which was likely a factor in his campaign against the Scottish ruler, William the Lion. John's easy success against the Scots, however, convinced any possible conspirators that the time was not yet ripe for action.

The next conflict between barons and the king came again in the North during the summer of 1212 with an abortive revolt, which led to the flight of Robert fitz Walter and Eustace de Vesci. John had heard rumours of a baronial plot to kill him, planned to coincide with his projected Welsh expedition, forcing him in mid-August 1212 to disband the large army he had gathered for an invasion of North Wales. His demand for hostages of barons suspected of being parties to the plot caused Robert fitz Walter to flee to the French court and Eustace de Vesci to take refuge in Scotland. John moved quickly to seize their castles and to outlaw them and their followers, some of whom were prominent clerics. Robert fitz Walter met exiled English bishops at Paris, where he posed as a devoted son of the Church suffering for refusal to serve an excommunicate king. The result was that the peace settlement between John and Innocent III provided for the conspirators' safe return to England along with clerical exiles and restoration of their confiscated lands.

This 1212 plot led to a crucial loss of political initiative for John; the plots and rumours of plots pushed him into contradictory policies. Early in 1213 and in 1214, he pulled back slightly from his previous harsh political and financial policies. He named commissioners to investigate wrong-doing by royal officials in Yorkshire and Lincolnshire. He made changes in some sheriffs of northern shires, replacing them with local men, and he revised his financial policy of increasing the sheriffs' increments. Also, John made moves to conciliate some individuals he had alienated, negotiating new schedules for paying debts to Jews, for example. Then in November 1213, he made vague promises to northern barons 'to restore their ancient liberties'.[1] At the same time, however, John's suspicions roused him to demand from some barons charters of fealty, custody of castles, and surrender of hostages. These repressive steps, coupled with the king's continued fierce money-raising tactics to finance the planned campaign on the Continent, aroused new fears among the baronage.

By 1213 and 1214 John's tenants in the North of England were raising an outcry against military service in Poitou, arguing that their overseas service was limited to Normandy and Brittany only. Knights throughout early thirteenth-century Europe were expressing similar demands for limits on feudal military service outside their kingdoms. John was never hesitant about disciplining his men for default of service, and only last minute persuasion prevented a military campaign to punish those northerners who had rejected their 1213 summons. When the Poitevin expedition finally got underway early in 1214, a few northern barons again refused to serve.

John's alarm at growing baronial opposition in 1212–13 played a part in his decision to end his long struggle with the pope. Settlement of the Canterbury succession dispute meant the return of exiled clergy and Stephen Langton's arrival in England, and it also brought back to the kingdom the embittered barons who had fled after the 1212 conspiracy. Soon the 'Northerners', a nucleus of future rebel barons, was forming against the king. As baronial resentment of John's rule flared, they found ideological support from clerics. The new archbishop, Stephen Langton, almost as soon as he arrived in England, sought influence among the barons, instructing them about their lawful rights; and John soon suspected that the primate would be too hostile towards him to act as a neutral mediator.

Historians have variously depicted the rebel leadership as bold defenders of English liberties against an oppressive

---

1. Holt, J.C. (1992) *Magna Carta*, 2nd edn, Cambridge UP, p. 222.

Angevin political system, or as bumbling feudal reactionaries incapable of formulating a coherent reform
programme. The baronial leaders fail to inspire much
confidence; few can be credited with any strong sense
of responsibility or public service. Perhaps proof is
their absence from any place among the statesmen of
young Henry III, in contrast to royalist barons who
were prominent in restoring England to peace and
order after John's death. Certainly rebel leaders such
as Robert fitz Walter or Eustace de Vesci fail to command
trust; each had earlier 'shown himself to be both a traitor
and a coward'.[2] Both had been implicated in plots against
John as early as the summer of 1212, when they fled the
kingdom; but they won authorization to return as part of
the 1213 Canterbury succession settlement.

The rebels chose the East Anglian baron, Robert fitz
Walter, as their military leader once they renounced
their oaths of fealty in May 1215. His earlier resort to
violence against the abbot of St Albans in a quarrel over
patronage of a priory gives little hint of respect for law
and custom; only after failing to win his claim by force
did he bring a lawsuit. Robert's lack of co-operation after
Magna Carta also casts doubts on his statesmanship. An
extremist who stood in the way of implementation of
the settlement made in June 1215, his refusal to return
London to the king as agreed at Runnymede contributed
to a renewal of fighting. Other barons among the rebel
leadership appear to fit into a similar pattern. Neither
would Roger de Montbegon nor Robert de Ros, members
of the group of twenty-five executors of Magna Carta,
display deep loyalty to the principle of rule of law in
1220. Montbegon defied the shire court when its decision
went against him and got away with flouting its authority
because 'he was a great man and a baron of the lord
king'.[3] Robert de Ros, convicted of disseizin by itinerant
justices, used an armed band to fight off the sheriff's men
attempting to carry out the judgment.

2. Norgate, K. (1902) *John Lackland*, Macmillan, p. 219.
3. Holt, J.C. (1961) *The Northerners: A Study in the Reign of King John*,
   Oxford UP, p. 6; citing Shirley, W.W. (ed.) (1862–6) *Royal Letters
   of Henry III*, Rolls Series, vol. 1, p. 104.

It will not do to depict the entire English baronage, however, as feudal reactionaries, illiterate louts, lacking any sense of public responsibility, and concerned only with their own selfish goals. By the early thirteenth century, barons and knights had attained 'pragmatic literacy', enabling them to read simple Latin charters or Anglo-Norman romances. Their literacy gave them access without clerical assistance to key documents such as the *Leges Edwardi Confessoris* or the coronation charters of Henry I, Stephen, and Henry II, which were copied in French versions around 1215. Scholars today appreciate the experience in government that Angevin innovations had given many barons and knights, so-called 'self-government by the king's command'.[4] A number of the lesser ranking rebels, such as Robert de Ros, Simon of Kyme, or Thomas of Moulton, had experience in royal office in the shires. Among the baronial leadership, however, few seem to have had much experience in government other than Saher de Quency, earl of Winchester, who had frequented John's court, witnessing many royal charters, and Roger Bigod, earl of Norfolk, who had served Richard I at the exchequer and on judicial eyres.

While baronial leaders nursed personal grievances against the king, convinced that he, his father or brother, had cheated them out of inherited lands, castles, or other privileges, some of the rebels showed a capacity to look beyond class or personal gain to the public good. They were capable of fashioning out of their feudal background a conviction that the king must govern *per judicium* and *per consilium*. Practical experience in law courts as jurors and as litigants enabled them to see John's arbitrary practices for what they were and gave them a healthy respect for principle of 'due process of law'. They could grasp their clerical colleagues' learned precedents and together forge a reform programme. Whatever the source of the barons' programme, their citation of good old law predating Henry II was useful propaganda, making a contrast with the Angevins' wicked novelties. Furthermore, some rebels

---

4. White, A.B. (1933) *Self-Government by the king's Command*, Minnesota UP, Minneapolis.

could see a practical need to appeal to moderate barons, loyal to the monarchical principle, yet alarmed by John's arbitrary rule.

In any case, by the early thirteenth century, it was not uncommon for communities to purchase charters of liberties or privileges. London had a short-lived commune in 1191, and a decade later, many English towns and a few shires were securing collective grants of liberties. A few years before Peter de Brus joined the rebellion, he had granted his knights and free tenants of Langbargh in Cleveland, Yorkshire, a charter of liberties. Another northern lord, Earl Ranulf of Chester, a royalist stalwart during the rebellion, sometime in 1215 granted his Cheshire tenants a charter with features similar to Magna Carta's. The novelty was the barons' demand that the whole land – *communa totius terrae* – secure a charter of liberties.[5]

Scholars have looked beyond the rebel barons, most often to Stephen Langton, for statesmanship that could supply the political principles underlying the Great Charter. Historians' support for the archbishop as author of the reform programme comes from Roger of Wendover, like so much of the received view of John's reign. The chronicler pictured Langton as early as August 1213 pressing for the laws of Henry I as a basis for a programme of political reform. A condition of lifting John's excommunication in July 1213 was a renewal of the promises in his coronation oath to protect the Church and to rule justly in accordance with the good old law. Not long afterwards, Stephen Langton met with two of John's highest officials, Geoffrey fitz Peter and Peter des Roches, in an early August council at St Albans. Apparently its purpose was to work out details for compensating the English Church for damages suffered during the interdict, but Stephen may have sought some additional implementation of John's oath. According to Roger of Wendover, this August council moved toward broader reform, declaring that the laws of Henry I should be observed and that sheriffs, foresters, and other royal officers should refrain from inflicting injuries

5. Magna Carta, Chap. 61.

or extortions. Comparison of the St Albans chronicle's account with other chronicles leads most scholars to reject the discussion of Henry I's laws as Wendover's embellishment. His version of the St Albans council contains a 'core of truth', however;[6] for John did promise some limited reforms and make some minor concessions in 1213.

According to Wendover, another discussion of the laws of Henry I took place at London in late August 1213, with the archbishop again figuring prominently. The chronicler repeated rumours of a sermon Langton preached at St Paul's, after which he took aside a group of barons to show them in secret Henry I's coronation charter, suggesting it as a means for recovering their 'long-lost liberties'.[7] Supposedly this newly-discovered charter would be the basis for the Articles of the Barons and Magna Carta. Many scholars tend to doubt this story also; most fail to find any baronial discussion of Henry I's Charter before the winter of 1214–15.

Later in October 1213, a group of barons met with the papal legate, Nicholas of Tusculum, who was on a mission to mediate their quarrel with the king. Possibly at this time they set forth a series of demands recorded as the 'Unknown Charter of Liberties', surviving only in a copy discovered later in Philip Augustus's archives at Paris. The Unknown Charter is not in fact a charter, but a copy of Henry I's Charter plus a short document that seems to be someone's notes, either observations on promises made informally on the king's behalf or baronial proposals. Although its main points are much the same as the barons' programme of 1215 and incorporated in Magna Carta, some of its demands are more far-reaching; for example, a royal promise to limit military obligations outside England only to Normandy and Brittany. Although it is difficult to determine this document's exact date in negotiations, most scholars connect it with discontent over the collection of scutage in autumn 1214 or with discussions early in 1215.

6. Holt (1992) p. 215.
7. Roger of Wendover. Hewlett, H.G. (ed.) (1886–9) *Chronica Rogeri de Wendover* ... *Flores Historiarum* (3 vols), Rolls Series, vol. 2, p. 84; translation, Warren, W.L. (1961) *King John*, California UP, Berkeley, Ca./Eyre Methuen, p. 228.

The clause about overseas military service (7) may confirm a 1213 date, however, since John's preparations for his continental expedition at that time had ignited it into a burning issue.[8]

Once John returned from Poitou in October 1214, following the collapse of his grand continental strategy, his standing in England was at a low point. Clearly, his weakness would embolden his baronial opponents, yet he courted conflict by attempting to collect scutage at a higher rate than ever. Not long after John's return to England, he received requests for reform. According to Roger of Wendover, hostile barons gathered at Bury St Edmunds in November to discuss their grievances. Before leaving the Abbey, they pledged themselves yet again – in Wendover's version – to seek reforms, basing their demands on Henry I's coronation charter; and they asked the king to confirm his predecessors' charters and his own coronation oath. Regardless of the details, discontent was becoming so apparent that John summoned a council at London on the feast of the Epiphany, 6 January 1215.

By then hostile barons had formed a sworn association or *conjuratio*, binding themselves together to seek redress. At the London meeting, John again put off answering their demands, which he maintained they had made disrespectfully and with threat of force. He postponed any decision on the barons' proposals until a meeting just after Easter at Northampton. His opponents maintained that at the London council he not only refused to recognize 'their ancient and customary liberties', but sought their promise in writing 'never again to demand such liberties from him or his successors'.[9]

---

8. For text of the Unknown Charter, see Rothwell, H. (ed.) (1975) *English Historical Documents*, vol. 3, *1189–1327*, Eyre & Spottiswoode, Cambridge, pp. 310–11.
9. Cheney, C.R. (1979) *Innocent III and England*, Hiersemann, Stuttgart, p. 268, citing Barnwell Chronicle. Stubbs, W. (ed.) (1872–3) *Memoriale Walteri de Coventria* (2 vols), Rolls Series, vol. 2, p. 218; *Chronica Majora*. Luard, H.R. (ed.) (1872–84) *Matthaei Parisiensis Chronica Majora* (7 vols), Rolls Series, vol. 2, p. 584; and *Rymer's Foedera*. Clarke, A., Caley, J., Bayley, F., Holbrooke, F., Clarke, F.W. (eds) (1816–30, 1869) *Foedera, Conventiones, litterae, etc.* or *Rymer's Foedera, 1066–1383* (4 vols in 7), Record Commission, vol. 1, p. 120.

The king showed an indecision in facing the threat of rebellion following the Epiphany council of 1215 that recalls his response to Philip Augustus's threat to Normandy in 1202–03. He began preparations for war, sending to Poitou for a force 'of barons and bachelors',[10] and reinforcing castle garrisons. A Poitevin force landed in Ireland in February, but John reversed himself and wrote that he would not need them. While his policy in early 1215 appears 'hopelessly feeble and vacillating'.[11] he recognized that delaying tactics served him better than direct confrontation. The king dismissed the Poitevins in order to appear reasonable and to retain moderate barons' support; above all, he wanted to keep within the letter of the law, rejecting first resort to force in order to ensure support from his new overlord, the pope.

The king's letters to Innocent III present his own conduct as reasonable and conciliatory while picturing the barons as totally uncompromising. John sought to placate some opponents with individual concessions, winning over many English churchmen with his grant of free episcopal elections, and he appealed to the papacy's powerful protection. He sent a royal clerk to Rome in February, and his representatives there had greater success than did the inexperienced agents whom the barons sent to present their case at the papal *curia* or did Stephen Langton, whose standing with Innocent III was steadily declining. Early in March John took up the crusader's cross, 'a master-stroke of diplomacy' that placed him and his property under the Church's special protection.[12] The pope saw the threat of rebellion in England as an obstacle to his proposed crusade, and he suspected that the archbishop of Canterbury supported John's opponents. Langton was refusing to carry out the king's request that he excommunicate the rebels.

10. *Rot. Lit. Pat.* Hardy, T.D. (ed.) (1835) *Rotuli Litterarum Patentium 1201–1216*, Record Commission, p. 130.
11. Painter, S. (1949) *The Reign of King John*, Johns Hopkins UP, Baltimore, p. 302.
12. Cheney, C.R.(1955–6) 'The Eve of Magna Carta', *Bulletin John Rylands library*, 38, p. 313. Reprinted in Cheney (1982) *The Papacy and England in the 12th–14th Centuries*, Variorum, Aldershot.

Negotiations went on almost continuously from January to June 1215. Royal agents – Stephen Langton and William Marshal – were meeting with rebel representatives at Oxford in late February. Shortly after John took the cross, he offered major concessions that the barons rejected, promising to abolish evil customs introduced by himself or his brother and to submit his father's customs to judgment of his men, 'if any of them were burdensome'.[13] Later John met some of the dissidents at Oxford on 13 April, but again they reached no agreement. The barons mustered at Stamford to march in arms south to Northampton for their meeting with John on the Sunday following Easter (26 April). Open conflict came, however, when the barons arrived in force for the great council at Brackley near Northampton to present a schedule of non-negotiable demands. They had taken advantage of the time since the London council to prepare a programme that would strengthen their political position. The king failed to keep his appointment, however, and they sent their demands to him at nearby Wallingford. He had no intention of making any concessions that would threaten what he considered the crown's traditional rights, and he expected statements of papal support for his monarchical prerogatives to arrive soon from Rome.

Three papal letters did arrive at the end of April, too late to prevent an open break between king and barons. One was addressed to the barons, advising them to abandon conspiracies and force, to petition the king respectfully for redress, giving proof of their loyalty; a second addressed to the archbishop of Canterbury, and the bishops, berated them for their failure to mediate and accused them of favouring the barons; a third addressed to John does not survive. Apparently Innocent forwarded proposed terms of agreement, a *triplex forma pacis*, either in the missing letter or as an addendum.

On 5 May the rebels formally renounced their fealty and chose as their commander John's longtime enemy, Robert fitz Walter, who took a preposterous title 'Marshal

13. Holt (1961) p. 112, citing *Rymer's Foedera*. Clarke, Caley, Bayley, Holbrooke, Clarke (1816–30, 1869) vol. 1, p. 129.

of the host of God and Holy Church'. Yet the king continued to propose concessions for a peaceful solution, and on 9 May he agreed to abide by the findings of eight arbitrators, four nominated by him and four by the barons, with the pope presiding. He added that he would not take any action against the barons 'except by the law of our realm or by judgment of their peers in our court'.[14] While John was admitting that his opponents had legitimate complaints, he made such an offer not so much out of a sincere wish for reconciliation as to strengthen his moral position in the eyes of the uncommitted and of the pope. Throughout the spring of 1215, he had sought to preserve papal support by placing his actions in a legal and moral context that would be impregnable. By May, however, the barons had already withdrawn their homage and were no longer interested in arbitration. They could see no reason to expect impartial judgment from proceedings in either the king's court or at the papal *curia*. Soon after the barons' defiance, the king moved to prepare for war, and he commanded that the rebels' lands be seized and chattels sold.

John had outmanoeuvred the barons with his delays and concessions, making them appear as the ones rejecting legal process and resorting to force. Armed rebellion began with their failed siege of Northampton Castle, soon followed by their successful occupation of London on 17 May. Although John had just granted the citizens of London a new charter (9 May), a faction of Londoners remained resentful on account of his earlier actions; and they co-operated with the rebel leader Robert fitz Walter, lord of Baynard's Castle, the city's chief fortification after the Tower. Once London was opened to the barons, the military situation changed sharply, and rebel success brought fence-sitters into their camp. John had gathered forces and strengthened fortifications, but he failed to move quickly; he missed his opportunity to crush the rebels, and now their possession of London would make repressing their revolt more difficult. By

14. *Rot. Chart.* Hardy, T.D. (ed.) (1837) *Rotuli Chartarum, 1199–1216,* Record Commission, p. 209. Cited by Warren (1961) p. 234.

late May, John saw himself almost deserted; he knew that he must negotiate, and he asked the archbishop of Canterbury to arrange a truce. Both Langton and such leading royalist barons as William Marshal were urging the king to seek a settlement.

By the end of May, John decided to come to terms with the rebels in order to buy time, and safe-conducts issued by him imply meetings with baronial agents. As Sir James Holt writes, 'Throughout, even when he sealed Magna Carta, John had not the slightest intention of giving in or permanently abandoning the powers which the Angevin kings had come to enjoy.'[15] The king seemed to have custom on his side; he was fighting in defence of traditional monarchical prerogatives, while the barons were the revolutionaries, trying to impose limitations on royal power. John could assume that his overlord the pope would pronounce invalid any concessions seriously threatening monarchical power and would impose spiritual sanctions on the rebel barons. Innocent III had little patience for armed rebellions; he insisted that the English barons only seek satisfaction after proving their loyalty and then humbly petitioning their king, or failing that, addressing petitions to him, their feudal overlord.

Negotiations got underway at Runnymede near Windsor Castle in early June 1215. The 'Articles of the Barons' was a preliminary agreement prepared before the meeting by a chancery clerk. Beginning 'These are the articles that the barons ask for and the lord King grants',[16] it was a product of weeks of negotiations between rebel and royal agents. Apparently Stephen Langton acted as a mediator between the two groups, since the 'Articles' later turned up in the archiepiscopal archives at Canterbury. Most of its clauses appear in Magna Carta with hardly any change, and it provided the basis for final discussions on a few disputed points and for formal drafting of the Charter. Indeed, John had his seal affixed to it on 10 June as a sign to barons not present at Runnymede that he accepted

15. Holt (1992) p. 228.
16. Rothwell (1975) vol. 3, p. 311.

its provisions. One dispute left to be resolved was their insistence that the king disavow any right to appeal to the pope. John resisted, unwilling to deny his overlord's authority; instead, he promised that he would not seek annulment of the agreement 'from anyone', in place of 'from the lord pope'.[17] Of course, he did exactly what the barons suspected and promptly petitioned Innocent III to revoke the Charter.

The Great Charter can be seen as little more than 'the Articles of the Barons carefully worked over by highly intelligent men with a thorough knowledge of the English government'.[18] Clearly the precision of language in the final draft of the Charter depends on the skill of royal chancery clerks. Moderate royalists must have contributed constructively to drafting the Articles and Magna Carta; indeed, the preamble acknowledging those by whose counsel the king was granting the Charter lists the archbishop of Canterbury, other bishops, including two *familiares regis*, Henry, archbishop of Dublin, and Peter des Roches, bishop of Winchester, four royalist earls, and several royal officials, but no prominent rebels. The list shows that men embodying much of the kingdom's accumulated wisdom stood at the king's side, counselling moderation. In the view of one authority, the Charter reflects the views of 'the moderate barons, the bishops, and the trained administrators'.[19] Their prominence in the difficult days following John's death, promptly reissuing Magna Carta as a means of conciliating the rebels, points to their statesmanship.

Final agreement was reached on terms by 19 June, when the rebel barons made a 'firm peace' with their king, symbolized by exchanging the kiss of peace and renewing homage to him. The barons' return to peace had to precede John's granting of the Charter so that it

---

17. *Magna Carta*, Chap. 61; Holt (1992) pp. 472–3; Galbraith, V.H. (1967) 'A Draft of Magna Carta', *Proceedings of the British Academy*, 53, p. 351.
18. Painter (1949) p. 316.
19. Powicke, F.M. (1929) 'England: Richard I and John'. Chapter 7 in Tanner, J.R., Prévite-Orton, C.W., Brooke, Z.N. (eds) *Cambridge Medieval History*, vol. 6, Cambridge UP, p. 245.

should not appear to be extracted from him by threat of force; otherwise,it would have been patently invalid. They then selected their twenty-five executors of the agreement, who were to enforce John's adherence. Sometime between 19 and 24 June, chancery clerks drafted and sealed copies of the document we know as Magna Carta. Four of these copies still survive. Soon John was moving, however reluctantly, to put some of the Charter's promises into effect, restoring rebels' lands and castles.

. . .

THE GREAT CHARTER AND ITS MEANING

King John agreed to the terms stated in Magna Carta at Runnymede by 19 June 1215. Official copies drafted a few days later by chancery clerks took a form that is significant; they are in the shape of a royal charter, a solemn grant from the king to 'all the free men of our realm' given freely and in perpetuity.[20] Its language gives no hint that its promises had been made under duress, a fact that would have rendered it invalid if admitted. Although the first version of the Great Charter remained in effect only a few weeks, its reissue following John's death in autumn 1216 and the definitive reissue of 1225 made it perpetual, the first of England's statutes and a cornerstone of the British constitution. It only gained the descriptive title of 'great' or 'large' with its 1217 reissue to differentiate from a smaller charter, the Forest Charter, issued at the same time. Demands for confirmations of its promises made it a rallying cry throughout the later Middle Ages and again in the seventeenth century, whenever the English felt themselves oppressed by a tyrannical ruler.

Obviously, much myth has grown up about such a document, due largely to anachronistic interpretations of Sir Edward Coke and other seventeenth-century lawyers seeking a weapon against absolutism. These accretions must be cleared away in order to understand its meaning in King John's time. Since the rise of the 'scientific' school

20. Holt (1992) pp. 448–51 app. vi, with Latin and English on facing pages. All citations of the Great Charter are from Holt's work.

of history in the late nineteenth century, two extremes in viewing the Charter have defined discussion of its meaning. One school follows traditional interpretations, seeing the makers of Magna Carta – whether the barons themselves or Stephen Langton and churchmen – as visionaries, formulating a document that could evolve into a strong protector of the English people's liberties. An opposing group of scholars sees the Great Charter in its medieval context, and they judge it a feudal document representing the barons' reactionary outlook, an obstacle to strong and effective central government. One writer at the beginning of the twentieth century saw the Charter as a 'positive nuisance and stumbling-block',[21] mainly aimed at protecting the barons' privileged position within a collapsing feudal structure. Such views still survive in some modern studies of King John and Magna Carta.

The barons sought to restore the 'good old law' of their grandfathers' time as they understood it. They had some notion of principles of good government, a desire for a king who would rule *per consilium* and *per judicium*. Left alone to frame a document, however, the baronial rebels might have drafted little more than a shopping list of baronial complaints and demands, a charter lacking any broad principles. Somehow they broadened their base of support by adopting a reform programme that appealed to groups beyond the feudal baronage, to the English Church, to knights, and to lesser-ranking freemen. The actual shaping of the settlement was the work of 'a mixed bag of rebels, royalists, and moderates'.[22] The negotiations of Stephen Langton, moderate barons, bishops, and royal administrators resulted in a document containing important constitutional principles.

Certainly the rebel barons had concrete feudal grievances against King John that they wanted remedied, but the Great Charter cannot be classed as simply a feudal document. The list of baronial grievances was broadened into a reform

---

21. Jenks, E. (1902) 'The Myth of Magna Carta', *Independent Review*, 4. Reprinted in Holt, J.C. (ed.) (1972) *Magna Carta and the Idea of Liberty*, John Wiley, New York, NY, p. 27.
22. Cheney (1979) p. 376.

programme of benefit to groups below the baronage. This
should not come as a great surprise, since barons, knights,
and lesser free landholders had many connections. They
came together to do business in courts of shire and honor
and before the royal justices, but stronger bonds were those
of family. Members of the knightly class often were kinsmen
of barons, descendants of younger sons of baronial families;
and smaller freeholders were often the kin of knights,
descendants of knightly landholders' younger sons who
had inherited less than a knight's fee. In terms of lands
possessed, such smallholders were little different from the
more prosperous peasants. Yet all would have considered
themselves superior to their peasants who actually laboured
in the fields and connected in some fashion to the knightly
class, bound by family ties to higher ranking members of
their shire's society. Many knights had grievances against
King John, and they joined the rebellion sometimes even
when their own lords remained loyal to the king.

Since both barons and knights possessed urban property
and engaged directly or indirectly in commerce, they had
contacts with merchants in the towns. Furthermore, this
group possessed resources useful to the rebels; the
barons' occupation of London clearly had given them
great advantage in the civil war. Not surprisingly, the
Charter also included concessions to the townspeople,
ratifying the 'liberties and free customs' of London and
other cities, boroughs, towns, and ports (Chapter 13).
Magna Carta, then, had to take account of complaints of
those below the baronage in rank, their knightly tenants,
lesser freeholders, and burgesses.

The 1215 version of Magna Carta consists of sixty-
three chapters, ranging over a wide number of topics.
It is a practical, detailed document, aimed at remedying
specific problems, not at applying philosophical principles.
Although drafted hastily, its articles fall rather logically
into five chief areas. A chapter concerning the Church's
rights stands first, perhaps following the example of
Henry I's coronation charter. Its protection of the rights
and liberties of the English Church contained little that
was new, merely committing John to promises already
made in his 1214 charter for free episcopal and abbatial
elections.

Second come fifteen articles dealing with the feudal concerns of King John's barons. They attempted to define feudal custom, limiting his increasing demands for various aids and scutages (Chapters 12 and 14), setting figures of £100 on relief payments for baronies and 100 shillings for knights' fees (Chapter 2), and banning relief payments by youths whose estates had been in royal custody while they were minors (Chapter 3). They also sought to remedy abuses of the royal right of wardship and marriage, such as excessive exploitation of wards' property during their wardship (Chapters 4 and 5) or requiring widowed ladies to marry against their will (Chapters 6 and 8).

A third group of chapters dealt with administrative matters; for example, ten treat finances. One chapter banned demands that sheriffs pay increments (25), while others defined proper methods for collecting crown debts or debts to Jews (Chapters 9–11). Three chapters dealt with the 'evil customs' of royal forest administration (Chapters 44, 47, 48). A number of these administrative chapters centred on the functioning of the common law courts. Only one chapter, article 34 limiting the writ *praecipe*, shows baronial resentment of the growth of royal jurisdiction at the expense of their honor courts. Its aim was to simplify the procedure by which a lord could claim a suit for his own court, but in fact did little to restrict the royal courts' jurisdiction. Most of the articles treating judicial matters indicate the popularity of the common law courts and the barons' interest in ensuring the people's ease of access to them. One chapter (19) required far more visits to the shires by itinerant justices than was practicable, calling for assizes to be taken in all counties four times a year; and another required that common pleas be held in some fixed place (Chapter 17). These two chapters clearly indicate criticism of John's concentration of all justice at his itinerant court *coram rege*.

A fourth group of chapters sought to guarantee that the king carried out his promises, creating machinery of enforcement. One of these articles required John to remove his aliens from office (Chapter 50), and another required removal of alien soldiers from the kingdom (Chapter 51). The most important of these chapters (61) established a committee of twenty-five

barons to share power with John, with the sanction
of renewing warfare if he refused to carry out his
promises. Of course, even moderate royalists found this
an unacceptable interference with royal authority; and
co-operation between the monarch and the twenty-five
barons would prove impossible, leading to resumption
of civil war by late summer 1215. The last chapter (63)
declared that the king had sworn an oath to observe in
good faith all the promises in the earlier articles and
would not seek release from them. The barons already
anticipated that John would seek papal annulment of the
agreement, and they hoped by this statement to head off
such action.

A final group of chapters laid down general principles
of lasting significance, and these deserve a close examina-
tion. While the underlying assumptions of Magna Carta
are conservative and thoroughly feudal, some of the
barons' feudal assumptions were capable of being expanded. Out of the lord-vassal relationship arose concepts
of government that still shape our fundamental views on
relations between government and the governed. It is, of
course, necessary to recognize that the term 'feudal' is
not simply an adjective for anything archaic, antiquated,
or reactionary, as it was used first by eighteenth-century
philosophes and then by Marxists. Four basic assumptions
appear in the Great Charter that are feudal in origin,
but have remained important in Anglo-American political
thought ever since 1215.

First, Magna Carta sought to protect the position
of the *liber homo* or free man, that is, knights and
smaller landholders who were capable of bearing arms.
While the Charter shared similarities with charters of
liberties granted by continental princes, its definition of
a free man is far broader, granting greater protection
to non-noble subjects than contemporary charters in
other countries. Late twelfth-century English law had
adopted a broad definition, linking knights and free
tenants together without much distinction, since they were
already linked closely in society. 'Knight' was a term with
military or social meaning, not indicating legally defined
status. The significant distinction was between freedom
and serfdom, and much of the early thirteenth-century

English population consisted of unfree peasants without the right to security of their persons or property. The free man had special privileges denied the non-free, including the right to bear arms, but most notably protection from arbitrary seizure of his land or corporal punishment by his lord. Recognition of the free man's privileges is given in Chapter 39 of the Charter, 'No free man shall be taken or imprisoned or dispossessed or outlawed or exiled or in any way ruined, nor will we [the king] go or send against him, except by the lawful judgements of his peers or by the law of the land.'

Stacks of learned papers and books have sought to clarify the meaning of that final phrase *legale judicium parium vel per legem terre*. The pair of terms did not have a precise legal definition, and different people meant different things by them. Judgment by peers certainly did not mean trial by jury or procedure by inquest or assize in all instances; most likely it meant for the barons a proceeding in a court consisting of their social equals. They wanted their trials held before fellow magnates, not before lowborn royal officials at the bench or exchequer. Royal justices applied the term *lex terre* to traditional procedures of shire courts, while litigants used the term and such similar ones as *consuetudo regni* more loosely. The barons apparently meant the common law actions developed for their tenants since Henry II's reforms, but which were not available to them against their feudal lord, the king. Article 39 did not entitle free men to trial by jury as opponents of the early Stuart kings would assume, but it did guarantee what the barons called government *per judicium* and constitutional lawyers today call 'due process of law', a privilege that the unfree did not enjoy. It protected the free from extralegal or illegal treatment by the king and his agents, enjoining him to proceed against them only by the writs and assizes of the common law courts or by combat, the ordeal, or compurgation, ancient processes of the shire and honor courts. In short, the king was to be bound by the law in his dealings with his free subjects.

Immediately following this clause and relating more clearly to demands for government *per judicium* is Chapter 40, 'To no one will we sell, to no one will we deny or delay right or justice.' Several additional articles sought to put the principle of due process into effect, providing redress to victims of arbitrary acts by John and his predecessors. Chapter 52 demanded full justice to anyone 'disseised or deprived without lawful judgement of his peers' of lands, castles, or liberties. Other chapters outlawed royal agents' arbitrary seizures of property for the king's works (28, 30, 31). Two chapters afforded protection against arbitrary amercements. Barons were only to be amerced by their peers (Chapter 21); a free man was to be amerced by testimony of his neighbours 'in accordance with the degree of the offence' and 'saving his livelihood' (Chapter 20). Even the livelihoods of the non-free were protected from amercements that would take their agricultural implements.

A second fundamental feudal principle that became a part of the Charter is the lord's obligation to take counsel with his vassals, the knights owing him military service. Since the barons were the king's tenants-in-chief, his immediate vassals, they expected him to seek their counsel. This was the principle of government *per consilium* which had featured prominently among their demands; and it represents a rejection of what would be called in the United States today 'executive privilege', a ruler's penchant for deciding important issues secretly on the advice of intimate advisers of his own choosing rather than relying upon recognized spokesmen for the community at large. Two chapters of Magna Carta (12 and 14) hint at this demand for government *per consilium*. In them, King John promised, 'No scutage or aid is to be levied in our realm except by the common counsel of our realm . . .'

It is sometimes carelessly asserted that these two articles set forth the principle of parliamentary approval of taxation or 'no taxation without representation', but such an interpretation encounters many difficulties. First, the chapters refer only to feudal payments by the king's tenants, not general taxes paid by the whole population, although the line between gracious aids, tallages, and general levies had become blurred. Second, they set forth only a requirement that the king take counsel, as would any feudal lord before collecting an aid from his vassals; no reference to consent or assent appears. The novelty here was a baronial demand that the king seek counsel before imposing a scutage, which he previously had imposed on his own initiative as a substitute for their feudal military obligation. Perhaps John's levying of scutages apart from actual military campaigns had blurred this point. Finally, Chapter 14 makes clear that the 'common counsel of the realm' is to be obtained from the prelates of the English church, the earls and greater barons, who were to be summoned individually, and from 'all those who hold of us in chief'. The barons were still thinking of the kingdom as a great feudal honor, with themselves comprising its honor court. This assembly summoned to give counsel was clearly a body of feudal magnates, not a band of intimates from the royal household; but neither did it contain representatives of knights or other ranks of English society below the baronage, even though its deliberations allegedly represented the 'common counsel of the realm'.

Magna Carta consisted chiefly of concessions to specific groups or more widely to all the king's free subjects, not recognition of abstract rights belonging to the *regnum* as a whole. A radical trend of thought came into the Charter, however, with references to the *communa tocius terre* and *communa consilium regni*. This concept of the kingdom as a 'commune' or corporate body of all free men capable of coercing the king was new and clearly threatening to royal supremacy. The barons considered themselves capable of acting for 'the community of the realm', when giving counsel to the king. The problem of securing consent from the whole body of the king's subjects would not be solved until Parliaments, containing representatives of the knights and burgesses, made their appearance in the fourteenth century. Nonetheless, Chapters 12 and 14 of the Charter are 'the first definition in northern Europe of a large secular assembly intended to set limits to royal power'.[23]

A third key aspect of feudal tradition implicit in the Great Charter is its contractual nature; the tie

23. Langmuir, G. (1972) 'Per Commune Consilium Regni in Magna Carta', *Studia Gratiana*, 15, p. 483.

between lord and vassal had the character of a contract, whether written down in a charter or not. The ceremony of homage and fealty implies acceptance of certain obligations by each party towards the other. The lord was obliged to proceed in any dispute against his man *per judicium*; a court composed of the lord and his men would define the contract's terms and determine whether one party was failing to carry out his responsibilities, a *judicium parium* in other words. The barons clearly saw the Charter in such a context, as an attempt to state King John's contractual obligations. Magna Carta represents an important stage in the growth of the contract theory of government; the feudal notion of contract between lord and vassal was already beginning to be expanded to the larger ruler-subject relationship.

Seventeenth-century common lawyers and parliamentarians would see the Great Charter as a fundamental contract between the ruler and the ruled. Memories of its many confirmations during the later thirteenth and fourteenth centuries influenced the contract doctrine that justified the Glorious Revolution of 1688–89. Many saw James II's deposition as simply a repetition of the events of 1215, re-enacting the barons' rebellion against an unjust ruler. The North American colonists in 1776 applied the same doctrine, derived from the feudal contract, to their rebellion. The Declaration of Independence rejected George III's rule on grounds that the king, by his arbitrary acts, had broken the contract by which he ruled his American subjects.

The difficulty for John's contemporaries was finding a means of enforcing this contract on him, and this brings up a fourth feudal principle which the barons applied in the enforcing provision of the Charter (Chapter 61). Feudal custom sanctioned vassals' right to renounce their fealty, proclaim their defiance, and take up arms against their lord if he failed to keep his part of the bargain. Of course, defiance originally implied an isolated, individual act, not the work of a corporate body of barons. The feudal right of rebellion against a lord had several sources, among them far older teachings of subjects' right to resist an unjust ruler. The barons knew no other way to enforce John's adherence to his promises, except to threaten him with renewal of civil war. Once again, feudal concepts of the lord-vassal relationship were being transferred to the larger ruler-subject relationship. Trying to put that threat into language that would mask the fact of warfare, Chapter 61 turns to the royal courts' legal vocabulary; the twenty-five 'shall distrain and distress . . . seizing castles, lands and possessions'. They aimed to act, in effect, as a feudal court, and two chapters refer to their role as judges in disputes over restoration of lands and other rights to John's victims (52, 55). This language of distraining and bringing to trial their lord the king was a subterfuge, aimed at legalizing baronial resort to force without risking forfeiture of their lands as rebels. Not surprisingly, the king and even his most moderate supporters saw the security clause as an unacceptable limitation on monarchical power.

Magna Carta was in force for less than three months, and by autumn 1215 it was a dead letter; fighting had broken out between royalist and baronial forces in late summer, and continued for a year after John's death in October 1216. As Christopher Cheney wrote, the Charter 'was a compromise accepted grudgingly by a king of autocratic temper and a group of embittered, bellicose barons'.[24] Another agreement made between John and baronial leaders at Runnymede was a source of bickering by both sides. Its provisions for the barons' continued possession of London and for Stephen Langton's custody of the Tower until 15 August show their distrust of the king, while their refusal to surrender the city on the specified date strengthened John's suspicion of them. Given the mutual mistrust, attempts to implement the Charter were bound to fail and both sides engaged in preparations for war in the summer. King John persuaded his new supporter, Innocent III, that the Charter infringed upon his God-given rights as monarch, and the pope obligingly annulled it in August.

The real significance of Magna Carta lies not in 1215, then, but in the early years of the reign of John's son, Henry III. Only a nine year-old boy when he succeeded

24. Cheney (1979) p. 375.

to the English throne, the council ruling in his name chose to reissue the Charter, with a few revisions, in November 1216. It was a gesture designed to win over some of the rebel barons whose quarrel had been a personal one with John, not with his son or with the institution of monarchy. Magna Carta by then had the approval of the young king's protector and overlord, Pope Honorius III, committed to its support by his legate on the scene in England. Young Henry's counsellors again reissued the Charter in 1217 once peace was restored, with more revisions, and then in its definitive version in 1225 with the most objectionable clauses omitted or replaced. These reissues show that Magna Carta was coming to be considered the fundamental law of the land, a kind of contract between the king and his subjects. The Charter was no myth for litigants in Henry III's common law courts, for they called on its provisions when conducting their suits. The royal judges in 1234 reversed Henry's extralegal pursuit of his fallen justiciar, Hubert de Burgh, and arbitrary seizure of his lands, delivering a message to the king that he was subject to the law of the land.

In the thirteenth and fourteenth centuries, Magna Carta became a banner to rally those discontented with royal government. Their dissatisfaction expressed itself in cries for its confirmation, and it was confirmed about thirty times during the later Middle Ages. Each reissue of the Great Charter required re-interpretation of its clauses to fit changing circumstances, and this enabled the document to grow and take on new meaning. Under Edward III, for example, an act of Parliament in 1354 enormously expanded the number of people protected by Chapter 39; instead of 'no free man' to be denied due process of law, it was now 'no Man, of what Estate or Condition that he be'.[25] Another of Edward III's statutes in 1368 declared Magna Carta the fundamental law of the land, stating that 'if any Statute be made to the contrary, that shall be holden for none'.[26] Under the Yorkists and Tudors, the Charter no longer had a central place in

25. Statute of 1354. Luders, A. *et al.* (eds) (1810–28) *Statutes of the Realm* (11 vols) (reprint, 1963), Record Commission, vol. 1, p. 345.
26. Statute of 1368. Luders, A. *et al.* (eds) (1810) vol. 1, p. 388.

discussions about the character of English government. Yet it was not completely forgotten, for it continued to be studied at the Inns of Court; and among the earliest printed books in England were editions of ancient laws, including the Great Charter. It came forward again during the conflict of Sir Edward Coke and other common lawyers with the early Stuart kings; Coke said, 'Magna Carta is such a fellow that he will have no sovereign.'[27]

. . .

RENEWED CIVIL WAR AND FRENCH INVASION

Neither side genuinely sought to put into effect the scheme for power-sharing by king and baronial committee of twenty-five that Chapter 61 of Magna Carta called for, and by late summer 1215 renewed civil war was in the air. John carried out its provisions as reluctantly as he could and promptly sought papal release from his promises. Even so, he saw that once he went to war, he would need to appear to be defending himself against the barons' unreasonable interpretations of his promises, not against the Charter itself, if he were to win over moderates. This was easy for him to do, since the Great Charter was in the main a moderate document. Shortly after 19 June, John began restoring properties of those whom he had arbitrarily dispossessed, as provided in Chapter 52. The sticking-point was the security clause (Chapter 61) that gave the committee of twenty-five barons the sanction of making war on the king, alarming moderates who accepted the monarchical principle. That clause, 'surely the most fantastic surrender of any English king to his subjects',[28] led to papal condemnation of the entire Charter.

The recent rebels' acts did not allay John's suspicions, for they had not sought even an appearance of neutrality in electing the twenty-five. In naming the committee, they failed to turn to respected moderates, such as Stephen Langton or William Marshal; instead, all chosen had fought on the rebel side, although not all were longtime foes of

27. Coke's statement quoted by Cam, H. (1965) 'Magna Carta – event or document?' (Selden Society Lecture). Reprinted in Holt (1972) p. 114.
28. Galbraith, V.H. (1966) 'Runnymede Revisited', *Proceedings of the American Philosophical Society*, 110, p. 308.

the king. The more radical rebels found Magna Carta too moderate and showed little enthusiasm for disbanding their armed forces, and when they were to meet with John at Oxford in mid-July, some stayed away. Wherever they were in control, they prevented royal officials from performing their tasks and continued to operate their own rival administration, set up the previous spring. John refused to meet the barons again at Oxford on 20 August, but sent agents to insist that they abandon London.

Papal release of the king from the promises of Magna Carta made civil war certain. On 24 August 1215, Innocent III freed the king from observing the Great Charter, which he described as 'not only shameful and demeaning but also illegal and unjust, thereby lessening unduly and impairing [the king's] rights and dignity'. His earlier letter excommunicating unnamed 'disturbers of the king and kingdom' was published by the end of August.[29] Three prominent ecclesiastics acting as papal agents in England issued letters on 5 September attacking the barons' whole programme for 'despoiling the king of his royal dignity',[30] and they nullified all the twenty-fives' enactments. A papal interdict on rebel lands followed in December. All this gave the rebels what appears in retrospect a moral advantage; they were fighting to preserve the Great Charter. They had one clear military advantage, their possession of London, their only major fortification. An agreement between King John and the rebel commander Robert fitz Walter, also made in late June at Runnymede, had specified that the barons would hold the city until 15 August, by which time the king was to have fulfilled his promises. No one knew what would happen once this agreement expired with the Charter's terms still unfulfilled. The barons' refusal to surrender London in accord with the June terms was a major stumbling block, preventing peace.

29. Cheney, C.R., Semple W.H. (ed. and trans.) (1953) *Selected Letters of Pope Innocent III concerning England (1198–1216)*, Thomas Nelson (Medieval Texts), Walton-on-Thames, pp. 215, 208, letter of 7 July.
30. Powicke, F.M. (1929) 'The Bull "Miramur plurimum" and a Letter to Archbishop Stephen Langton, 5 September 1215', *English Historical Review*, 44, p. 92.

John spent the summer of 1215 visiting royal castles, seeing that they were stocked, garrisoned, and ready for conflict; and he sent agents abroad to enlist additional troops. Among the royal strongholds that the king wished to resupply was Rochester, a royal castle, although in perpetual custody of the archbishop of Canterbury and actually held by Reginald de Cornhill, a longtime royal agent in Kent. When John began to doubt Cornhill's loyalty and sought to install his own man as constable, Stephen Langton refused to co-operate on grounds that he was protecting Canterbury's rights over the fortress. His obstinacy allowed rebel forces to take control of Rochester Castle, and John's failure to recover London and Rochester soon set off the second civil war.

The king had powerful advantages. He had the support of the only barons who could field a significant feudal force, Irish and Welsh marcher lords such as William Marshal and Ranulf of Chester. Other royalist barons were the earl of Arundel (or Sussex), who held castles in Norfolk and Sussex; the earl of Warenne (or Surrey), an important lord in Norfolk and the North as well as in Surrey; and the earl of Salisbury, the king's half-brother and longtime stalwart. A belt of royalist-controlled castles across the North cut off the northern barons from their fellow rebels in the South. Royalist control of the countryside could also supply money to hire a mercenary army, especially engineers needed to conduct sieges, while the rebels had few men skilled at attacking or defending strongpoints. John's importation of mercenaries was a mixed blessing, however; while the foreigners gave him an effective fighting force, they fuelled resentments among the English just as they had earlier among the Normans.

John had the strong support of the papacy and of most of his bishops, although he found the archbishop of Canterbury to be 'a notorious and barefaced traitor to us'.[31] John skilfully played upon his position as a papal vassal and upon Innocent III's pride in his lordship over England, writing to the pope that the barons who 'were

31. P.R.Q. Ancient Correspondence, i.6. Translation, Galbraith, V.H. (1948) *Studies in the Public Records*, Thomas Nelson, Walton-on-Thames, p. 136.

devoted to us before we undertook to submit ourselves
and our land to your lordship, now – on account of
this, so they publicly state – rise up violently against
us'.[32] By midsummer 1215, Innocent, concerned for
his crusade and exasperated by Langton's refusal to
excommunicate the rebels, accepted John's opinion of
his archbishop; he denounced Langton and some of
his fellow-bishops as accomplices of 'the disturbers of
the kingdom' and partners in 'a wicked conspiracy'.[33]
Soon the papal commissioners in England suspended
the archbishop from his functions, and he departed
for Rome to attend and appeal to the fourth Lateran
Council. The only bishop left to side openly with the
baronial party was Giles de Braose of Hereford, one with
powerful personal motives for opposing a king who had so
cruelly persecuted his family. A few radical English clerks,
including Langton's own brother and his steward, actively
supported the rebel side, however.

The rebel barons also sought foreign support, appealing
in early autumn to Louis, son of Philip Augustus. This
invitation to a foreign prince proved that the rebel barons
were a faction, no longer representative of the community
of the realm, a propaganda plus for King John. Louis's
father was not eager to break his truce with John, and
he lacked confidence in the English barons. Also he
preferred to avoid another quarrel with the pope, who
sent his legate to the French court to oppose Louis's
proposed expedition against a papal vassal and who
excommunicated the prince in the spring of 1216. Yet
Philip probably supported his son privately, while publicly
appearing to avoid involvement with the expedition.

Louis put forward specious claims to the English crown
based on the French royal court's supposed condemnation
of John after his murder of his nephew, Arthur of
Brittany, and his own right through his marriage to
Blanche of Castile, John's niece. Both claims were barely
decent cover for a campaign of conquest in England and
could not have been taken seriously by contemporaries.
It is not at all certain that the French court actually

32. *Rot. Lit. Pat.* Hardy (1835) p. 182.
33. Cheney, Semple (1953) p. 207, no. 80.

had condemned John for Arthur's death; and even if it had, the judgment would have had no effect in England, an independent kingdom never subject to French overlordship. Louis had no hereditary claim except a very remote one through his wife, which not even French rules of succession would have recognized. Other descendants of Henry II's daughters had claims equal to Blanche's; and Eleanor of Brittany, Arthur's sister who remained imprisoned in England for her entire life, had a stronger claim through her father. Nonetheless, Louis went ahead with plans to aid the English rebels, although he could not cross the Channel immediately. He sent some knights in late November to London, where they awaited his arrival, unhappy at the lack of wine and quarrelling with their English hosts.

While the rebel barons proved indecisive in confronting King John in early stages of the civil war, his own success showed his greater capability and experience in warfare that many historians have seriously underestimated, mis-led by his supposed title of 'Softsword'. His task was to isolate the rebels in London, to control the southeast coast in order to stop French aid from reinforcing the rebels, and to keep contacts open with Flanders, a source of hired soldiers. While he was at Dover, royalists in the West would threaten London from another direction. In autumn 1215 he largely succeeded in these efforts. While waiting for continental mercenary forces to land at Dover, the king saw that royal castles were provisioned and prepared for conflict. He was at Dover on 1 September, awaiting arrival of Flemish mercenaries, when a storm arose to disperse their ships and drown most of them. The rebels occupied Rochester Castle, which Stephen Langton had refused to render to the king, in order to prevent the king from reaching London.

John's seven-week siege of Rochester, ended by its garrison's surrender on 30 November 1215, confirmed his deserved reputation as a castle-breaker. It was 'one of the greatest [siege] operations in England up to that time'.[34] First, John destroyed the bridge spanning the

34. Brown, R.A. (1986) *Rochester Castle*, 2nd edn, English Heritage, pp. 10–11.

Medway, isolating the rebels from London. His engineers had five great stone-slinging devices, but they gained entry to the castle by mining under one of the corner towers and then building a fire fed by forty fat pigs to burn the tunnel props. This tumbled down a great section of the tower, opening the keep to the royalists. Rochester's fall revealed to John's opponents their insecurity behind fortress walls, and other castles surrendered without putting up much resistance. The Barnwell Chronicler writes, 'Our age has not known a siege so hard pressed nor so strongly resisted,' and after Rochester, 'Few cared to put their trust in castles.'[35] Royalist success at Rochester caused some rebels to seek peace with the king in December 1215 and January 1216.

After the fall of Rochester, John decided in December to divide his army into two parts. He sent one band under William Longsword and some mercenary captains into counties just north and east of London to besiege rebels' castles and to devastate their lands. This force encountered little opposition from the rebels based at London, and by the new year they had overrun lower East Anglia and had driven the enemy from its shelter in the Isle of Ely. John marched with another force to harry rebel-controlled counties in the North, and by Christmas he had reached Nottingham, destroying as much rebel property as possible and spreading terror in his path. A number of rebel strongholds surrendered to him; according to Roger of Wendover, only one castle (Helmsley) remained in rebel hands in the North. John also had to repel the Scottish king's invasion of the previous autumn, which had reached Newcastle-on-Tyne by January 1216. He chased Alexander II back across the Tweed, butchering and burning throughout Northumberland on his march back to the South.

The king had reached Suffolk and Essex by March 1216, taking Framlingham, Colchester, and Castle Hedingham. In three months, John had come close to achieving complete control over the east side of the

---

35. Barnwell Chronicle. Stubbs (1872–3) vol. 2, p. 227; translation, Brown (1986) p. 10.

country, either retaking or razing all rebel castles except a few isolated holdouts. The rebel barons remained idle, 'unsuccessful amateurs without the knowledge or resources for modern warfare';[36] but they stubbornly held out behind the walls of London, waiting for additional French forces to come to their aid. The following May Prince Louis himself would arrive in England at the head of a large army. Until Louis's arrival, John had held firm control over the South and West, and elsewhere only isolated castles defied him. If significant French aid to the rebels had not arrived, King John could simply have camped outside London and waited for their surrender.

John spent late April and early May 1216 gathering an army in Kent in preparation for Prince Louis's invasion. His chief defence was his navy waiting off Dover to destroy the French fleet at Calais, but a storm wrecked many ships and dispersed the others in mid-May, only days before Louis's landing. Louis was able to land in England unopposed on 21 May, for John dared not risk a pitched battle. This is not necessarily an instance of John's reputed lack of boldness. He may have had doubts about the loyalty of his largely foreign force, many of whom, recruited in French domains, acknowledged Philip Augustus as overlord. John could not be sure that his mercenaries might not go over to the Capetian heir, if the fighting turned in his favour. Instead, the king withdrew along the coast to Dover, leaving Louis to take Rochester; then he marched overland to Winchester. When the French followed in pursuit, taking Winchester on 14 June, John withdrew to Corfe Castle, Dorset. French success in pushing the king westward had a powerful political impact, leading some royalist supporters to abandon him; among them were four earls including Salisbury, his half-brother.

John's reign after Louis's landing was 'a tumult of confusion and civil war'.[37] The king spent July and

36. Brown, R.A. (1989) *Castles, Conquest and Charters: Collected Papers*, Boydell & Brewer, Woodbridge, p. 204. Reprinted from (1951) 'Framlingham Castle and Bigod 1154–1216', *Proceedings of the Suffolk Institute of Archaeology*, 25.
37. Poole, A.L. (1955) *From Domesday Book to Magna Carta*, 2nd edn, Oxford UP, p. 484.

August roaming with his Poitevin mercenaries in the West between Corfe at the Channel coast and Shrewsbury near the Welsh border, where he kept busy resupplying castles and seeking allies within the kingdom and without. One of his mainstays, William Marshal, had great strength in the marches of Wales and while there the king negotiated with Welsh chieftains. French and rebel forces tried without much success to expand their control beyond the northern and southeastern counties. Even in those regions royalist castellans at Windsor, Dover, Lincoln, and in the bishopric of Durham continued to withstand sieges. Rebel forces invaded East Anglia, but seem to have captured few of the castles in royalist hands. A new threat to John appeared in August when Alexander II of Scotland began marching south once more, this time seeking to link with Louis and the rebels. By September, he had arrived at Dover, where he did homage to the French pretender.

The autumn of 1216 saw John furiously energetic, even though illness hampered him. In September, he marched with his army from the West down the Thames valley to take the offensive. While it appeared that he planned to relieve the besieged royalists at Windsor castle, he actually aimed at East Anglia, hoping to meet the Scottish king on his way north. John did retake Cambridge and several Essex castles, resulting in some respite for Windsor as its besiegers took off in pursuit of the king. He then moved north to make a lightning raid on Lincoln, under rebel siege; and he remained in the region until 4 October, in Powicke's words, 'in an orgy of reckless ferocity in the fenlands and Lincolnshire'.[38] He turned south once more on a raid into Norfolk, where loyal townsfolk at Lynn welcomed him; but by 11 October he left there and headed back towards Lincolnshire once more.

John was seriously ill by now; and unable to travel further, he took refuge at the bishop of Lincoln's castle, Newark, where he died on 19 October 1216. Only a few days before his death, he had suffered the humiliation of losing his baggage train with his household goods to the high tide in the Wash. The exchequer had not functioned since the spring of 1215, leaving the

---

38. Powicke (1929) p. 250.

king's itinerant wardrobe as the closest equivalent to a central revenue office; nonetheless, the decentralized castle treasures succeeded in keeping the royalist army supplied despite the exchequer's collapse. John depended upon his constables to collect whatever they needed from the shires, sending to the castle treasuries sums not spent on the spot. The king was forced to spend the last year of his life, not in supervising a complex government, but 'like a condottiere living from hand to mouth on the country'.[39] Yet he died with dignity, receiving the Church's consolation, making a will, and requesting burial in the church of his patron St Wulfstan. He sought to ensure his son's succession, entrusting little Henry III to the pope and to William Marshal.

The situation on King John's death was stalemated; he controlled the west of England and could move freely about the Midlands. Even within the rebel-held southeast, royal castles such as Windsor and Dover were still holding out. He had loyal support from his foreign military captains, who were ensconced in strongholds throughout the country, and from two of the greatest magnates, the earls of Pembroke and Chester, who controlled the Welsh marches. Some of his supporters who had gone over to Louis's side had returned to his allegiance, most notably his half-brother, William Longsword. The citizens of southeastern port towns remained loyal, although compelled against their wills to take oaths to the French prince. John also enjoyed the moral support of the English episcopate, abbots of the great religious houses, and the papacy. It was possible that the king could have overcome the French-rebel forces whose alliance had been undergoing strains, which he could have exploited had he lived; they were now confined to the southeast, with pockets in East Anglia and the North. John's last raid into Lincolnshire before his death destroyed any danger of united French-Scottish action. King John died in 1216 not decisively defeated, after having fought a combination of English rebels and French invaders to a standstill.

39. Barlow, F. *The Feudal Kingdom of England 1042–1216*, 4th edn, Longman, p. 392.

Chapter 9

JOHN, HIS CONTEMPORARIES AND OUR CONTEMPORARIES

King John died a failure, no doubt even in his own eyes, having failed to recover Normandy, the chief task that he set for himself, and having provoked a baronial rebellion that left his son's succession threatened. His contemporaries had little doubt about his place in history, and English chroniclers writing not long after his death depicted him as the worst of their kings. In comparing John with other monarchs of their time, they found him to fall far short. His arch-enemy, Philip Augustus, enjoyed the advantage of the Saint Denis school of history working to foster a favourable royal image, while the most influential English chroniclers, the St Albans monks, would write with an anti-royal bias. The Victorians continued to follow these monastic chroniclers, not only applying standards based on traditional morality and Christian piety, but also adding Protestant family virtues as standards for judging John.

Above all, John's lack of military success accounts for his continuing poor historical reputation. His ill-repute results chiefly from one campaign, his disastrous failed defence of Normandy, 1202–04, and it is partially deserved. Yet John's military record on his death is hardly one of cowardice or incompetence; he was a capable enough strategist and skilled in siegecraft. His strategy for recovering his lost duchy came incredibly close to success in 1214. John died in 1216 unbeaten in battle, having outmanoeuvred a combination of English rebel barons and their French allies. A royalist victory, eventually won in the name of his young son, might have proven difficult but not impossible for him, had he lived longer.

While John's failure as a military commander cannot be accounted to deficiency in courage or in military science, he can be blamed for moral and personal failings. Yet the collapse of John's schemes and consequent civil war can be seen as due also to larger, structural problems, not solely a result of personal failure as a leader. Since Sir Maurice Powicke first wrote in 1913, scholars have continued to doubt that the Angevins could have held on to Normandy militarily even had Richard Lionheart lived longer to lead its defence. They find Philip Augustus's superior financial resources an overwhelming advantage, and they see too many cultural and political forces weakening the Angevin 'empire' and pulling John's Norman and Loire Valley subjects into the Capetian orbit.

Certainly John saw the financial problems that had plagued his two predecessors reach a crisis point, and his desperate search for money to match Philip Augustus's military expenditures is the defining characteristic of his reign. It led to oppressive financial measures that pressed harder on his English subjects than had his father and brother's policies. He involved himself personally in revenue-raising much more than had Henry II or Richard I, and his activity aroused animosity that had been deflected earlier to the king's 'evil counsellors'. Lady Stenton concluded from her study of the 1208 pipe roll, 'That the king himself was personally interested in the details of extracting money from his subjects is suggested both by the venom which was engendered against him personally and by such record evidence as can occasionally be produced.'[1] The poverty of Henry III's government during his early minority affords a perspective on John's preoccupation with money, forcing us to consider the possibility that his brazen financial demands and brutal pursuit of crown debtors were necessary. After the civil war ended in 1217, both magnates and local notables proved reluctant to fulfil their financial obligations to the royal government. Sheriffs had become habituated

---

1. Stenton, D.M. (general ed.) (1933–64) *Great Roll of the Pipe, 1–17 John*, Pipe Roll Society, new ser. 23, pp. xvi–xvii [Pipe Roll 10 John].

to collecting and spending money without accounting at the exchequer, and they were excluding justices on eyre from their shires. The inability of the boy-king's guardians to raise revenues pushed the government towards bankruptcy by 1220.

Doubtless John's disagreeable personality prevented him from winning the support of the nobility, which was still the military caste and possessor of much of the kingdom's wealth in the early thirteenth century. His suspicion and dislike, even contempt, for his barons and his extralegal actions fed the fear and mistrust of many, especially those who were crown debtors. Some rebels' prompt switch to the royalist side after John's death shows that their quarrel was due more to personal distrust of him than to ideological disputes over the nature of England's government. Yet a basic change in England's government, the growth of administrative monarchy, was also significant as a source of baronial discontent. The 'country' barons felt their local authority slipping into the hands of royal *familiares* or *curiales*, often men on the margins of the knightly class, who possessed new administrative skills. Even in warfare, John's recruitment of hired captains reduced his dependence on his great men, and at the same time, the confidence he placed in mercenaries aroused the magnates' resentment.

Disputes between king and baronage over the royal power were real, then. Some barons had a conviction that the monarch must be compelled to rule *per consilium* and *per judicium*. The actions of other magnates during the civil war and the early minority, however, show them taking advantage of a weakened royal government to shake off financial obligations and to shift the balance of power in the kingdom from the monarch back to themselves. A recent study of Henry III's minority finds that 'the passage of power and resources to the great regional governors had . . . taken place on a large scale'.[2] Clearly some sought to turn back the clock, converting their baronies into great liberties; the young king's uncle,

2. Carpenter, D.A. (1990) *The Minority of Henry III*, California UP, Berkeley, Ca./Methuen, p. 120.

Earl William Longsword, sold his loyalty at a high price, seeking palatine powers in several shires. The earls and barons preferred a situation like that of Stephen's reign, when they had ruled the localities by means of private castles and hereditary shrievalties.

Because England lacked a constitution, King John and his barons could hold conflicting views on the government for the kingdom and on their proper places in it. It is no accident that the Tudors admired John; he appealed to them not only because of his opposition to the papacy, but also because of his authoritarian concept of monarchy. His statements about the *corona* or the *dignitas regis*, coupled with his adoption of an elaborate court ceremonial, indicate a lofty idea of kingship that has not been given its proper place by students of his reign. While he and his barons both acknowledged the weight of law and custom, he felt that history sanctioned longstanding royal rights and privileges. John, like his son later, turned to the Anglo-Saxon past for support of his pretensions. His authoritarian tendencies point toward Henry III's proto-absolutist notions, and his use of display and splendour to foster a majestic image of monarchy foreshadows his successor's similar attempts to shore up his prestige through patronage of artists and builders.

John faced economic, social, and political changes in his lifetime that resulted in crises to confound even a leader possessing the virtues of a philosopher-king. Although he had ability with potential for great accomplishments, his own character had serious faults that contained the seeds of failure. He proved clever enough at political manoeuvring, but often pressed beyond accepted bounds, exhibiting morally suspect conduct and undermining any advantage initially gained. His jealousy and suspicion were perhaps implanted by the uncertainty of his prospects for land or title during his childhood and youth; yet they led to behaviour that passed the limits of acceptable conduct for nobles, revealing a lack of any chivalric sense of personal honour. A ruler such as John who maintained power through cruelty and fear, who behaved boorishly, and who proved greedy for his subjects' wealth, was unlikely to prove an inspiring leader. While English chroniclers may have exaggerated John's moral flaws, he cannot escape some personal responsibility for his failures.

An essential test of greatness in a ruler that monastic chroniclers, concentrating on conventional piety, over-looked is leadership – the ability to inspire one's followers to achievements beyond their limits and to accept sacrifices for the common good. This was a quality present in such World War II leaders as Winston Churchill or Franklin D. Roosevelt, or possibly in a postwar US president, John F. Kennedy. Can we measure this quality of inspiring leadership among medieval monarchs? In an age of primitive communications, leaders could not address their subjects directly; to accomplish their aims, they had to inspire a band of devoted followers, not simply fighting men and clerics in administrative offices, but also the politically articulate classes. Clearly, Richard Lionheart possessed the quality of inspiring his subjects. Basic to winning support of the baronage and the increasingly important knightly class was earning their trust. John trusted few men, however, and was himself untrust-worthy.

Very much a part of this inspirational aspect of leadership is a sense of purpose or vision, an agenda or programme that galvanizes one's followers. Henry II seems always to have had before him an image of his grandfather Henry I's forceful yet just rule. The crusading ideal coupled with chivalric pursuit of glory through combat inspired Richard Lionheart. For Philip Augustus, it was restoring French monarchy to the greatness of the Carolingians, making it equal or surpass the Angevins. Others set John's agenda for him: Philip ensured his preoccupation with recovery of his continental possessions, Innocent III forced him to defend royal rights over the English Church, and rebel barons forced him to fight for the royal prerogative.

In the late twentieth century, our perspective differs not only from medieval chroniclers' but also from historians who wrote less than a century ago. When the world has endured dictators willing to sacrifice millions of lives for some ideological vision, John appears far less fearsome than he did to nineteenth-century academics. Compared to Hitler, Stalin, or Pol Pot, he seems quite tame and earlier generations' denunciations of him ludicrously disproportionate. Neither the Austin canon William of Newburgh's labelling John an 'enemy of nature' nor Bishop Stubbs' later description of him as a man 'who had defied God by word and deed all his life' is convincing in today's context.[3] He appears not as a monster of superhuman evil, but merely as a twisted and complex personality, yet a man with ability and potential for greatness, whose own flaws prevented him from living up to the reputations of his brother, Richard I, or his rival, Philip Augustus.

Certainly John was capable and dedicated to the work of kingship, in many ways a worthy successor to his father Henry II and great-grandfather Henry I. Even a nineteenth-century writer who denounced John with his age's moralistic bombast admitted that he was 'the ablest and most ruthless of the Angevins'.[4] Recent research rejecting chronicle accounts in favour of record evidence has led some scholars to hail him as an administrative genius. His personal attention to the work of his courts led Lady Stenton, for example, to discount the rebel barons' conviction that the king tampered with justice for selfish ends and to conclude that he deserves more praise than blame for his tireless activity in hearing pleas.

It seems impossible to avoid an ambivalent attitude towards King John. One authority's description of his rule in Gascony seems applicable to his reign as a whole; she finds the king's policy showing 'a curious combination of shrewdness and slackness, of ability and ineptitude.'[5] While John's reign was a failure, with the shattering of his scheme for recovery of his continental lands making a baronial uprising inevitable in England,

3. William of Newburgh. Howlett, R. (ed.) (1885–90) *Historia Rerum Anglicarum of William of Newburgh*. In *Chronicles, Stephen, Henry II and Richard I* (4 vols), Rolls Series, vol. 1, p. 390; Stubbs, W. (1874–8) *The constitutional History of England* (3 vols), Oxford UP, vol. 1, p. 534; Hassall, A. (ed.) (1902) *William Stubbs' Historical Introductions to the Rolls Series*. Reprint Haskell House, NY, p. 487.
4. Green, J.H. (no date) *A History of the English People*, American Book Company, New York, NY, p. 123.
5. Lodge, E.C. (1926) *Gascony under English Rule*, Methuen, p. 23.

he had some successes and even came tantalizingly close to accomplishing his goal of regaining Normandy and then defeating the rebel barons. His attention to financial details and adoption of harsh money-raising measures achieved its purpose of accumulating a huge surplus to spend on the 1214 campaign. His handling of the Canterbury succession crisis was masterful, securing for him and his young son the papacy's solid support. John's efforts in the British Isles, 1209–12, strengthened the English monarch's position as overlord of his Gaelic neighbours, and they give a preview of Edward I's policies. The Barnwell chronicler wrote at the peak of John's power, 'There is now no one in Ireland, Scotland and Wales who does not obey the command of the king of England; that, as is well known, is more than any of his ancestors had achieved.'[6]

King John seems most comparable to some twentieth-century US presidents, who had important goals and some great achievements, but whose psychological make-up cost them popular support and limited their successes. Two recent American presidents – Lyndon B. Johnson and Richard M. Nixon – with personality flaws that seem similar to John's, arouse the same ambivalence. Like them, John could inspire loyalty among capable administrative officials; some, such as Hubert Walter and Geoffrey fitz Peter, had served his father and brother well, while such others as William Marshal and Hubert de Burgh would distinguish themselves establishing Henry III's government on a sound basis. John and the two presidents could be brilliant in political operations, clever at evaluating their prospects, exploiting their enemies' weaknesses, spreading discord and leaving opponents in disarray. Yet he also resembles them in an almost paranoid sense of insecurity, deep suspicion of associates, jealousy of others' achievements, preoccupation

---

6. Barnwell Chronicle. Stubbs, W. (ed.) (1982–3) *Memoriale Walteri de Coventria* (2 vols), Rolls Series, vol. 2, p. 203; translation, Davies, R.R. (1990) *Domination and Conquest*, Cambridge UP, p. 82.

with secrecy, and predilection for devious plotting over open search for consensus. He shares with Johnson and Nixon personality flaws that prevented him from winning the trust of his most important subjects, much less their enthusiasm for his projects and their willingness to help him pay for them.

BIBLIOGRAPHY

The place of publication is London unless otherwise stated.

. . .

PRIMARY SOURCES

Literary sources

Appleby, J.T. (ed. and trans.) (1963) *The Chronicle of Richard Devizes*, Thomas Nelson (Medieval Texts), Walton-on-Thames.

Brewer, J.S., Dimcock, J.F., Warner, G.F. (eds) (1861–91) *Giraldi Cambrensis Opera* (8 vols), Rolls Series [Gerald of Wales].

Douie, D.L., Farmer, H. (eds and trans.) (1961–2) *The Life of St Hugh of Lincoln* (2 vols), Thomas Nelson (Medieval Texts), Walton-on-Thames.

Johnson, C. (ed. and trans.) (1950, 1983) corrections by F.E.L. Carter and D.E. Greenway, *Dialogus de Scaccario*, Oxford UP (Oxford Medieval Texts).

Hall, G.D.G. (1965) (ed. and trans.) *Tractatus de Legibus et Consuetudinibus Regni Anglie qui Glanvilla vocatur*, Thomas Nelson (Medieval Texts), Walton-on-Thames.

Howlett, R. (ed.) (1885–90) *Historia Rerum Anglicarum of William of Newburgh*. In *Chronicles, Stephen, Henry II and Richard I* (4 vols), Rolls Series.

Hewlett, H.G. (ed.) (1886–9) *Chronica Rogeri de Wendover . . . Flores Historiarum* (3 vols), Rolls Series [Roger of Wendover].

Luard, H.R. (ed.) (1864–9) *Annales Monastici* (5 vols), Rolls Series.

Luard, H.R. (ed.) (1872–84) *Matthaei Parisiensis Chronica Majora* (7 vols), Rolls Series [Matthew Paris].

Meyer, P. (ed.) (1891–1901) *Histoire de Guillaume le Maréchal* (3 vols), Société de l'Histoire de France, Paris.

Stevenson, J. (ed.) (1875) *Radulphi de Coggeshall Chronicon Anglicanum*, Rolls Series [Ralph of Coggeshall].

Stubbs, W. (ed.) (1867) *Gesta Regis Henrici secundi Benedicti Abbatis* (2 vols), Rolls Series [Benedict of Peterborough, rightly Roger of Howden].

Stubbs, W. (ed.) (1868–71) *Chronica Rogeri de Hovedene* (4 vols), Rolls Series [Roger of Howden].

Stubbs, W. (ed.) (1872–3) *Memoriale Walteri de Coventria* (2 vols), Rolls Series [Barnwell Chronicle].

Stubbs, W. (ed.) (1876) *Radulphi de Diceto, Opera Historica* (2 vols), Rolls Series [Ralph Diceto or of Diss].

Stubbs, W. (ed.) (1879–80) *Gervase of Canterbury, Historical Works* (2 vols), Rolls Series.

Record materials

Brown, R.A. (ed.) (1957) *Memoranda Roll 10 John*, Pipe Roll Society, new ser. 31.

Cheney, C.R., Semple, W.H. (eds and trans.) (1953) *Selected Letters of Pope Innocent III concerning England (1198–1216)*, Thomas Nelson (Medieval Texts), Walton-on-Thames.

Clarke, A., Caley, J., Bayley, F., Holbrooke, F., Clarke, F.W. (eds) (1816–30, 1869) *Foedera, Conventiones, Litterae, etc.* or *Rymer's Foedera, 1066–1383* (4 vols in 7), Record Commission.

Flower, C.T. (ed.) (1923–) *Curia Regis Rolls* (17 vols in course), HMSO.

Hardy, T.D. (ed.) (1833–4) *Rotuli Litterarum Clausarum* (2 vols), Record Commission [*Rot. Lit. Claus.*].

Hardy, T.D. (ed.) (1835) *Rotuli Litterarum Patentium 1201–1216*, Record Commission [*Rot. Lit. Pat.*].

Hardy, T.D. (1835a) *Rotuli de Oblatis et Finibus*, Record Commission [*Rot. de Obl. et Fin.*].

Hardy, T.D. (ed.) (1837) *Rotuli Chartarum, 1199–1216*, Record Commission [*Rot. Chart.*].

Hardy, T.D. (ed.) (1844) *Rotuli de Liberate ac de Misis et Praestitis*, Record Commision [*Rot. de Lib. ac de Mis.*].

Richardson, H.G. (ed.) (1943) *Memoranda Roll 1 John*, Pipe Roll Society, new ser. 21.

Stenton, D.M. (general ed.) (1933–64) *Great Roll of the Pipe, 1–17 John*, Pipe Roll Society, new ser. 10, 12–16, 18–20, 22–4, 26, 28, 30, 35, 37.

Stubbs, W. (ed.) (1913) *Select Charters and Other Illustrations of English Constitutional History*, 9th edn, Clarendon Press, Oxford.

Translations

Douglas, D.C., Greenaway, G.W. (eds) (1968) *English Historical Documents*, vol. 2, *1042–1189*, Eyre and Spottiswoode, Cambridge.

Rothwell, H. (ed.) (1975) *English Historical Documents*, vol. 3, *1189–1327*, Eyre & Spottiswoode, Cambridge.

. . .

BIBLIOGRAPHICAL AND HISTORIOGRAPHICAL AIDS

Altschul, M. (1969) *Anglo-Norman England 1066–1154*, Cambridge UP (Conference on British Studies Bibliographical Handbooks).

Elton, G.R. (1969) *England: 1200–1640*, Cornell UP, Ithaca, NY (The Sources of History series).

Gransden, A. (1974) *Historical Writing in England c. 550–1307*, Cornell UP, Ithaca, NY.

Graves, E.B. (1975) *A Bibliography of English History to 1485*, Oxford UP.

Wilkinson, B. (1978) *The High Middle Ages in England 1154–1377*, Cambridge UP (Conference on British Studies Bibliographical Handbooks).

. . .

GENERAL HISTORIES

Barlow, F. (1988) *The Feudal Kingdom of England 1042–1216*, 4th edn, Longman.

Brooke, C.N.L. (1961) *From Alfred to Henry III 871–1272*, Thomas Nelson (A History of England, vol. 2), Walton-on-Thames.

Clanchy, M.T. (1983) *England and its Rulers 1066–1272*, Fontana

Poole. A.L. (1955) *From Domesday Book to Magna Carta*, 2nd edn, Oxford UP (Oxford History of England, vol. 3).

Stenton, D.M. (1952) *English Society in the Early Middle Ages*, 2nd edn, Penguin (Pelican History of England, vol. 3), Harmondsworth.

. . .

CONSTITUTIONAL AND LEGAL HISTORY

Clanchy, M.T. (1979) *From Memory to Written Record: England 1066–1307*, Harvard UP, Cambridge, Mass.

Flower, C.T. (1943) *Introduction to the Curia Regis Rolls*, Selden Society, 62.

Holt, J.C. (1985) *Magna Carta and Medieval Government*, Hambledon Press. Reprints of previously published articles, including his unpublished Hinkley Lecture, 'The Origins of the Constitutional Tradition in England'.

Holt, J.C. (1992) *Magna Carta*, 2nd edn, Cambridge UP.

Jolliffe, J.E.A. (1961) *The Constitutional History of Mediaeval England*, 4th edn, A. & C. Black.

Kemp, B. (1973) 'Exchequer and bench in the later twelfth century – separate or identical tribunals?', *English Historical Review*, 88.

Milsom, S.F.C. (1976) *The Legal Framework of English Feudalism*, Cambridge UP.

Palmer, R.C. (1981) 'The feudal framework of English law', *University of Michigan Law Review*, 79.

Richardson, H.G., Sayles, G.O. (1963) *The Governance of Mediaeval England*, Edinburgh UP.

Stenton, D.M. (1964) *English Justice between the Norman Conquest and the Great Charter*, American Philosophical Society, Philadelphia.

Turner, R.V. (1977) 'The origins of Common Pleas and King's Bench', *American Journal of Legal History*, 21.

Van Caenegem, R.C. (1988) *The Birth of the English Common Law*, 2nd edn, Cambridge UP.

Warren, W.L. (1987) *The Governance of Norman and Angevin England 1086–1272*, Edward Arnold.

. . .

ADMINISTRATION

Brooks, F.W. (1925) 'William of Wrotham and the Office of the Keeper of the King's Ports and Galleys', *English Historical Review*, 49.

Brown, R.A. (1989) *Castles, Conquest and Charters: Collected Papers*, Boydell & Brewer, Woodbridge.

Carpenter, D. (1976) 'The decline of the curial sheriff 1194–1285', *English Historical Review*, 91.

Harris, B.E. (1964) 'King John and the sheriffs' farm', *English Historical Reivew*, 79.

Jolliffe, J.E.A. (1948) 'The chamber and castle treasuries under King John'. In Hunt, R.W., Pantin, W.A., Southern, R.W. (eds) *Studies in Medieval History presented to F.M. Powicke*, Oxford UP.

Morris, W.A. (1927) *The Medieval English Sheriff to 1300*, Manchester UP.

Powell, W.R. (1956) 'The administration of the Navy and the Stannaries, 1189–1216', *English Historical Review*, 71.

Tout, T.F.T. (1920–33) *Chapters in the Administrative History of Medieval England* (6 vols), Manchester UP.

West, F.J. (1966) *The Justiciarship in England 1066–1232*, Cambridge UP.

Young, C.R. (1976, 1979) *The Royal Forests of Medieval England*, Pennsylvania UP, Philadelphia/Leicester UP.

Individual Royal Servants

Cazel, F.A. (1989) 'Intertwined careers: Hubert de Burgh and Peter des Roches', *Haskins Society Journal*, 1.

Cheney, C.R. (1967) *Hubert Walter*, Thomas Nelson, Walton-on-Thames.

Holt, J.C. (1952) 'Philip Mark and the shrievalty of Nottinghamshire and Derbyshire in the early thirteenth century', *Transactions of the Thoroton Society*, 66.

Richardson, H.G. (1932) 'William of Ely, the King's Treasurer, 1195–1215', *Transactions of the Royal Historical Society* 4th ser., 15.

Turner, R.V. (1985) *The English Judiciary from Glanvill to Bracton c. 1176–1239*, Cambridge UP.

Turner, R.V. (1988) *Men Raised from the Dust: Administrative Service and Upward Mobility in Angevin England*, Pennsylvania UP, Philadelphia.

Weiss, M. (1974) 'The castellan: The early career of Hubert de Burgh', *Viator*, 5.

Young, C.R. (1967) *Hubert Walter, Lord of Canterbury and Lord of England*, Duke UP, Durham, NC.

. . .

ANGLO-NORMAN BACKGROUND

Chibnall, M. (1986) *Anglo-Norman England 1066–1166*, Blackwell, Oxford.

Green, J.A. (1986) *The Government of England under Henry I*, Cambridge UP.

Hollister, C.W. (1976) 'Normandy, France, and the Anglo-Norman *Regnum*', *Speculum*, 51. Reprinted in Hollister (1986) *Monarchy, Magnates and Institutions in the Anglo-Norman World*, Hambledon Press.

Hollister, C.W., Baldwin, J.W. (1978) 'The rise of administrative kingship: Henry I and Philip Augustus', *American Historical Review*, 83. Reprinted in *Monarchy, Magnates and Institutions*.

Hollister, C.W. (1986) *Monarchy, Magnates and Institutions in the Anglo-Norman World*, Hambledon Press. Reprints of previously published articles.

Le Patourel, J. (1976) *The Norman Empire*, Oxford UP.

Southern, R.W. (1970) 'The Place of Henry I in English history'. In Southern (1970) *Medieval Humanism and Other Studies*, Harper & Row, New York, NY/Blackwell, Oxford.

. . .

CAPETIAN COMPARISONS

Baldwin, J.W. (1986) *The Government of Philip Augustus*, California UP, Berkeley, Ca.

Baldwin, J.W. (1986a) 'The Capetian court at work under Philip Augustus'. In Haymes, E. (ed.) *The Medieval Court in Europe*, Wilhelm Fink Verlag, Munich.

Baldwin, J.W., Nortier, M. (1980) 'Contributions à l'étude des finances de Philippe Auguste', *Bibliothèque de l'Ecole des Chartes*, 138.

Bautier, R.H. (ed.) (1982) *La France de Philippe Auguste, le temps de mutations*, Paris (Colloques internationaux du CNRS 602).

Duby, G. (1990) *The Legend of Bouvines*. Translated by Tihanyi, C., Polity Press. French edn (1973) *La Dimanche de Bouvines*, Gallimard, Paris.

Dunbabin, J. (1985) *France in the Making 842–1180*, Oxford UP.

Fawtier, R. (1960) *The Capetian Kings of France*. Translated by Butler, L., Adam, R.J., Macmillan.

Hallam, E.M. (1980) *Capetian France 987–1328*, Longman.

Lewis, A.W. (1981) *Royal Succession in Capetian France: Studies on Familial Order and the State*, Harvard UP, Cambridge, Mass.

Lot, F., Fawtier, R. (1932) *Le premier budget de la monarchie française, le compte général de 1202–1203*, Paris (Bibliotèque de l'Ecole des Hautes Etudes, 259).

. . .

ANGEVIN ENGLAND

Appleby, J.T. (1965) *England without Richard, 1189–1199*, Cornell UP, Ithaca, NY.

Brundage, J.A. (1974) *Richard Lion Heart*, Scribners, New York, NY.

Carpenter, D. (1990) *The Minority of Henry III*, California UP, Berkeley, Ca/Methuen.

Crouch, D. (1990) *William Marshal: Court, Career and Chivalry in the Angevin Empire, 1147–1219*, Longman.

Gillingham, J. (1978) *Richard the Lionheart*, Weidenfeld & Nicolson.

Gillingham, J. (1984a) 'Richard I and the science of war in the Middle Ages'. In Gillingham, J., Holt, J.C. (eds) (1984) *War and Government in the Middle Ages, Essays in Honour of J.O. Prestwich*, Boydell & Brewer, Woodbridge.

Holt, J.C. (1981) 'Ricardus Rex Anglorum et Dux Normannorum', *Accademia Nazionale dei Lincei*, 253. Reprinted in Holt (1985) *Magna Carta and Medieval Government*, Hambledon Press.

Jolliffe, J.E.A. (1956) *Angevin Kingship*, A & C Black.

Painter, S. (1933) *William Marshal*, Johns Hopkins UP, Baltimore.

Painter, S. (1961) *Feudalism and Liberty, Articles and Addresses of Sidney Painter*. Edited by Cazel, F.A., Johns Hopkins UP, Baltimore.

Powicke, F.M. (1960) *The Loss of Normandy*, 2nd edn, Manchester UP.

Powicke, F.M. (1929) 'England: Richard I and John'.

Chapter 7 in Tanner, J.R., Prévite-Orton, C.W., Brooke, Z.N. (eds) *Cambridge Medieval History* vol. 6, *Victory of the Papacy*, Cambridge UP.

Warren, W.L. (1973) *Henry II*, California UP, Berkeley, Ca./Eyre Methuen.

. . .

THE BRITISH ISLES

Bartlett, R., MacKay, A. (eds) (1989) *Medieval Frontier Societies*, Oxford UP.

Crouch, D. (1988) 'Strategies of lordship in Angevin England and the career of William Marshal'. In Harper-Bill, C., Harvey, R. (eds) *The Ideals and Practice of Medieval Knighthood*, vol. 2, Boydell & Brewer, Woodbridge (Papers from the Third Strawberry Hill Conference).

Ireland

Flanagan, M.T. (1989) *Irish Society, Anglo-Norman Settlers, Angevin Kingship: Interactions in Ireland in the Late Twelfth Century*, Oxford UP.

Martin, F.X. (1987) 'John, Lord of Ireland, 1185–1216'. Chapter 5 in Cosgrove, A. (ed.) *A New History of Ireland*, vol. 2, *Medieval Ireland 1169–1534*, Oxford UP.

Warren, W.L. (1976) 'John in Ireland 1185'. In Bossy, J., Jupp, P. (eds) *Essays Presented to Michael Roberts*, Blackstaff Press, Dundonald.

Warren, W.L. (1981) 'King John and Ireland'. In Lydon, J. (ed.) *England and Ireland in the Later Middle Ages, Essays in Honour of Jocelyn Otway-Ruthven*, Irish Academic Press, Dublin.

Scotland

Barrow, G.W.S. (1973) *The Kingdom of the Scots: Government, Church and Society from the eleventh to the fourteenth Century*, Edward Arnold.

Duncan, A.A.M. (1975) *Scotland: The Making of the Kingdom*, Barnes & Noble, New York, NY (The Edinburgh History of Scotland, vol. 2).

Stones, E.L.G. (ed. and trans.) (1965) *Anglo-Scottish Relations 1174–1328: Some Selected Documents*, Oxford UP (Oxford Medieval Texts).

Wales

Davies, R.R. (1979) 'Kings, lords and liberties in the march of Wales, 1066–1272', *Transactions of the Royal Historical Society*, 5th ser., 29.

Davies, R.R. (1987) *The Age of Conquest: Wales 1063–1415*, Oxford UP (Oxford History of Wales, vol. 2).

Davies, R.R. (1990) *Domination and Conquest: The Experience of Ireland, Scotland and Wales 1100–1300*, Cambridge UP.

Walker, D. (1990) *Medieval Wales*, Cambridge UP.

. . .

KING JOHN AND HIS REPUTATION

Appleby, J.T. (1958) *John, King of England*, Cornell UP Ithaca, NY.

Bartlett, R. (1982) *Gerald of Wales 1146–1223*, Oxford UP.

Galbraith, V.H. (1945) 'Good kings and bad kings in English history', *History*, 30. Reprinted in Galbraith, V.H. (1982) *Kings and Chroniclers: Essays in English Medieval History*, Hambledon Press.

Galbraith, V.H. (1944) 'Roger Wendover and Matthew Paris' (David Murray Foundation Lecture no. 11). Reprinted in Galbraith (1982) *Kings and Chroniclers*, Hambledon Press.

Gransden, A. (1975) 'Propaganda in English medieval historiography', *Journal of Medieval History*, 1.

Hollister, C.W. (1961) 'King John and the Historians', *Journal of British Studies*, 1.

Holt, J.C. (1963) 'King John'. Historical Association (General Studies 53). Reprinted in Holt (1985) *Magna Carta and Medieval Government*, Hambledon Press.

Levin, C. (1988) *Propaganda in the English Reformation: Heroic and Villainous Images of King John*, Andrew Mellen, Lewiston, Maine.

Norgate, K. (1902) *John Lackland*, Macmillan

Painter, S. (1949) *The Reign of King John*, Johns Hopkins UP, Baltimore.

Warren, W.L. (1961) *King John*, California UP, Berkeley Ca./Eyre Methuen.

Warren, W.L. (1989) 'Painter's *King John* – Forty Years On', *The Haskins Society Journal*, 1.

. . .

YOUNG JOHN IN HIS BROTHERS' SHADOWS

Aries, P. (1960) *L'Enfant et la vie familiale sous l'Ancien Régime* (reprint 1973), Librarie Plon, Paris. Translated by Baldic, R. (1962) *Centuries of Childhood* (reprint 1979), Penguin, Harmondsworth.

Bachrach, B. (1984) 'Henry II and the Angevin tradition of family hostility', *Albion*, 16.

Brown, E.A.R. (1976) 'Eleanor of Aquitaine: parent, queen, duchess'. In Kibler, W.W. (ed.) *Eleanor of Aquitaine, Patron and Politician*, Texas UP, Austin.

Duby, G. (1964) 'Les "jeunes" dans la société aristocratique dans la France du Nord-Ouest au XIIe siècle', *Annales*, 27. Translated by Postan, C. 'Youth in aristocratic society: northwestern France in the twelfth century'. In (1974) *The Chivalrous Society*, Edward Arnold.

Herlihy, D. (1978) 'Medieval children'. In Ladner, B.K., Philips, K.R. (eds) *Essays on Medieval Civilization* Texas, UP, Austin (Webb Memorial Lectures, 12).

Herlihy, D. (1985) *Medieval Households*, Harvard UP, Cambridge, Mass.

Labande, E.-R. (1952) 'Pour une image véridique d'Aliénor d'Aquitaine', *Bulletin de la Société des Antiquaires de l'Ouest*, 4th ser., 2. Reprinted in Labande (1973) *Histoire de l'Europe occidentale XIe-XIVe siècles*, Variorum, Aldershot.

McLaughlin, M.M. (1974) 'Survivors and surrogates: children and parents from the ninth to the thirteenth century'. In De Mause, L. (ed.) *History of Childhood*, Psychohistory Press, New York, NY.

Orme, N. (1984) *From Childhood to Chivalry: The Education of the English Kings and Aristocracy 1066–1530*, Methuen.

Pollock, L. (1983) *Forgotten Children: Parent-Child Relations from 1500 to 1900*, Cambridge UP.

Turner, R.V. (1988) 'Eleanor of Aquitaine and her

children: an inquiry into medieval family attachment', *Journal of Medieval History*, 14.

Turner, R.V. (1990) 'The children of Anglo-Norman royalty and their upbringing', *Medieval Prosopography*, 11.

John's Succession

Holt, J.C. (1986) 'Aliénor d'Aquitaine, Jean sans Terre et la succession de 1199', *Cahiers de Civilisation médiévale*, 29.

Holt, J.C. (1990) 'The *Casus Regis*: the law and politics of succession in the Plantagenet dominions 1185–1247'. In King, E.B., Ridyard, S.J. (eds) *Law in Mediaeval Life and Thought*, University of the South UP, Sewanee, Tenn. (Sewanee Mediaeval Studies 5).

Wilkinson, B. (1944) 'The government of England during the absence of Richard I on the Third Crusade', *Bulletin John Rylands Library*, 28.

. . .

THE ANGEVIN EMPIRE

Bachrach, B. (1978) 'The idea of Angevin Empire', *Albion*, 10.

Bachrach, B. (1988) 'The Angevin economy, 960–1060: ancient or feudal?', *Studies in Medieval and Renaissance History*, new ser., 10, AMS Press, New York, NY.

Boussard, J. (1938) *Le comté d'Anjou sous Henri Plantegenêt et ses fils 1151–1204*, Bibliothèque de l'Ecole des Hautes Etudes, Paris (Section des sciences historiques et philosophiques 271.

Boussard, J. (1955) 'Les influences anglaises dans le développement des grandes charges de l'Empire Plantegenêt', *Annales de Normandie*, 5.

Boussard, J. (1956) *Le gouvernement d'Henri II Plantegenêt*, Librarie d'Argences, Paris.

Boussard, J. (1963) 'Aspects particuliers de la féodalité dans l'empire Plantegenêt, *Bulletin de la Société des Antiquaires de l'Ouest*, 4th ser., 7.

Chaplais, P. (1955) 'Le Traité de Paris de 1259 et l'inféodation de la Gascogne allodiale', *Le Moyen Age*,

61. Reprinted (1981) *Essays in Medieval Diplomacy and Administration*, Hambledon Press.

Gillingham, J. (1984) *The Angevin Empire*, Holmes & Meier, New York, NY/Edward Arnold.

Hajdu, R. (1978) 'Castles, castellans and the structure of politics in Poitou, 1152–1271', *Journal of Medieval History*, 4.

Haskins, C.H. (1918) *Norman Institutions*, Harvard UP, Cambridge, Mass.

Higounet, C. (1971) *Histoire de l'Aquitaine*, Privat, Toulouse.

Le Patourel, J. (1984) *Feudal Empires, Norman and Plantagenet*, Hambledon Press. Includes reprints of (1965) 'The Plantagenet Dominions', *History*, 50; also 'Angevin successions and the Angevin Empire', unpublished paper.

Norgate, K. (1887) *England under the Angevin Kings* (2 vols). Reprinted in 1969, Haskell House, New York, NY.

Painter, S. (1955) 'The Houses of Lusignan and Chatellerault, 1150–1250', *Speculum*, 30. Reprinted in Painter (1961) *Feudalism and Liberty, Articles and Addresses of Sidney Painter* (edited by Cazel, F.A.), Johns Hopkins UP, Baltimore.

Painter, S. (1956) 'Castellans of the plain of Poitou in the eleventh and twelfth centuries', *Speculum*, 31. Reprinted in Painter (1961) *Feudalism and Liberty*.

Painter, S. (1957) 'The Lords of Lusignan in the eleventh and twelfth centuries', *Speculum*, 32. Reprinted in Painter (1961) *Feudalism and Liberty*.

Powicke, F.M. (1906) 'The Angevin administration of Normandy', *English Historical Review*, 21–2.

Renouard, Y. (1965) *Bordeaux sous les rois d'Angleterre*, Féderation historique du Sud-Ouest, Bordeaux (Historie de Bordeaux, vol. 3).

Law of Succession and Inheritance

Hollister, C.W., Keefe, T.K. (1973) 'The making of the Angevin empire', *Journal of British Studies*, 12.

Holt, J.C. (1972) 'Politics and property in early medieval England', *Past and Present*, no. 57.

Holt, J.C. (1983) 'Feudal society and the family in

early medieval England: II. notions of patrimony', *Transactions of the Royal Historical Society*, 5th ser., 33.

Keefe, T.K. (1974) 'Geoffrey Plantagenet's will and the Angevin succession' *Albion*, 6.

Le Patourel, J. (1984) 'Angevin successions and the Angevin Empire'. In le Patourel, *Feudal Empires, Norman and Plantagenet*, Hambledon Press.

. . .

FINANCIAL CRISIS

Bolton, J.L. (1980) *The Medieval English Economy 1150–1500*, J.M. Dent (Everyman's University Library).

Coss, P. (1975) 'Sir Geoffrey de Langley and the crisis of the knightly class in thirteenth-century England', *Past and Present*, no. 68.

Feeney, B. (1985) 'The effects of John's scutages on East Anglian subjects', *Reading Medieval Studies*, II.

Harris, B.E. (1964) 'King John and the sheriffs' farms', *English Historical Review*, 79.

Harriss, G.L. (1975) *King, Parliament and Public Finance in Medieval England to 1369*, Oxford UP.

Harvey, P.D.A. (1973) 'The English inflation of 1180–1220', *Past and Present*, no. 61.

Holt, J.C. (1961) *The Northerners: A Study in the Reign of King John*, Oxford UP.

Mayhew, N.J. (1984) 'Frappes de monnaies et hausse des prix en Angleterre de 1180 à 1220'. In Day, J. (ed.) *Etudes d'Histoire monétaire*, Lille UP, Lille.

Miller, E., Hatcher, J. (1978) *Medieval England: Society and Economic Change 1086–1348*, Longman.

Mitchell, S.K. (1914) *Studies in Taxation under John and Henry III*, Yale UP, New Haven, Conn.

Palmer, R.C. (1985) 'The economic and cultural impact of origins of property: 1180–1220', *Law and History Review*, 3.

Poole, A.L. (1946) *The Obligations of Society in the 12th and 13th Centuries*, Oxford UP.

Postan, M.M. (1975) *The Medieval Economy and Society, an Economic History of Britain in the Middle Ages*, Penguin Books, Harmondsworth.

Prestwich, J.O. (1954) 'War and finance in the Anglo-Norman realm', *Transactions of the Royal Historical Society*, 5th ser., 4.

Reynolds, S. (1977) *An Introduction to the History of English Medieval Towns*, Oxford UP.

Richardson, H.G. (1960) *The English Jewry under the Angevin Kings*, Methuen.

. . .

THE LOSS OF NORMANDY

Brown, R.A. (1955) 'Royal castle-building in England, 1154–1216, *English Historical Review*, 70.

Brown, R.A. (1959) 'A list of castles, 1154–1216', *English Historical Review*, 74. Both the above are reprinted in Brown (1989) *Castles, Conquest and Charters: Collected Papers*, Boydell & Brewer, Woodbridge.

Contamine, P. (1984) *War in the Middle Ages*. Translated by Jones, M., Blackwell, Oxford.

Coulson, C. (1984) 'Fortress-policy in Capetian tradition and Angevin practice: aspects of the conquest of Normandy by Philip II', *Anglo-Norman Studies*, 6.

Gillingham, J. (1984a) 'Richard I and the science of war in the Middle Ages'. In Gillingham, J., Holt, J.C. (eds) (1987) *War and Government in the Middle Ages*, Boydell & Brewer, Woodbridge.

Gillingham, J. (1987) 'War and chivalry in the *History of William the Marshal*'. In Coss, P.R., Lloyd, S.D. (eds) *Thirteenth Century England II*, Boydell & Brewer, Woodbridge.

Holt, J.C. (1975) 'The end of the Anglo-Norman realm', *Proceedings of the British Academy*, 61. Reprinted in Holt (1985) *Magna Carta and Medieval Government*, Hambledon Press.

Holt, J.C. (1987) 'The loss of Normandy and royal finances'. In Gillingham, J., Holt, J.C. (eds) *War and Government in the Middle Ages*, Boydell & Brewer, Woodbridge.

Legge, M.D. (1982) 'William Marshal and Arthur of Brittany', *Bulletin of the Institute of Historical Research*, 55.

Musset, L. (1982) 'Quelques problèmes posés par l'annexion de la Normandie au domaine royal français'. In Bautier, R.-H. (ed.) *La France de Philippe Auguste, le temps de mutations*, Paris (Colloques internationaux du CNRS 602).

Petit-Dutaillis, C. (1925) *Le Désheritment de Jean sans Terre et le meurtre d'Arthur de Bretagne*, F. Alcan, Paris.

Painter, S. (1948, 1952) 'The marriage of Isabelle of Angouleme' II, *English Historical Review* 63, 67. Reprinted in Painter, S. (1961) *Feudalism and Liberty, Articles and Addresses of Sidney Painter* (edited by Cazel, F.A.), Johns Hopkins UP, Baltimore.

Richardson, H.G. (1946) 'The marriage and coronation of Isabelle of Angoulême', *English Historical Review*, 61.

Richardson, H.G. (1950) 'King John and Isabelle of Angoulême', *English Historical Review*, 65.

Richardson, H.G. (1967) 'The marriage of Isabelle of Angoulême: a problem of canon law', *Studia Gratiana*, 12.

Southern, R.W. (1970) 'England's first entry into Europe'. In Southern (1970) *Medieval Humanism and Other Studies*, Harper & Row, New York, NY/Blackwell, Oxford.

Verbruggen, J.F. (1977) *The Art of Warfare in Western Europe during the Middle Ages*. Translated by Willard, S., Southern, S.C.M., North Holland, Amsterdam.

· · ·

THE CANTERBURY SUCCESSION CRISIS

Brooke, Z.N. (1931) *The English Church and the Papacy from the Conquest to the Reign of John*, Cambridge UP.

Cheney, C.R. (1956) *From Becket to Langton: English Church Government 1170–1213*, Manchester UP.

Cheney, C.R. (1979) *Innocent III and England*, Hiersemann, Stuttgart.

Cheney, C.R. (1982) *The Papacy and England in the 12th–14th Centuries*, Variorum, Aldershot. Includes reprints of (1948) 'King John and the papal interdict', *Bulletin John Rylands Library*, 31; (1949) 'King John's reaction to the interdict on England', *Transactions of the Royal Historical Society*, 4th ser., 31; (1966) 'A recent view of the general interdict on England', *Studies in Church History*, 3; (1948) 'The alleged deposition of King John'. In Hunt, R.W., Pantin, W.A., Southern, R.W. (eds) *Studies in Mediaeval History Presented to F.M. Powicke*, Oxford UP.

Johnstone, H. (1929) 'Poor-relief in the royal households of 13th-century England', *Speculum*, 4.

Knowles, D. (1938) 'The Canterbury election of 1205–6', *English Historical Review*, 53.

Knowles, D. (1963) *The Monastic Order in England 940–1216*, 2nd edn, Cambridge UP.

Powicke, F.M. (1927) 'Alexander of St Albans: a literary muddle'. In Davis, H.W.C. (ed.) *Essays in History Presented to Reginald Lane Poole*, Oxford UP.

Powicke, F.M. (1928) *Stephen Langton*, Oxford UP.

Roberts, P.B. (1968) *Studies in the Sermons of Stephen Langton*, Pontifical Institute of Mediaeval Studies, Toronto.

Southern, R.W. (1970a) *Western Society and the Church in the Middle Ages*, Penguin Books (Pelican History of the Church, vol. 2), Harmondsworth.

Watt, J.A. (1988) 'Spiritual and temporal power'. In Burns, J.H. (ed.) *Cambridge History of Medieval Political Thought c. 350–c. 1450*, Cambridge UP.

Young, C.R. (1960) 'King John of England: an illustration of the medieval practice of charity', *Church History*, 29.

Continental Background

Packard, S.R. (1922) 'King John and the Norman church', *Harvard Theological Review*, 15.

Shaw, I.P. (1951) 'The ecclesiastical policy of Henry II on the continent', *Church Quarterly Review*, 151.

Walker, D. (1982) 'Crown and episcopacy under the Normans and Angevins', *Anglo-Norman Studies*, 5.

. . .

JOHN AND THE BARONS

Coss, P.R. (1991) *Lordship, Knighthood and Locality: A Study in English Society c. 1180–c. 1290*, Cambridge UP.

Crouch, D., Carpenter, D.A., Coss, P.R. (1991) 'Debate: bastard feudalism revised', *Past and Present*, no. 131.

Holt, J.C. (1992) *Magna Carta* 2nd edn, Cambridge UP; also Holt (1961) *The Northerners: A Study in the Reign of King John*, Oxford UP.

Keefe, T.K. (1983) *Feudal Assessments and the Political Community under Henry II and his Sons*, California UP, Berkeley, Ca.

Keefe, T.K. (1981) 'Henry II and the earls: The Pipe Roll evidence', *Albion*, 13.

Lally, J.E. (1976) 'Secular patronage at the court of Henry II', *Bulletin of the Institute of Historical Research*, 49.

Painter, S. (1943) *Studies in the History of the English Feudal Barony*, Johns Hopkins UP, Baltimore.

Turner, R.V. (1990) 'Changing perceptions of the new administrative class in Anglo-Norman and Angevin England: the *curiales* and their conservative critics', *Journal of British Studies*, 29.

Walker, S.S. (1979) 'Feudal constraint and free consent in the making of marriages in medieval England: widows in the king's gift'. In Cook, T., Lacel, C. (eds) *Historical Papers, Saskatoon 1979*, Canadian Historical Association, Ottawa.

Waugh, S.L. (1988) *The Lordship of England: Royal Wardships and Marriages in English Society and Politics, 1217–1327*, Princeton UP, Princeton.

Individual barons

Alexander, J.W. (1983) *Ranulf of Chester, a Relic of the Conquest*, Georgia UP, Athens, Ga.

Golding, B. (1983) 'Simon of Kyme, the making of a rebel', *Nottingham Medieval Studies*, 27.

Harris, B.E. (1975) 'Ranulph III earl of Chester', *Journal of the Chester Archaeological Society*, 58.

Painter, S. (1961) 'The Earl of Clare: Richard de Clare, Earl of Hertford'. In *Feudalism and Liberty, Articles and Addresses of Sidney Painter* (edited by Cazel, F.A.), Johns Hopkins UP, Baltimore.

Turner, R.V. (1973) 'William de Forz, Count of Aumale', *Proceedings of the American Philosophical Society*, 115.

Vine, M.J. (1975) 'Two Yorkshire rebels: Peter de Brus and Richard de Percy', *Yorkshire Archaeological Journal*, 47.

Political Thought

Burns, J.H. (ed.) (1988) *The Cambridge History of Medieval Political Thought*. Chapter 9, Van Caenegem, R.C., 'Government, law and society'; Chapter 10, Nelson, J., 'Kingship and empire'; Chapter 12, Luscombe, D.E., Evans, G.R., 'The twelfth-century renaissance'; Chapter

15, Pennington, K., 'Law, legislative authority and theories of government, 1150–1200; Cambridge UP.

Kantorowicz, E. (1957) *The King's Two Bodies*, Princeton UP, Princeton.

Post, G. (1964) *Studies in Medieval Legal Thought: Public Law and the State*, Princeton UP, Princeton.

Rosenthal, J.T. (1967) 'The king's "wicked advisers" and medieval baronial rebellions', *Political Science Quarterly*, 82.

Turner, R.V. (1990) 'Henry II's legal reforms: feudal or royalist?' *Sewanee Mediaeval Studies*, 3.

Ullmann, W. (1961) *Principles of Government and Politics in the Middle Ages*, Methuen.

John and Justice

Holt, J.C. (1992) *Magna Carta*, 2nd edn, Chapter 5, Justice and Jurisdiction, Cambridge UP.

Loengaard, J.S. (1985) 'Of the gift of her husband: English dower and its consquences in the year 1200'. In Kirshner, J., Wemple, S.F. (eds) *Women of the Medieval World*, Blackwell, Oxford.

Stenton, D.M. (1958) 'King John and the courts of justice', *Proceedings of the British Academy*, 44. Reprinted in (1964) *English Justice, 1066–1215* (Raleigh Lecture).

Turner, R.V. (1968) *The King and his Courts: The Role of John and Henry III in the Administration of Justice, 1199–1240*, Cornell UP, Ithaca, NY.

Turner, R.V. (1968a) 'The royal courts treat disseizin by the king: John and Henry III, 1199–1240', *American Journal of Legal History*, 12.

Turner, R.V. (1989) 'The Mandeville inheritance, 1189–1236: its legal, political and social context', *Haskins Society Journal*, 1.

Turner, R.V. (1990) 'Exercise of the king's will in inheritance of baronies: the example of King John and William Briwerre', *Albion*, 22.

. . .

MAGNA CARTA AND CIVIL WAR

Cheney, C.R. (1955–6) 'The eve of Magna Carta', *Bull John Rylands Library*, 38. Reprinted in Cheney (1982) *The Papacy and England*, Variorum, Aldershot.

Cheney, C.R. (1965) 'The Church and Magna Carta', *Theology*, 68. Reprinted in Cheney (1982) *The Papacy and England*, Variorum, Aldershot.

Cheney, C.R. (1967–8) 'The twenty-five barons of Magna Carta', *Bull John Rylands Library*, 50. Reprinted in Cheney (1982) *The Papacy and England in the 12th–14th Centuries*, Variorum, Aldershot.

Clanchy, M.T. (1985) 'Magna Carta and the common pleas'. In Mayr-Harting, H.M.R.E., Moore, R.I. (eds) *Studies in Medieval History Presented to R.H.C. Davis*, Hambledon Press.

Galbraith, V.H. (1966) 'Runnymede revisited', *Proceedings of the American Philosophical Society*, 110.

Holt, J.C. (1955) 'The barons and the Great Charter', *English Historical Review* 70. Reprinted in Holt (1985) *Magna Carta and Medieval Government*, Hambledon Press.

Holt, J.C. (1960) 'Rights and liberties in Magna Carta', *Album Helen Cam*, vol. 1, Nauwelaerts, Louvain (Studies Presented to the International Commission for the History of Representative and Parliamentary Institutions, 23. Reprinted in Holt (1985) *Magna Carta and Medieval Government*, Hambledon Press.

Holt, J.C. (1965) *The Origins of Magna Carta*, Virginia UP, Charlottesville. Reprinted in Holt (1985) *Magna Carta and Medieval Government*, Hambledon Press.

Holt, J.C. (ed.) (1972) *Magna Carta and the Idea of Liberty*, John Wiley, New York, NY (Major Issues in History).

Holt, J.C. (1972a) 'Magna Carta and the origins of statute law', *Studia Gratiana*, 15. Reprinted in Holt (1985) *Magna Carta and Medieval Government*, Hambledon Press.

Holt, J.C. (1992) *Magna Carta* 2nd edn, Cambridge UP. Contains texts of various editions of the Charter and its forerunners.

Hurnard, N.D. (1948) 'Magna Carta, Clause 34'. In Hunt, R.W., Pantin, W.A., Southern, R.W. (eds) (1948) *Studies in Medieval History Presented to F.M. Powicke*, Oxford UP.

Langmuir, G. (1972) 'Per Commune Consilium Regni in Magna Carta', *Studia Gratiana*, 15.

Maldon, H.E. (ed.) (1917) *Magna Carta Commemoration Essays*, Royal Historical Society. See especially Powicke, F.M. 'Per Judicium Parium'.

Miller, E. (1962) 'The background of Magna Carta', *Past and Present*, no. 23.

Painter, S. (1947) 'Magna Carta', *American Historical Review*, 53. Reprinted in Painter (1961) *Feudalism and Liberty, Articles and Addresses of Sidney Painter* (edited by Cazel, F.A.), Johns Hopkins UP, Baltimore.

Subsequent History of Magna Carta

Stenton, D.M. (1965) *After Runnymede, Magna Carta in the Middle Ages*, Virginia UP, Charlottesville.

Thompson, F. (1925) *The First Century of Magna Carta*, Minnesota UP, Minneapolis.

Thompson, F. (1948) *Magna Carta: Its Role in the Making of the English Constitution, 1300–1629*, Minnesota UP, Minneapolis.

Post Magna Carta Civil War

Holt, J.C. (1961a) 'King John's disaster in the Wash', *Nottingham Medieval Studies*, 5. Reprinted in Holt (1985) *Magna Carta and Medieval Government*, Hambledon Press.

Richardson, H.G. (1945–6) 'The morrow of the Great Charter', *Bull. John Rylands Library*, 29.

Rowlands, I.W. (1989) 'King John, Stephen Langton and Rochester Castle 1213–15'. In Harper-Bill, C., Holdsworth, C.J., Nelson, J.L. (eds) *Studies in Medieval History presented to R. Allen Brown*, Boydell & Brewer, Woodbridge.

GENEALOGICAL TABLE
AND MAPS

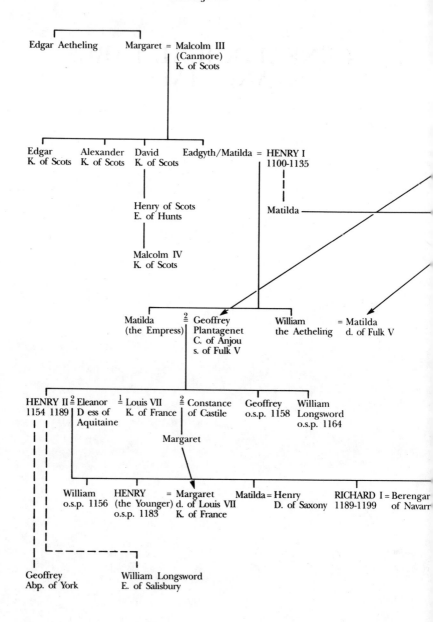

The Angevin Kings

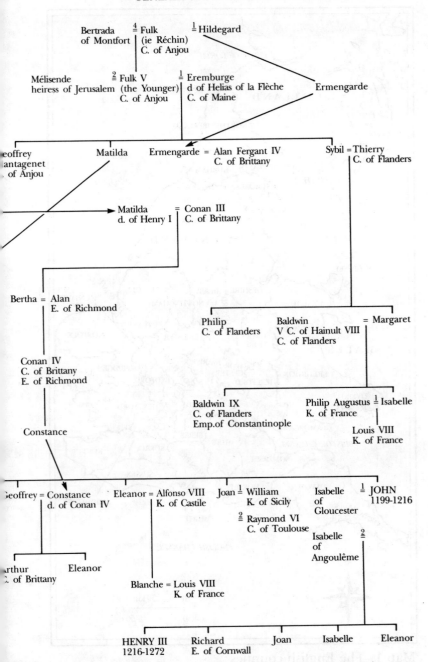

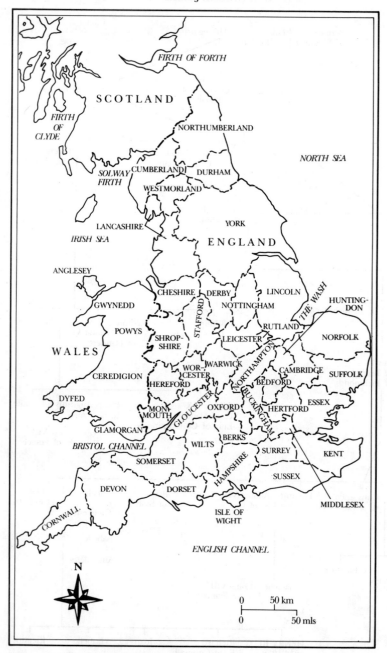

Map 1: The English counties

After Smith, G. (1966) *A History of England*, Scribners, New York

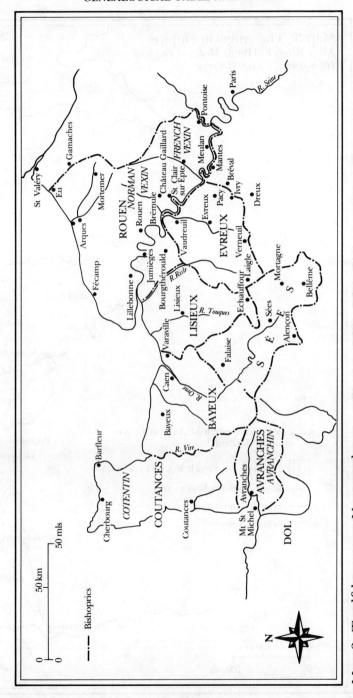

Map 2: Twelfth-century Normandy
After Hallam, E.M. (1990) *Capetian France 987–1328*, Longman, London

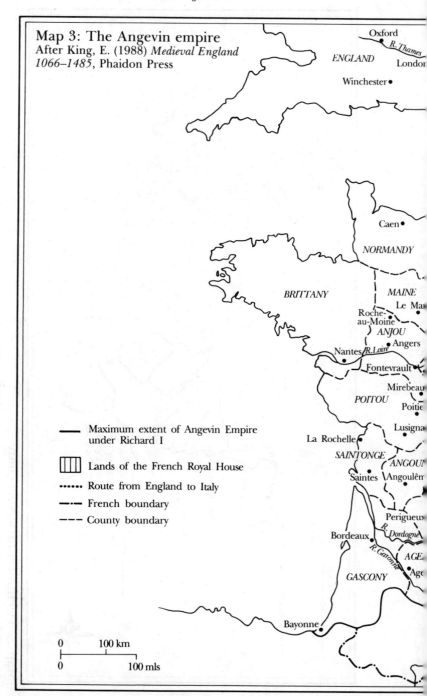

Map 3: The Angevin empire
After King, E. (1988) *Medieval England 1066–1485*, Phaidon Press

Oxford
R. Thames
ENGLAND
London
Winchester

Caen
NORMANDY
MAINE
Le Mar
BRITTANY
Roche-au-Moine
ANJOU
Angers
Nantes R. Loire
Fontevrault
Mirebeau
POITOU
Poitie

Maximum extent of Angevin Empire under Richard I

Lusigna
La Rochelle
SAINTONGE
ANGOUI
Saintes
Angoulêm

Lands of the French Royal House

Route from England to Italy

French boundary

County boundary

Perigueu
Bordeaux
R. Dordogn
R. Garonne
AGE
GASCONY
Age

Bayonne

0   100 km
0   100 mls

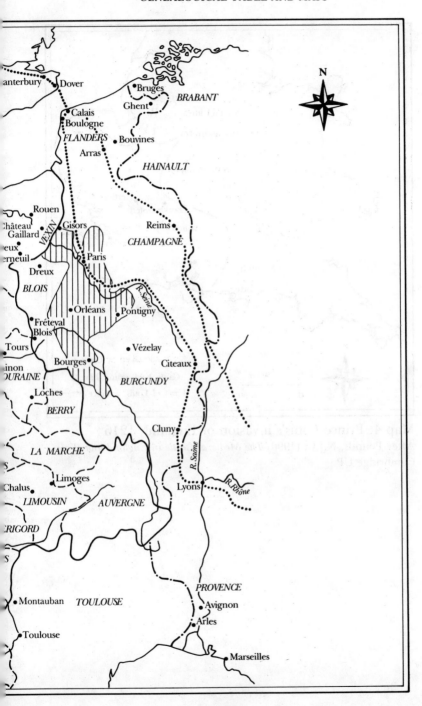

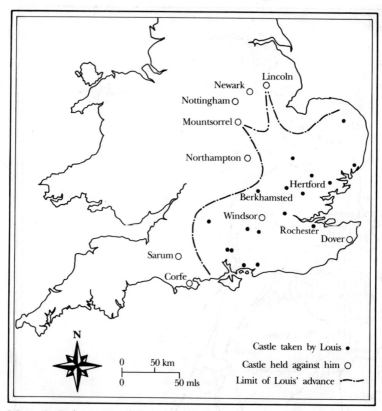

Map 4: Prince Louis's invasion of England, 1216
After Pounds, N.J.C. (1990) *The Medieval Castle in England and Wales*,
Cambridge UP

INDEX

The following abbreviations have been employed: abb = abbot; abp = archbishop; abpc = archbishopric; bp = bishop; bpc = bishopric; cath = cathedral; chap = chapter; css = countess; ct = count; co = county; dk = duke; dr = daughter; e = earl; emp = emperor; illegit = illegitimate; k = king; qn = queen; vct = viscount; w = wife.